THE DETRANSITION DIARIES

Jennifer Lahl and Kallie Fell

The Detransition Diaries

IGNATIUS PRESS   SAN FRANCISCO

Cover photograph © iStock/Getty Images

Cover design by John Herreid

© 2024 by Ignatius Press, San Francisco
All rights reserved
ISBN 978-1-62164-637-2 (PB)
ISBN 978-1-64229-276-3 (eBook)
Library of Congress Control Number 2023935057
Printed in the United States of America ∞

To Kellie-Jay Keen, who never loses

CONTENTS

Foreword   9

Introduction   15

1   The Rise of the Gender-Affirmation Movement   21

2   Lessons Not Learned from Medical Abuses
    of the Past   45

3   Helena   66

4   Grace   77

5   Nick   88

6   Cat   100

7   Chloe   114

8   Torren   124

9   Rachel   134

10 Why Is the Trend Higher among Adolescent
    Girls?   145

11 Lasting and Irreversible Damage   175

Conclusion: How Does This Dark Moment in
Medical History End?   207

Acknowledgments   227

Index   233

FOREWORD

Every once in a while you meet someone who can only be described as a force of nature, a fearless person who will do whatever it takes to make sure that justice is done.

These are the types of people who ensure that the abused and the exploited are seen, heard, and given a voice. They speak for those who have been forgotten and discarded, particularly those whose stories are not often considered and who have faced injustices that are rarely if ever scrutinized or that are perversely renamed and portrayed as progressive and good.

Jennifer Lahl is one such fearless force of nature whom I'm proud to call a friend, and she embodies this honorable and relentless justice-seeking ethos. In the coming pages she tackles a thorny issue that I doubt even she knew she would be broaching in her decades-long efforts in the trenches advocating for sound biomedical ethics and helping countless women who have been exploited.

If you ask her, the debate over the experimental medicalization of gender—which is known by the deceptive euphemism "gender-affirming care"—was never something she thought she would find herself addressing, as her primary focus has been fighting the scourge of the artificial reproductive technology industry. Her pioneering, razor-sharp work unveiling the horrors imposed upon college-age girls who are hustled for their eggs and revealing how vulnerable women are preyed upon by commercial surrogacy operators is extraordinary and deserves much more attention than it has received. See her films *Eggsploitation, Breeders: A Subclass of Women* and *Big Fertility: It's All About the Money.*

But gender ideology is a particularly parasitic kudzu, and when it invaded the space she was diligently working in, she knew this fight was also hers to take on. The way it intruded itself into her work was that youth who considered themselves trans were being offered fertility preservation measures, such as freezing and banking their gametes before beginning the medicalization that would render them permanently sterile. This was one of the disturbing realities she highlighted in her powerful documentary film *Trans Mission: What's the Rush to Reassign Gender?* (released in June 2021).

In this book, the stories of three women who were harmed by this brutal medicalization (and were featured in her most recent film of the same name, released on September 19, 2022) are told in greater depth, as are the harrowing experiences of two other women and two men who also detransitioned. Remarkably, these men and women have bravely related their own mistakes and failures as well as the medical malfeasance of which they were victims.

Together with the eminently thoughtful Kallie Fell, Jennifer has penned a wonderful account detailing the journeys of troubled young people who were put through what I sometimes call "the gender meat grinder". Each story has its own uniquely distressing dimensions, and yet they all contain eerily similar threads. These young people were all affirmed in their own conception of their "gender identity" and were not challenged or safeguarded by those who held themselves out to be professionals.

The real costs of such astonishing institutional hijacking by gender ideology, and the mental and bodily injury with which many detransitioners will live for the rest of their lives, are most grievously seen in Chloe's story, who was transitioned as a minor. Historians will look back on this period in time and wonder how it was that powerful institutions overflowing with educated people sporting impressive credentials could have furthered such brutality.

As is typical of her, with every issue she confronts, Jennifer has done her homework. Few could have imagined the sordid legacies that figures such as Alfred Kinsey and John Money have left, and how the medical and psychological horrors they unleashed gave rise to the contemporary dogma that has infected once-respectable institutions.

She also highlights the brave voices of people who, like her, have been resisting this highly unethical experiment on vulnerable people for years. What Jennifer Lahl is to bioethics, Drs. Paul Hruz and Quentin Van Meter are to pediatric endocrinology and Dr. André Van Mol is to family medicine, for example. As you read the first chapter, which chronicles the forces that have led to the exploitative medicalization of gender dysphoria that we have seen erupt, and before you hear from those who have been harmed, please remember just how important it is to do whatever you can in your respective sphere of influence for good. It really matters.

In another equally informative chapter, coauthor Kallie Fell impressively details the dearth of sound research in this arena, the gaps in the relevant endocrinology and psychology literature, and the perilously flimsy basis on which hormones are being prescribed and how readily medically unnecessary surgeries are being performed on physically healthy bodies. Readers will especially appreciate her distilled explanation of how junk studies are so often bandied about as though they are authoritative in contradistinction to the actual science. She also explains the devastating effects this experimental medicalization has wrought on young people, including the long-term risks of hormone use, reproductive regret, and complications that arise from various surgeries.

When I was reading the book you're about to read and absorbing each detransitioner's story, I could not stop shaking my head in dismay, hearing how synthetic cross-sex hormones hijacked their endocrine systems and deleteriously impacted their mental and physical health. It's all too familiar and so maddening. I was devastated to read about how easy it was for them to obtain these controlled substances and about the haste with which therapists wrote referral letters so that their healthy bodies could be carved up in pursuit of a physiological impossibility.

But as Grace Lidinsky-Smith, who is one of the detransitioners featured in both the film and the book, so poignantly said, "I want people to know that there is life after detransition."

But although the accounts that are movingly retold here (a few of which elaborate on the three testimonies in the film) are harrowing indeed, the book points to that very real hope these young people have for the future despite the damage done to their bodies.

As an investigative journalist who has been on the frontlines of this difficult beat for years, I'll be the first to say that this topic is not for the faint of heart. But the truth must be told, and it is vitally important that what has happened to detransitioners, especially to detrans females—since they're the predominant demographic who have been harmed—be documented journalistically. For years, the corporate press has run with a manipulative narrative that has stifled their voices. Legacy media outlets have systematically ignored their perspectives, diminished their stories, and insisted with an ardent certainty that only a minuscule number of people regret undergoing hormonal and surgical transitioning.

This moving book works to reverse this silencing of people who regret their medicalized transition and captures several personal glimpses of how it was allowed to happen.

In my own work documenting the devastating damage caused by false ideology surrounding gender in recent years, I've often prayed that God would open my eyes and ears so that I could see and hear the cries of those who are suffering—especially where the suffering wasn't immediately obvious, where the cries were hidden or misunderstood. It's a scary prayer to pray because some of the hidden misery one discovers reveals layer upon layer of darkness. But darkness always, always yields to light, and telling the truth, no matter how difficult, is always worth it.

Finally, these young people's cries of anguish, which were seized upon by an industry that irreversibly harmed them and in some cases left them likely sterile and permanently disfigured, are being given the hearing they deserve. The stories told in this book will probably anger you. They will also surely inspire you.

And when the full history of this horrific medical scandal is written, Jennifer Lahl and Kallie Fell will have left an unmistakably important mark.

Brandon Showalter
Senior Investigative Reporter
The Christian Post
July 31, 2023

INTRODUCTION

We are nurses who happen to make movies. This book is partially based on our 2022 film, *The Detransition Diaries: Saving Our Sisters*, made in collaboration with the Center for Bioethics and Culture Network. The work we do is, in part, to challenge the medical industry when it loses its connection to the ancient precept of ethical medicine: "Do no harm."

When we released our documentary film *Trans Mission: What's the Rush to Reassign Gender?* we wanted the film to be sharply focused on the debate on the ethics of allowing children to block their puberty, take cross-sex hormones, and undergo what is called sexual-reassignment surgery, all of which can cause irreparable harm. If we've learned anything from our history and from what happens when medicine loses its way or becomes untethered from an ethical framework that recognizes the dignity of the human person, it is that the dismantling of medical ethics causes human civilization to devolve into a state of collapse ruled only by the principle of the survival of the fittest. We must recall our history lessons exposing the exploitation of and abuses committed against individuals or groups and apply them to the modern transgender movement. As philosopher George Santayana said, "Those who cannot remember the past are condemned to repeat it."[1]

[1] George Santayana, *The Life of Reason, Introduction and Reason in Common Sense*, ed. Marianne S. Wokeck and Martin A. Coleman (Cambridge, MA: The MIT Press, 1905/2011), 172.

Much of our previous work focuses on fertility and infertility, so when we learned that children, before they are put on a path to "transition" to the opposite sex, are offered so-called fertility preservation technologies, such as the freezing of female ova for future use, we knew we had to weigh in on this urgent debate, using the powerful medium of film. It is unconscionable that children are rendered infertile by "transitioning therapies" while also being promised that they can reproduce later, and it is alarming how little publicized this common occurrence is. During the global COVID-19 pandemic we therefore set out to make *Trans Mission*, which involved the navigation of mandates, closures, social distancing, and shelter-in-place orders. The film was released in June of 2021.

Upon the film's release, we learned a great deal from the reactions and comments of the audience. First, viewers found it easy to connect with the parents we interviewed in the film who have gender-confused children and live with the fear of losing them to the radical transgender movement. These parents share how they received little or no support from teachers, doctors, counselors, and even members of their own family. These anguished mothers and fathers were desperately trying to save their children from making disastrous decisions at a time when they lacked the maturity to weigh their long-term consequences, while having to fight the reckless professionals who were playing fast and loose with their responsibility to do good and not harm to their patients.

Second, it was clear that the audience connected strongly with the "detransition voices". Detransitioners are those who had bought into the lie that they could transition to the opposite sex and who now regret the terrible decisions they made, decisions that are often associated with irreversible consequences and that they were oftentimes encouraged by others to make. The power of these first-account personal testimonies should not be underestimated, and they should never be discounted.

A few weeks before *Trans Mission* was released, *60 Minutes* aired a program titled *Health Care Challenges for Transgender Youth*, which included interviews with some detransitioners who said that they had been pushed into harmful "gender-affirmation" therapies instead of receiving the healthcare that they needed.[2] Lesley Stahl, the host of this program, received severe criticism for interviewing these people. For example, GLAAD (originally the Gay & Lesbian Alliance against Defamation) dismissed the inclusion of detransitioner voices as "fearmongering".[3] It seemed to us that some transgender activists will not tolerate any suggestion that there are people who once considered themselves trans who now regret having undergone procedures that did permanent damage to their body. It was then that the idea for our film *The Detransition Diaries: Saving Our Sisters* was born.

In the meantime, more and more detransitioners have been coming forward with their stories. Additionally, there is a growing number of people who have been working inside transgender clinics, believing that the work they were doing was good, important, and helpful to those in need, who now regret their contribution to the transition industry. Jamie Reed is one such person. In her words a "queer woman" "married to a transman", Reed left her job at the Washington University Transgender Center at

---

[2] *60 Minutes*, season 53, episode 6, "Health Care Challenges for Transgender Youth", featuring Lesley Stahl, aired May 23, 2021, on CBS, 13:42, https://www.cbsnews.com/video/transgender-health-care-60-minutes-video-2021-05-23.

[3] GLAAD (@GLAAD), "Tonight @60Minutes @LesleyRStahl aired a shameful segment fearmongering about trans youth", Twitter, May 23, 2021, 11:11 p.m., https://twitter.com/glaad/status/1396665047645138945?lang=en.

St. Louis Children's Hospital after coming to the conclusion that the clinic was doing irreparable harm to vulnerable young people.[4] Reed's decision to speak out has raised the stakes of this debate, and both Missouri Attorney General Andrew Bailey and U.S. Senator Josh Hawley have begun investigations into the clinic's practices.

Just before this book went to print, Washington University released a press release announcing that its physicians "will no longer prescribe puberty blockers or cross-sex hormones to minors for purposes of gender transition". The reason for this change in course? "Missouri's newly enacted law regarding transgender care has created a new legal claim for patients who received these medications as minors. This legal claim creates unsustainable liability for health-care professionals and makes it untenable for us to continue to provide comprehensive transgender care for minor patients without subjecting the university and our providers to an unacceptable level of liability."[5]

We are confident that we are seeing the tip of the iceberg. There will be more and more people, like those in this book, speaking out about their regrets about transitioning or participating in transgender medical practices. Their stories will spark more investigations, laws, and lawsuits, which will create "unstainable liability" for practicing so-called transgender medicine on minors.

While the principles presented and supported in this book apply to any attempt to transition medically, through the use of hormones and/or surgery, and although we

[4]Jamie Reed, "I Thought I Was Saving Trans Kids. Now I'm Blowing the Whistle", *The Free Press* (blog), *Substack*, February 9, 2023, https://www.thefp.com/p/i-thought-i-was-saving-trans-kids.

[5]Washington University in St. Louis, *The Source*, "Statement on Washington University Transgender Center", September 11, 2023, https://source.wustl.edu.

have included the stories of two men, this book has a special focus on girls and young women who have gender dysphoria and on the societal pressures they experience. For reasons we explore in chapter 3, adolescent girls are disproportionately affected by transgender ideology. We present the stories of young women interviewed for our film *The Detransition Diaries: Saving Our Sisters* who made the decision to transition, regretted that decision, and then reversed course to detransition. We explain how they were persuaded to make a decision they would later regret and how the same thing can happen to other vulnerable young people who will hear, and might well believe, the lies they are being told—such as "If you don't love your body, you must be trans" or "Once you transition, all your problems will go away." Parents are being told another lie: "If you don't allow your child to transition, she will kill herself." It is our hope that readers will come to understand how these regrettable decisions were made so that they can help others, such as family members and friends, avoid making them.

We were thrilled with the offer from Ignatius Press to bring these stories to life in book format. While film is an important genre of storytelling, books allow for the expansion of ideas and a deeper analysis of modern-day problems. To understand the problem of gender dysphoria and to discuss humane ways to treat it, certain facts must be first established: (1) biological sex is real and innate, (2) no one can change his or her sex, and (3) gender dysphoria is real, and the people diagnosed with it need to be treated with care and respect, while being offered appropriate professional help instead of being pressured by financially or politically motivated people into accepting puberty blockers, cross-sex hormones, or surgeries. While we use the word "transition" to describe the process whereby people

seek medical treatments in an attempt to bring their appearance closer to that of the opposite sex, we do not intend
to imply that we believe it is ever possible for a person to
change biological sex. Words matter and truth is important, and we will refer to people by their natal sex, which is
the only sex people can have. Men will be called "he" or
"him", and women will be called "she" or "her", even if
we are referring to a person who believes his or her sex to
be otherwise.

Once people accept the truth about sex and realize the
dangers of denying it, the right course of treatment for
young people with gender dysphoria can be found, a treatment that truly does no harm.

The Rise of the Gender-Affirmation Movement

While this chapter is not an exhaustive account of when and how gender ideology began, it identifies some crucial chronological markers as a way of explaining how we got here. Some of these markers are the significant figures who have led the movement; others are the organizations that have captured institutions and professionals in academia, medicine, and elsewhere. And it would be remiss of us to fail to highlight the voices in the wilderness who have been standing up and speaking truth to the powerful influencers trying to erase biology and blur the distinction between male and female.

Einar Wegener

A Danish painter born in the late 1800s, Einar Wegener found that he enjoyed cross-dressing when his wife, Gerda, who was also a painter, would have him model for her wearing her clothes.[1] Wegener fit the definition

---

[1] Rainer Herrn and Annette F. Timm, "Elbe, Lili (1882–1931)", in *Global Encyclopedia of Lesbian, Gay, Bisexual, Transgender, and Queer (LGBTQ) History*, ed. Howard Chiang et al. (Farmington Hills, MI: Charles Scribner's Sons, 2019), 1:500–2.

of the term "transvestite", coined in 1910, meaning a person who dresses in clothing stereotypically associated with the opposite sex.[2] Once Wegener discovered that he liked wearing feminine clothes, he went on to assume a "female" persona. He changed his name to Lili Elbe, and his wife introduced him to people as Einar's cousin.[3]

Ultimately, Wegener was the first man to undergo what is now called sex-reassignment surgery, and his marriage was annulled under Danish law. In trying to achieve a woman's body, and even to conceive a child and give birth, he underwent four operations, but he ultimately died of an infection from, and rejection of, a transplanted uterus in 1931.[4]

Wegener's failure to achieve what he wanted through surgery has not stopped the idea of men receiving uterine transplants from gradually gaining ground. In the largest study of its kind, researchers found that more than 90 percent of 182 "transgender women" (that is, men) believed that a uterine transplant might improve their quality of life, alleviate their dysphoric symptoms, and enhance their feelings of femininity.[5] These men reported a "desire to

[2] Stephen Whittle, "A Brief History of Transgender Issues", *The Guardian*, June 2, 2010, https://www.theguardian.com/lifeandstyle/2010/jun/02/brief -history-transgender-issues. See also Vern L. Bullough and Bonnie Bullough, *Cross Dressing, Sex, and Gender* (Philadelphia: University of Pennsylvania Press, 1993), 207–22.

[3] Herrn and Timm, "Elbe, Lili", 1:500.

[4] David Cox, "The Danish Girl and the Sexologist: A Story of Sexual Pioneers", *The Guardian*, January 13, 2016, https://theguardian.com/science/blog /2016/jan/13/magnus-hirschfeld-groundbreaking-sexologist-the-danish-girl -lili-elbe. See also Jennifer Lahl, "Can Men Really Have Babies?", The Center for Bioethics and Culture Network (CBC), May 17, 2022, https://cbc -network.org/2022/05/can-men-really-have-babies.

[5] Benjamin P. Jones et al., "Perceptions and Motivations for Uterus Transplant in Transgender Women", *JAMA Network Open* 4, no. 1 (January 20, 2021), https://doi.org/10.1001/jamanetworkopen.2020.34561.

have physiologic experiences unique to cisgender women, such as menstruation and gestation, as well as potentially having a physiologically functioning transplanted vagina".[6] The study found that these men "may expect the ability to menstruate to enhance satisfaction with their desired gender and uterus transplant and anticipate improvements in perceptions of their femininity".[7]

Yet, uterine transplants into *female* bodies for the purpose of childbearing are still experimental, having met with only modest success. The first reported uterine transplant in a woman was performed in Saudi Arabia in 2000; it was unsuccessful, and the uterus was removed after three months. Sweden reported the first successful uterine transplant producing a live birth, but the baby was born two months premature. In 2016, the first uterine transplant was performed in the United States, but the transplant caused life-threatening complications that required the uterus to be surgically removed two weeks after transplantation. In 2017, Brazil documented the world's first-known woman to receive a womb transplant from a deceased donor and then give birth (she gave birth via cesarean section to a six-pound girl).[8] To date, it is estimated that approximately eighty uterine transplants, mostly taken from living donors, have been performed worldwide, "resulting in more than 40 births".[9] For the twenty women who received a uterine transplant at Baylor University Medical Center from 2016

[6] Jones et al., "Uterus Transplant", 1.

[7] Jones et al., "Uterus Transplant", 7.

[8] Kate Kelland, "World's First Baby Born Via Womb Transplant from Dead Donor", Reuters, December 4, 2018, https://www.reuters.com/article /us-health-womb-transplant-idUSKBN1O32WS.

[9] Mats Brännström, Michael A. Belfort, and Jean Marc Ayoubi, "Uterus Transplantation Worldwide: Clinical Activities and Outcomes", *Current Opinion in Organ Transplantation* 26, no. 6 (2021), https://doi.org/10.1097/MOT .0000000000000936.

to 2019, the live birth rate per attempted transplant was 55 percent.[10] Since recipients of transplanted organs must take immunosuppressant antirejection medication for the rest of their lives, making them vulnerable to infectious diseases, transplanted uteruses have usually been removed after patients have had one or two children.[11]

Given this track record with women, whatever uterine transplants might be performed on men in the near future will be experimental and will likely end in failure. Men, by nature, are not meant to have uteruses in their bodies in order to have babies. And if men have uterine transplants simply in order to pretend to be women, or to feel feminine, they will likely need to remain on antirejection medications for the rest of their lives.

Harry Benjamin and George "Christine" Jorgensen

With Wegener's unsuccessful uterine transplant in 1931, men who felt as if they were actually women, or who at least thought that they would be happier as women, were mostly left with cross-dressing, or transvestism, to address their desires. The term "transsexualism" and the push to use medical treatments to change a person's sex did not gain traction until George "Christine" Jorgensen's so-called "sex change" in 1952, under the care of Dr. Harry

[10] Liza Johannesson et al., "Twelve Live Births after Uterus Transplantation in the Dallas Uterus Transplant Study", *Obstetrics & Gynecology* 137, no. 2 (2021), https://doi.org/10.1097/AOG.0000000000004244.

[11] Emily S. Rueb, "Second U.S. Baby to Be Born from a Dead Donor's Uterus Is Delivered", *The New York Times*, January 9, 2020, https://www.nytimes.com/2020/01/09/health/uterus-transplant-baby.html. See also Kallie Fell, "Let's Talk about Uterine Transplants", The Center for Bioethics and Culture Network (CBC), January 28, 2020, https://cbc-network.org/2020/01/lets-talk-about-uterine-transplants.

Benjamin, and the subsequent publication of Benjamin's *The Transsexual Phenomenon* in 1966.[12]

Generally considered a medical term, "transsexualism" has typically denoted at least the intention, if not the actual action, of changing one's physical appearance, by hormonal and surgical intervention, to resemble that of the opposite sex. The term "transgenderism", though used as far back as 1965 by Dr. John F. Oliven, did not become widespread until the early 1990s.[13] Today, the word "transgender" is used more often than "transsexual" and carries the added assumption that there are distinct male or female psyches, or souls, that are not always aligned with the physical, sexed bodies with which people are born.

Regardless of the choice of terms, Benjamin played a key role in promoting the idea that a person's sex or gender could be changed. He was born in Germany in 1884 and earned his medical degree in 1912. In 1913, he came to the United States as a clinical assistant to F. F. Friedmann, who had been working on a remedy for tuberculosis in the form of a "turtle vaccine".[14] What Benjamin had thought would be a grand mission turned out to be quackery. Friedmann's "cure" was exposed as a fraud, which American psychiatrist and psychoanalyst Ethel Spector Person has called "a scandal perhaps unparalleled in the annals of modern medicine".[15]

---

[12] Joanne Meyerowitz, *How Sex Changed: A History of Transsexuality in the United States* (Cambridge, MA: Harvard University Press, 2002/2004), 19, 49–50.

[13] Cristan Williams, "Transgender", *Transgender Studies Quarterly (TSQ)* 1, nos. 1–2 (May 1, 2014), https://doi.org/10.1215/23289252-2400136. See also Antar Martínez-Guzmán and Katherine Johnson, "Transgender, Overview", in *Encyclopedia of Critical Psychology*, ed. Thomas Teo (New York: Springer, 2014), 599, https://doi.org/10.1007/978-1-4614-5583-7.

[14] Ethel Spector Person, *The Sexual Century* (New Haven: Yale University Press, 1999), 352–55.

[15] Person, *Sexual Century*, 353.

Benjamin next latched onto the work of Austria's Eugen Steinach, who believed men could have more vim and vigor by having vasectomies. He followed Steinach's "sex change" operations on guinea pigs and became fascinated with transsexualism.[16] His views on gender dysphoria differed from those of most psychiatrists, who thought that patients who experienced these feelings had a significant psychopathology. In *The Transsexual Phenomenon*, Benjamin writes, "Psychotherapy with the aim of curing transsexualism, so that the patient will accept himself as a man, it must be repeated here, is a useless undertaking with present available methods. The mind of the transsexual cannot be changed in its false gender orientation. All attempts to this effect have failed."[17] Benjamin saw sex as a continuum and thought that the best approach to transsexualism was to change the body to "fit" the perceptions of the patient—in other words, "to adjust the body to the mind".

Benjamin had tested his theory on George "Christine" Jorgensen, the first American man to undergo what would now be called "sex-reassignment surgery".[18] Born in New York on May 30, 1926, Jorgensen began taking cross-sex hormones at the age of twenty-four. In 1950, he had his first surgery: an experimental operation to remove his male genitalia that the surgeon performed for free. Years later, Jorgensen had another operation to create a cavity imitating a vagina—a surgery that even today requires a lifetime of regular dilation to keep the cavity open.[19] After his years

---

[16] Person, *Sexual Century*, 356.

[17] Harry Benjamin, *The Transsexual Phenomenon* (New York: The Julian Press, Inc., 1966), 91.

[18] John T. McQuiston, "Christine Jorgensen of Sex-Change Fame Dies at 62", *The New York Times*, May 4, 1989, D22, https://www.nytimes.com/1989/05/04/obituaries/christine-jorgensen-62-is-dead-was-first-to-have-a-sex-change.html.

[19] "Vaginoplasty", Boston Children's Hospital, accessed June 29, 2023, https://www.childrenshospital.org/treatments/vaginoplasty.

of service in the U.S. military, Jorgensen's surgical transition made headlines all around the world, such as "Ex-GI Becomes Blonde Beauty: Operations Transform Bronx Youth".[20] Jorgensen died in 1989, at the age of sixty-two, from bladder and lung cancer.

Alfred Kinsey

Alfred Kinsey has been referred to as "one of the most influential Americans of the twentieth century" for his revolutionary ideas about sexual behavior.[21] He was born in 1894 and graduated from Bowdoin College in 1916 with high honors. His father wanted him to major in engineering, but after two years of study, Kinsey switched to biology. The elder Kinsey never forgave his son for this decision and refused to attend his commencement. Next, Kinsey studied applied biology at Harvard, where, in 1919, he completed his dissertation: a meticulous study of the evolutionary taxonomy of the gall wasp.[22]

The following year, Kinsey was invited to join the faculty of Indiana University, where he was asked to teach a course on marriage and the family. In 1940, the university gave Kinsey a choice: he could either continue teaching his course on marriage and the family or focus on his research in sexual expression. He opted for the latter. Kinsey published two major works: *Sexual Behavior in the Human Male*

[20] Marta V. Vicente, "The Medicalization of the Transsexual: Patient-Physician Narratives in the First Half of the Twentieth Century", *Journal of the History of Medicine and Allied Sciences* 76, no. 4 (2021): 412, https://doi.org/10.1093/jhmas/jrab037.

[21] Theodore M. Brown and Elizabeth Fee, "Alfred C. Kinsey: A Pioneer of Sex Research", *American Journal of Public Health* 93, no. 6 (2003): 896, https://doi.org/10.2105/ajph.93.6.896.

[22] James H. Jones, *Alfred C. Kinsey: A Life* (New York: W.W. Norton & Company, 1997/2004), 147.

in 1948, followed by *Sexual Behavior in the Human Female* in 1953, known as the Kinsey Reports.

Kinsey's methods of data collection, which involved asking questions about sexual orientation and sexual activity, were widely criticized. Biographer James H. Jones has written that, for Kinsey, his Institute for Sex Research became a kind of "sexual utopia", where Kinsey decreed that "men could have sex with each other; wives would be swapped freely; and wives, too, would be free to embrace whichever sexual partners they liked."[23] Exploring both his sadomasochistic and homosexual desires, Kinsey engaged in various sexual acts with members of the institute's inner circle, including filming such acts in the attic of his home.[24] In Jones' view, Kinsey was not just a scientist but "a reformer" seeking to deal with his personal "demons" while also making a "sexual revolution" in the repressive society in which he had lived.[25]

Critics like Judith Reisman, coauthor of *Kinsey, Sex, and Fraud: The Indoctrination of a People*, published in 1990, have argued that Kinsey's research was fraudulent and that his widespread influence has been harmful.[26] Defenders like American historian and sexologist Vern L. Bullough, however, have seen him as "a pioneer and trailblazer", dismissing Reisman's first book as "an extreme right-wing political tract, not a piece of research".[27] Kinsey and his

[23] Jones, *Alfred C. Kinsey*, 603.

[24] Jones, *Alfred C. Kinsey*, 605.

[25] Jones, *Alfred C. Kinsey*, 772. See also Brown and Fee, "Alfred C. Kinsey", 897.

[26] See Judith A. Reisman and Edward W. Eichel, *Kinsey, Sex, and Fraud: The Indoctrination of a People* (Lafayette, LA: Lochinvar Inc., 1990). See also Judith Reisman, *Kinsey: Crimes and Consequences*, 3rd ed. (Crestwood, KY: The Institute for Media Education, 2003).

[27] Vern L. Bullough, "Sex Will Never Be the Same: The Contributions of Alfred C. Kinsey", *Archives of Sexual Behavior* 33, no. 1 (2004): 285, https://doi.org/10.1023/B:ASEB.0000026627.24993.03.

works remain controversial. He blurred the lines of human sexuality, suggesting that sexuality is fluid and always evolving, to the extent that articles on him feature headlines such as "Liberator or Pervert?"[28] and "Fraud and Pervert".[29]

John Money

Born in New Zealand in 1921, John Money came to the United States to study when he was in his twenties. He received his Ph.D. in social relations from Harvard University in 1952, and in 1966 he founded the Gender Identity Clinic at Johns Hopkins, the first American medical center to venture into surgery as an attempt to treat gender dysphoria. Money is credited for the terms "gender identity" and "gender role", which he defined as "concepts liberated from biological determinism of sex on the one hand and separate from sexual functioning on the other".[30]

Money's views and research were not only unconventional but controversial. For example, he saw pedophilia as simply a sexual orientation, alongside heterosexuality, homosexuality, and bisexuality. "Paedophilia", Money wrote, "should just be accepted for its etymological

[28] Caleb Crain, "Doctor Strange Love: Alfred Kinsey: Liberator or Pervert? Hollywood Wades into the Fray", *The New York Times*, October 3, 2004, AR1, AR20, https://www.nytimes.com/2004/10/03/movies/alfred-kinsey-liberator -or-pervert.html.

[29] Robert Knight, "Fraud and Pervert Alfred C. Kinsey Returns", *The Washington Times*, September 24, 2022, https://www.washingtontimes.com /news/2022/sep/24/fraud-and-pervert-alfred-c-kinsey-returns.

[30] Anke A. Ehrhardt, "John Money, Ph.D.", *The Journal of Sex Research* 44, no. 3: 223–24, https://doi.org/10.1080/00224490701580741. Though psychiatrist and psychoanalyst Robert J. Stoller has been credited for coining "gender identity" in 1964, Money has been credited for a further development of this concept, his coinage of "gender role", which expanded to "gender-identity/ role". See also Terry Goldie, *The Man Who Invented Gender: Engaging the Ideas of John Money* (Vancouver, Canada: UBC Press, 2014).

meaning, which is simply the love of children."[31] It should come as no surprise that his work has appeared on the website of the North American Man Boy Love Association (NAMBLA).[32]

Perhaps Money is most famous for his experimentation on the Reimer twins, Bruce and Brian, who were born in Canada in 1965. After the observation that the twin boys urinated a lot, they were both diagnosed with phimosis—a tight foreskin. It was decided when they were eight months old that the two boys should be circumcised to alleviate this perceived problem. During what should have been a routine circumcision procedure, Bruce's penis was accidentally removed. Because of this tragic event, Brian's circumcision was canceled, and it was reported that his phimosis resolved on its own. The parents sought out the expertise of John Money, who recommended that Bruce undergo surgery to remove his testes and construct a "vulva"—and that he be raised as a girl. Money believed that sex and gender are malleable—influenced by upbringing and manipulatable by medical intervention—at a young age. According to Money's theory, rearing a male child with a "female" gender identity was possible, and, in Bruce's case, it was desirable.

At twenty-two months of age, Bruce had the surgery Money recommended. His parents changed his name to Brenda. As a teenager, he was put on estrogen so that he would develop breast tissue. Money continued to follow the twins, claiming that Brenda was very much the little girl and Brian the little boy and that the two children were well adjusted.

[31] John Money, "Interview: John Money", by Joseph Geraci and Donald Mader, *Paidika* number 7, vol. 2, no. 3 (Spring 1991): 3.

[32] Judith Reisman, "Strange Bedfellows", *The Washington Times*, August 21, 2002, https://washingtontimes.com/news/2002/aug/21/20020821-041050-7378r.

When the twins were thirty-two years old, Canadian journalist John Colapinto questioned the assessment that "the twins were reported to have grown into happy, well-adjusted children of opposite sex"[33] in "The True Story of John/Joan", a 1997 article in *Rolling Stone*. Following the article, Colapinto's book *As Nature Made Him: The Boy Who Was Raised as a Girl*, published in 2000, exposed further details of the case, including Money's treatment of the Reimer twins during therapy. Money would force the twins to engage in "sexual rehearsal play", which he saw as a natural way for the children to develop healthy "gender schemas". He would have the children, as young as six years old, strip naked, inspect each other's genitals, and simulate sexual intercourse. Sometimes Money would photograph the twins during these sessions. Both twins recalled that Money had "two sides to his personality" and would go from "mild-mannered" around the parents to "irritable or worse" if the twins showed any resistance to his treatments.[34]

At age fourteen, Bruce learned about the botched circumcision and what had been done afterward to make him resemble a girl. He decided then to live as a boy and took the name David. He lived a troubled life, and in 2004, at age thirty-nine, shot and killed himself. His brother, Brian, had died of a drug overdose in 2002.[35]

In 1979, Johns Hopkins closed the Gender Identity Clinic founded by Money. Instrumental in this decision was Dr. Paul R. McHugh, the hospital's psychiatrist-in-chief from

[33] John Colapinto, "The True Story of John/Joan", *Rolling Stone* (December 11, 1997), 56.

[34] John Colapinto, *As Nature Made Him: The Boy Who Was Raised as a Girl* (New York: HarperCollins Publishers, 2000/2006), 86–88.

[35] Jesse Walker, "The Death of David Reimer", *Reason*, May 24, 2004, https://reason.com/2004/05/24/the-death-of-david-reimer. See also John Colapinto, "Why Did David Reimer Commit Suicide?", *Slate*, June 3, 2004, https://slate.com/technology/2004/06/why-did-david-reimer-commit-suicide.html.

1975 to 2001, who explained that the medical center closed the clinic after a study that compared patients who had "sex-change" surgeries with those who did not. "Most of the surgically treated patients described themselves as 'satisfied' by the results, but their subsequent psycho-social adjustments were no better than those who didn't have the surgery." So, Johns Hopkins stopped doing the surgeries because "producing a 'satisfied' but still troubled patient seemed an inadequate reason for surgically amputating normal organs."[36]

To back up this decision, McHugh cites a 2011 long-term study by the Karolinska Institute in Sweden, which followed 324 people for up to thirty years who had surgery intended to reassign their sex. He writes, "The study revealed that beginning about 10 years after having the surgery, the transgendered began to experience increasing mental difficulties. Most shockingly, their suicide mortality rose almost 20-fold above the comparable nontransgender population."[37]

According to McHugh, men who think they are women and women who think they are men suffer from a "disorder of assumption", in which they assume they are different from what they have been given by nature—namely their maleness or femaleness—which is similar to "other kinds of disordered assumptions ... held by those who suffer from anorexia and bulimia nervosa, where the assumption that departs from physical reality is the belief by the dangerously thin that they are overweight".[38] The belief that one is or could be other than he really is, is a psychological, not a physiological or anatomical problem;

[36] Paul McHugh, "Transgender Surgery Isn't the Solution", updated version, *The Wall Street Journal*, May 13, 2016, https://www.wsj.com/articles/paul-mchugh-transgender-surgery-isnt-the-solution-1402615120.

[37] McHugh, "Transgender Surgery".

[38] McHugh, "Transgender Surgery".

thus, hormones and surgeries cannot cure it. It is unfortunate that Johns Hopkins has since reversed its decision and again offers surgeries such as "penile construction (phalloplasty/metoidioplasty),... top surgery (mastectomy or augmentation), [and] vaginal construction (vaginoplasty)[39] at its Center for Transgender and Gender Expansive Health, which opened in 2017.[40]

Psychiatrist Dr. Miriam Grossman traces back to John Money "the radical concept that maleness and femaleness are feelings, separate from anatomy and chromosomes. He was convinced we are born without gender, then conditioned by society to identify either as male or female." Grossman also notes that Money did not disapprove of pedophilia or incest, but instead believed that adult-child sex, even between persons related to each other, was just "a love affair between an age-discrepant couple". Learning about Money and also Kinsey, whom Grossman describes as suffering from a "psychopathology", she realized "how we had reached today's madness. It came from disturbed individuals with dangerous ideas, radical activists who wanted to create a society that would not only accept their pathology, but celebrate it. These men were pedophiles. It was in their interest to see children as miniature adults who enjoyed sexual contact, and had the right to consent to it, without other adults, or the law, interfering."[41]

---

[39] "Gender-Affirming Care", Center for Transgender and Gender Expansive Health, Johns Hopkins Medicine, accessed June 30, 2023, https://www.hopkinsmedicine.org/center-transgender-health.

[40] Mark Hamby, "Johns Hopkins Hospital Opens Center for Transgender Health", American Bar Association, April 15, 2017, https://www.americanbar.org/groups/litigation/committees/lgbt-law-litigator/practice/2017/johns-hopkins-hospital-opens-center-for-trangender-health.

[41] Miriam Grossman, "A Brief History of Sex Ed: How We Reached Today's Madness", Public Discourse, July 16, 2013, https://www.thepublicdiscourse.com/2013/07/10408.

Judith Butler

The work of Benjamin, Kinsey, and Money contributed in fundamental ways to the rise and spread of what we may identify today as the gender-affirmation movement, which encourages people, including minor children, to undergo transsexual treatments and surgeries in order to have bodies that match their feelings or aspirations about their genders. Another significant contribution to this movement has been made by Judith Butler, a professor of philosophy and literature at the University of California, Berkeley. Butler's *Gender Trouble: Feminism and the Subversion of Identity*, published in 1990, was foundational to the development of "queer theory", which is an analytical method that dismantles traditional assumptions about sex and gender. At first queer theorists said that, unlike biological sex, gender is not inherent to a person but is a social construct and therefore subject to a person's will. Butler, however, argued that even though biological traits exist, they do not constitute the essence of a person. Since the very idea of sex is socially conditioned, she wrote, there is no important distinction to be made between sex and gender. According to this view, people should be able to choose their identities and remake their bodies, without any reference to biological sex or social norms regarding sexual differentiation.[42] In the last three decades, queer theory has spread like wildfire in academia, and the result has been the trend in American institutions to deny the innateness and the uniqueness of biological sex and to promote transsexualism.

---

[42] For a discussion of Butler's theory of "gender performativity", see Abigail Favale, *The Genesis of Gender: A Christian Theory* (San Francisco: Ignatius Press, 2022), 72–76.

Janice Raymond

Among the earliest feminist critics of transsexualism was Janice G. Raymond, a professor emerita of medical ethics at the University of Massachusetts, Amherst. Beginning in 1977, Raymond criticized transsexualism (especially with regard to women) as "the ultimate homage to sex-role power".[43] Instead of seeking the development and the empowerment of women who want to pursue goals and activities traditionally thought to be suited only to men, powerful voices are telling them that perhaps they have a medically treatable problem: the wrong body. In doing so, they have created a "transsexual empire", which Raymond describes as "ultimately a medical empire, based on a patriarchal medical model. This medical model has provided a 'sacred canopy' of legitimations for transsexual treatment and surgery. In the name of therapy, it has medicalized moral and social questions of sex-role oppression, thereby erasing their deepest meaning."[44] Rather than working for real sexual equality, "transgenderism reduces gender [stereotype] resistance to wardrobes, hormones, surgery, and posturing."[45]

Raymond analyzes the development of the trans movement. She points to "strategic early alliances trans activists made with the mainstream LGB [lesbian, gay, and bisexual] organizations, such as the Human Rights Campaign, Lambda Legal, and GLAAD [formerly Gay and Lesbian

[43] Janice G. Raymond, "Transsexualism: The Ultimate Homage to Sex-Role Power", *Chrysalis* 1, no. 3 (1977).

[44] Janice G. Raymond, *The Transsexual Empire: The Making of the She-Male* (New York: Teachers College Press, 1979/1994), 119.

[45] Raymond, *Transsexual Empire*, xxv. See also Janice G. Raymond, "The Politics of Transgender", *Feminism & Psychology* 4, no. 4 (1994), https://doi.org/10.1177/0959353594044024.

Alliance Against Defamation], who gave them an equal place at the table and then allowed them to preside at the head where they hammered the 'T' into the original LGB." As a result, in a very short time, "we have all been plunged into the alphabet swamp of the LGBT+ environment and are sinking there."[46]

Transitioning Children

One of the fastest areas of growth in the trans movement has been so-called gender-affirming care for children. According to The Gender Mapping Project, which has been tracking the expansion of American pediatric gender clinics, ten years ago there were "a handful of gender clinics for children". Currently there are over four hundred in North America.[47] Alix Aharon, who manages the website, notes that the first gender clinic opened in 2007 at Boston Children's Hospital, "mainly seeing hypergender dysphoric young males who were expressing gender confusion and cross-dressing".[48] This was followed by a steady increase in these types of clinics, with "2014 being a big year for transgenderism". In a flashy cover story, Aharon observes, *Time* magazine declared 2014 "the transgender tipping point".[49]

"Tipping point" is indeed a good description. In 2015, Olympian and reality television personality Bruce Jenner

[46]Janice G. Raymond, *Doublethink: A Feminist Challenge to Transgenderism* (Mission Beach, Australia: Spinifex Press, 2021), 55.

[47]The Gender Mapping Project, accessed March 13, 2023, https://www.gendermapper.org.

[48]Alix Aharon, email message to author Jennifer Lahl, August 29, 2022.

[49]See Katy Steinmetz, "The Transgender Tipping Point", *Time*, May 29, 2014, https://time.com/135480/transgender-tipping-point.

declared himself a "woman",[50] and in 2020, actress Ellen Page announced she was a "man".[51] Page followed up this declaration with a double mastectomy in 2021.[52] Since 2013, the number of double mastectomies performed on girls in the United States has increased thirteen-fold.[53]

Michelle Forcier, M.D., M.P.H., an associate professor of pediatrics at Brown University and the assistant dean of admissions at Brown's Alpert Medical School, is an example that shows how acceptable trans treatments for children are becoming to our culture. She is an advocate of such treatment for children. The focus of her work is on sexual health issues for "lesbian, gay, bisexual, transgender, queer, and questioning youth with a focus on gender-nonconforming youth, puberty blockers and hormones".[54]

For our film *Trans Mission: What's the Rush to Reassign Gender?*, we asked Forcier about her care of minor patients. She claimed that puberty blockers and cross-sex hormones are safe and completely reversible and that they give parents and their children "time to figure things out". She said she encourages parents of minor children to "listen to your kid, accept your kid as they are, love them

[50] Daniel E. Slotnik, "In Interview, Jenner Says He Identifies as a Woman", *The New York Times*, April 25, 2015, B6, https://www.nytimes.com/2015/04/25/business/media/bruce-jenner-says-he-identifies-as-a-woman.html.

[51] Alexia Fernández, "Juno Oscar Nominee Elliot Page Comes Out as Transgender: 'My Joy Is Real, but It Is Also Fragile'", *People*, December 1, 2020, https://people.com/movies/elliot-page-comes-out-as-trans.

[52] Ale Russian, "Elliot Page Beams in Shirtless Poolside Shot: 'Trans BB's First Swim Trunks'", *People*, May 24, 2021, https://people.com/movies/elliot-page-beams-in-shirtless-pool-side-shot-trans-bbs-first-swim-trunks.

[53] Annie Tang et al., "Gender-Affirming Mastectomy Trends and Surgical Outcomes in Adolescents", *Annals of Plastic Surgery* 88, no. S4 (2022).

[54] "Michelle Forcier, MD, MPH", National LGBTQIA+ Health Education Center, accessed June 30, 2023, https://www.lgbtqiahealtheducation.org/us/faculty-advisory-board/michelle-forcier.

even if they're not who you expected them to be. Don't wait until they're eighteen to let them decide and be who they need to be. Don't deny them access to care that we know is safe and healthy." Forcier's clinic has a road map for the care of minor children on their "gender journey". It states that the child is directing treatment. According to Forcier, "The kid's driving the bus; the parent's in the front seat going, 'What's going to happen?' It's scary when your kid's driving the bus. We're in the back seat, and we have the road map, and we can help families and children select from a number of good, hopefully, options and avoiding [sic] the less good or the harmful options."[55]

Dr. Paul W. Hruz, a pediatric endocrinologist and a professor at Washington University School of Medicine in St. Louis, began looking more closely into transgender care when Washington University was planning to open a gender identity clinic for children in 2012. Hruz gathered information and raised many questions as to whether the approach being taken by the hospital was wise.[56] He argued that gender-related care must follow evidence-based principles applied to other areas of medicine. He also called for a clear risk-to-benefit calculus. But some strong advocates were pushing the clinic forward, he said, and his colleagues accepted their claim that children were in great need of trans medicine outlined by protocols being followed at the time. Financial considerations were also affecting the decision to start the clinic, he added. Ten years later, this clinic is being investigated

---

[55] Michelle Forcier, in *Trans Mission: What's the Rush to Reassign Gender?*, directed by Kallie Fell and Jennifer Lahl (Pleasant Hill, CA: Center for Bioethics and Culture Network [CBC], 2021), 12:38–13:07, https://www.youtube.com/watch?v=rUeqEoARKOA.

[56] Paul W. Hruz, interview by Jennifer Lahl, St. Louis, Missouri, January 21, 2021.

for alleged harms done to children. In its defense, it says that it has been giving "standard-based care".[57] Which standards of care? one may ask.

WPATH and the Dutch Protocol

WPATH

One set of standards being followed by American providers of gender treatments is that developed by the World Professional Association of Transgender Health (WPATH). John Money founded the organization in 1979 as the Harry Benjamin Foundation, also known as the Harry Benjamin International Gender Dysphoria Association. The WPATH guidelines have gone through many iterations. Its most recent update, "Standards of Care for the Health of Transgender and Gender Diverse People, version 8" (SOC8), was released on September 6, 2022 (published online on September 15, 2022).[58] In general, the sections on care for adolescents and children recommend that healthcare providers and parents support a young person's desire to transition to the opposite sex and move the child along in that direction with hormone treatments and surgeries in due course.

Dr. Quentin Van Meter is a pediatric endocrinologist in private practice in the Atlanta, Georgia, area. After medical school, he completed his fellowship in pediatric

---

[57] Jonah McKeown, "St. Louis Children's Transgender Clinic Refuses to Halt Operations Amid AG Investigation", Catholic News Agency, February 27, 2023, https://www.catholicnewsagency.com/news/253755/st-louis-children-s -transgender-clinic-refuses-to-halt-operations-amid-ag-investigation.

[58] Eli Coleman et al., "Standards of Care for the Health of Transgender and Gender Diverse People, Version 8", *International Journal of Transgender Health* 23, no. S1 (2022), https://doi.org/10.1080/26895269.2022.2100644.

endocrinology at Johns Hopkins, studying under Paul McHugh and John Money. He says that Money's concept of gender "was sort of the internal sexual identity that was established at some point in time", a view that Van Meter did not share.[59] He explains, "If you look at medical literature prior to 1950, 1960, gender wasn't a word in medicine; it was a linguistic term."

WPATH, says Van Meter, is an organization of activists who believe that a person should be able to change the appearance of his or her body from that of one sex to that the other and live as the opposite sex. "That is their goal. That is their agenda. Everyone who belongs to that, as far as I know, is an agenda-oriented person and loves this ideology and promotes this ideology."

James Esses, a barrister from the United Kingdom, adds to the concern that WPATH is driven by an agenda:

> There have long been concerns that the organization acts more as a partisan lobby group underpinned by gender ideology, instead of a body driven by medical evidence. Many of the senior members of WPATH identify as "trans" or "non-binary" themselves or are gender activists. Susie Green, the former CEO of the United Kingdom organization Mermaids, sits on the body responsible for revisions to the Standards of Care.[60]

Mermaids is an advocacy group for trans youth. In 2007, Susie Green took her son to Boston to receive puberty blockers and afterward lobbied the National Health Service to provide them in the United Kingdom, which they began doing in 2011. On her son's sixteenth birthday,

---

[59] Quentin Van Meter, in *Trans Mission*.

[60] James Esses, "What's Wrong with WPATH Version 8?", Sex Matters, September 20, 2022, https://sex-matters.org/posts/updates/wpath.

Green took him to Thailand for surgery to create a "neovagina",[61] and was caught on record saying that her son's genitals were "not much to work with", possibly, in part, because her son had taken puberty blockers.[62] Her son, formerly called Jack, now goes by the name of Jackie and was, in 2009, the youngest person to undergo the surgery.[63]

Before becoming an attorney, Esses was three years into his five-year training to become a psychotherapist when he was fired from his institution for holding views critical of gender ideology. He notes the language changes in WPATH documents and argues that they are meant to obfuscate what is really happening in trans medicine. For example, according to SOC8, clinicians and therapists are no longer to say "double mastectomy" but should instead refer to "chest masculinization surgery". No longer is it acceptable to say that someone was "born male" or "born female"; rather one must say that the person was "assigned male" or "assigned female" at birth. Binding of young girls' breasts and genital tucking for boys are described as "comfort care" and measures to reduce the risk of being "misgendered".

Esses notes that many of the surgeries WPATH recommends for adults and children are irreversible, such as "top" and "bottom" surgeries, voice surgery, and facial masculinization surgeries. He reports that their guidelines have removed any minimum age limit for a child to

[61] Jo Bartosch, "Mermaids: Leading Children up the Trans Path", sp!ked, July 3, 2020, https://www.spiked-online.com/2020/07/03/mermaids-leading-children -up-the-trans-path.

[62] *Transsexual Teen, Beauty Queen*, directed by Dan Murdoch (London: Renegade Pictures, September 9, 2012). For the clip of Green, see Graham Linehan, *Mermaids CEO Susie Green*, September 22, 2021, 0:09–0:12, https://youtu .be/ppzgLqWAOTc.

[63] Sue Reid, "Jackie Green at the Heart of a Controversy over Children Given Drugs to Change Sex", *Daily Mail*, November 25, 2016, https://www .dailymail.co.uk/news/article-3973036/Jackie-Green-heart-controversy-children -young-nine-given-drugs-change-sex.html.

be given puberty blockers, cross-sex hormones, or sex-reassignment surgery so long as that child has reached Tanner stage II of puberty, which can be as young as nine years old.[64] (Tanner stage II is when girls start to develop breasts, boys see an increase in penis size, and both start to develop pubic hair.)

The WPATH Standards of Care heavily influence other professional organizations, such as the American Academy of Pediatrics (AAP) and the Pediatric Endocrine Society (PES). Both the AAP and the PES recommend puberty blockers and cross-sex hormones for children, as well as surgeries, in the name of gender equity and inclusivity. Yet WPATH itself, in the most recent version of its guidelines, admits that "the number of studies is still low" and that "there are few outcome studies that follow youth into adulthood", adding that studies on people who regret their decision to transition have not yet been done.[65]

The Dutch Protocol

The twenty-five-year-old Dutch Protocol became the first international standard of care for adolescents diagnosed with gender dysphoria, and it was adopted by the first pediatric gender care clinic in the United States, the one at Boston Children's Hospital.[66] A case report by Peggy Cohen-Kettenis, a professor of gender development at the University Medical Center in Utrecht, the Netherlands, provided some of the basis for the protocol. It claims that blocking puberty was an appropriate intervention in a minor, because the pubertal processes would be too traumatic for young people who consider themselves trans to

[64] Esses, "WPATH Version 8".

[65] Coleman et al., "Standards of Care", S46.

[66] Quentin Van Meter, interview by Jennifer Lahl, Atlanta, Georgia, January 13, 2021.

endure.[67] It also claims that puberty suppression is reversible. Treating such people early, while they are still young, it argues, provides patients with better outcomes.

However, Michael Biggs, an associate professor of sociology at Oxford University, has recently looked at the Dutch Protocol through a critical lens and notes that it was based on a small sample of only seventy teenagers using "a small number of observations and incommensurable measures of gender dysphoria", adding that "a replication study conducted in Britain found no improvement."[68] Biggs is affiliated with the Society for Evidence-Based Gender Medicine (SEGM), an international organization of "over 100 clinicians and researchers concerned about the lack of quality evidence for the use of hormonal and surgical interventions as first-line treatment for young people with gender dysphoria".[69] As any medical researcher should agree, no protocol in any branch of medicine should be adopted as a standard of care without substantial evidence that it is needed, safe, and effective.

Yogyakarta Principles

In spite of the speculative nature of gender theories and the experimental nature of trans medicine, the worldwide

---

[67] P. T. Cohen-Kettenis and S. H. M. van Goozen, "Pubertal Delay as an Aid in Diagnosis and Treatment of a Transsexual Adolescent", *European Child & Adolescent Psychiatry* 7, no. 4 (1998), https://doi.org/10.1007/s007870050073. See also P. T. Cohen-Kettenis and S. H. M. van Goozen, "Sex Reassignment of Adolescent Transsexuals: A Follow-Up Study", *Journal of the American Academy of Child and Adolescent Psychiatry* 36, no. 2 (1997), https://doi.org/10.1097/00004583-199702000-00017.

[68] Michael Biggs, "The Dutch Protocol for Juvenile Transsexuals: Origins and Evidence", *Journal of Sex & Marital Therapy* 49, no. 4 (2023), https://doi.org/10.1080/0092623X.2022.2121238.

[69] "About Us", Society for Evidence-Based Gender Medicine (SEGM), accessed June 30, 2023, https://segm.org/about_us.

movement to cement transsexualism in social behavior and civil law is gaining momentum. In 2006, a group of international human rights advocates met in Yogyakarta, Indonesia, to set forth principles to protect people from abuse and discrimination based on sexual orientation or gender identity. Michael O'Flaherty writes that these principles "were developed against a backdrop of appalling human rights abuses perpetrated worldwide against persons on the basis of their sexual orientation or gender identity".[70] These principles are being used to establish international legal standards for human rights, with which national governments will be compelled to comply through international bodies such as the United Nations.

It is of course a worthy goal to protect vulnerable people from unjust treatment and violence. But the Yogyakarta Principles broadly define human rights to include, for example, the right not to be identified by sex in birth certificates and passports.[71] They would prevent gender dysphoria, as medically diagnosed, from being considered a mental illness. Instead, the principles demand that transsexualism be regarded as a form of gender diversity that must be accepted, embraced, and even celebrated as normal. Yet, as we have seen, these principles are the product of a political movement that is heavily influenced by the sexual predilections of its founders and based on insufficient and questionable medical evidence.

---

[70] Michael O'Flaherty, "The Yogyakarta Principles at Ten", *Nordic Journal of Human Rights* 33, no. 4 (2015): 281, https://doi.org/10.1080/18918131.2015.1127009.

[71] *The Yogyakarta Principles Plus 10*, November 10, 2017, 9, http://yogyakartaprinciples.org/wp-content/uploads/2017/11/A5_yogyakartaWEB-2.pdf.

2

Lessons Not Learned from
Medical Abuses of the Past

The first principle of medical ethics, "Do no harm", is in the ancient oath attributed to Hippocrates (460–370 B.C.), the father of Western medicine. The section where the physician promises not to administer poisons or abortifacients includes the words "I will do no harm or injustice." Some form of this oath has been taken by European and American medical school graduates for hundreds of years. Yet, there have been plenty of times when doctors have ignored this promise and done grave harm to many people. If we recount some of these dark moments in medical history, we will see parallels between the unethical medicine practiced then and some of the treatments being given to minors today in the name of gender-affirming care.

The first parallel between the present situation and the abuses of the past is the use of human beings as research subjects without their informed consent or even without their knowledge that they are part of an experiment. Sometimes the reason for the lack of informed consent is that those running the experiment have failed to disclose all the risks involved—either because the risks are not known or because revealing them would discourage people from freely participating in the research. An even more egregious violation takes place when the researcher does not bother with consent at all; the subjects in his study are coerced into cooperating and are treated as disposable objects without dignity or rights.

Nazi Germany

This same disregard for human dignity is seen in the medical abuses of the past in experimentation on people deemed "unfit". Let us begin with the doctors in Nazi Germany.

By the time Hitler came to power, eugenics was already a growing movement in the United States and the United Kingdom. In the late 1800s, Gregor Mendel, an Augustinian monk, had discovered genetic heredity in plants and developed Mendel's laws of inheritance, which drove further research in the United States on human genetic traits. The term "eugenics" was first used in Sir Francis Galton's *Inquiries into Human Faculty and Its Development*, published in 1883. It comes from the Greek word *eugenes*, meaning "good in stock".[1] An early image of the eugenics movement featured the "eugenics tree", used at the Second International Exhibition of Eugenics in 1921.[2] The word "eugenics" is prominently featured on its trunk, and the text declares, "Eugenics Is the Self Direction of Human Evolution" and "Like a Tree Eugenics Draws Its Materials From Many Sources and Organizes Them Into an Harmonious Entity." At the tree's roots are the words "genetics", "psychology", "biology", "law", "statistics", "politics",

[1] Francis Galton, *Inquiries into Human Faculty and Its Development* (London: Macmillan and Co., 1883), 24–25.

[2] Harry H. Laughlin, *The Second International Exhibition of Eugenics Held September 22 to October 22, 1921, in Connection with the Second International Congress of Eugenics in the American Museum of Natural History, New York* (Baltimore, MD: Williams & Wilkins Company, 1923), 15.

"religion", "psychiatry", "surgery", "medicine", "education", and "religion". Eugenics became a pseudoscience
that encompassed every area of life. County fairs hosted
"better babies contests", and governments launched sterilization programs.

Galton, a cousin of Charles Darwin, used the new word
"eugenics" to advocate, in scientific terms, the marriage of
those whom he saw as "the fit", even providing monetary
incentives to encourage it, and these ideas quickly took
root in government, science, education, and even religious
communities in both the United Kingdom and the United
States. Charles Davenport, a professor of zoology at the
University of Chicago, campaigned for funding from
the Carnegie Institution of Washington, incorporated in
1902, to establish a biological experiment station. In 1904,
he received his appointment as director of the Station for
Experimental Evolution in Cold Spring Harbor, New
York, which is widely known as a center of American
eugenics research in the early twentieth century.

But the documented links between Davenport, American eugenics, and German "racial hygiene" of the 1920s
and 1930s have been far less known.[3] The Eugenics
Record Office (ERO), established at Cold Spring Harbor in 1910, was founded by Davenport and funded by
the Carnegie Institution. It collected information such as
"inborn physical, mental and temperamental properties
to enable the family to trace the segregation and recom-
bination of inborn or heritable qualities".[4] Davenport

---

[3] Antoinette Sutto, "Cold Spring Harbor and German Eugenics in the 1930s",
Cold Spring Harbor Laboratory, September 23, 2021, https://www.cshl.edu
/archives-blog/cold-spring-harbor-and-german-eugenics-in-the-1930s.

[4] "Eugenics Record Office", Cold Spring Harbor Laboratory, accessed
June 30, 2023, https://www.cshl.edu/archives/institutional-collections/eugenics
-record-office.

appointed Harry H. Laughlin, a eugenicist educated in cell biology at Princeton University, who lobbied for "eugenic legislation to restrict immigration and sterilize 'defectives', educating the public on eugenic health, and disseminating eugenic ideas widely".[5]

An often forgotten, uncomfortable historical fact is that the atrocities carried out in Nazi Germany flowed from ideas that originated in the United States, where physicians, scientists, and lawmakers collaborated "to research and implement ways of decreasing the number of people considered to be hereditarily weak (negative eugenics) and increasing the number of people thought to be hereditarily strong (positive eugenics)".[6] The United States eugenics movement was not on the scale of the Nazi regime under Hitler, which aimed to "cleanse" the whole human race, but it was well underway, putting forth policies in science and medicine to stop those deemed "unfit" from reproducing. We should be attentive to this transition from seemingly noble goals to utter disregard for human dignity, which led immediately to atrocities against individuals. The mechanism by which this transition is effected is the denial of the right of the individual to be treated with the full dignity of a human person.

Another parallel between the rise of what is called "gender-affirming care" today and the trajectory of the abuses of the past has to do with the connection between ideology and political gain. The Nazis' medical human rights abuses in the twentieth century were a radical departure from the values Germany had previously upheld.

[5] "Eugenics Record Office".

[6] Michael A. Grodin, Erin L. Miller, and Johnathan I. Kelly, "The Nazi Physicians as Leaders in Eugenics and 'Euthanasia': Lessons for Today", *American Journal of Public Health* 108, no. 1 (2018): 54, https://doi.org/10.2105/AJPH.2017.304120.

Germany had not only been on the cutting edge of medical advances, but had established itself as a leader on the world stage of medical ethics. In fact, before the Nazis' rise to power, not only was informed consent required of human research subjects, but the foundations of the concept actually originated in German law, around 1900, with the Neisser case.[7]

The parallel we wish to draw here concerns an examination of how doctors in Germany, who up until this point had been exemplary in their practice of medical ethics, became capable of participating in such abuses. In the previous chapter on the history of the gender-affirmation movement, we saw groups and individuals associating themselves with unethical organizations and individuals to advance their own personal and political agendas. During the early twentieth century, doctors in Germany tended to be unemployed or underemployed, and this disenfranchisement led many to align themselves with the well-organized Nazi Party, in hopes of reattaining their prestige as medical professionals. The National Socialist German Physicians' League was formed in 1929 and "unified the goals of physicians and the State", with physicians "join[ing] the Nazi Party both earlier and in larger numbers than any other group of professionals".[8]

By 1942, thirty-eight thousand physicians had joined the ranks of the Nazi Party and were swept up in its ideology. The new pseudoscience of the eugenics movement

---

[7] Jochen Vollmann and Rolf Winau, "Informed Consent in Human Experimentation before the Nuremberg Code", *BMJ: British Medical Journal* 313, no. 7070 (1996): 1446, https://doi.org/10.1136/bmj.313.7070.1445. See also Jochen Vollmann, Rolf Winau, and J. H. Baron, "History of Informed Medical Consent", *The Lancet* 347, no. 8998 (February 10, 1996): 410, https://doi.org/10.1016/S0140-6736(96)90597-8.

[8] Vollmann and Winau, "Informed Consent", 53

was "cleansing" Germany of its Jewish inhabitants and others who were deemed "unfit": anyone whom the Nazi regime had designated as racially, physically, or mentally imperfect or weak. Physicians did what should always have been regarded as morally reprehensible, justifying and facilitating sterilization and euthanasia in order to "purify" the human race and leading the way in devaluing, dehumanizing, and murdering millions of human beings. According to the National World War II Museum, this number rose to "approximately six million European Jews and at least five million prisoners of war, Romany, Jehovah's Witnesses, homosexuals, and other victims".[9]

Among the most famous doctors within the Nazi regime was Josef Mengele, known as "the Angel of Death".[10] Mengele joined the Nazi Party in 1937, a year before he received his medical degree, and transferred to Auschwitz on May 30, 1943. He used this appointment to advance his career and establish himself as a scientist and researcher, having obtained his Ph.D. in anthropology and his M.D. in medicine. He is notorious for heinous experiments carried out on prisoners in the camps. Because of his training in genetics, he was fascinated with experimentation on fraternal and identical twins in order to understand genetic diseases and heredity. Tragically, he conducted much of this experimentation on children. None of his subjects were consenting volunteers. Mengele fled Auschwitz in 1945 when the Soviet Army was entering Poland and evaded capture. In the immediate postwar period, he was held in United States custody, but as the United States was "unaware that Mengele's name already stood on a list of

[9] "The Holocaust", National World War II Museum, accessed June 30, 2023, https://www.nationalww2museum.org/war/articles/holocaust.

[10] For a fuller analysis of Mengele, see Robert Jay Lifton, *The Nazi Doctors: Medical Killing and the Psychology of Genocide* (New York: Basic Books, 1986/2017), 337–83.

wanted war criminals", he was quickly released.[11] Until his death thirty-four years later, he lived mostly in Argentina.

In November of 1945, the Nuremberg Trials began. The four major allies—France, the Soviet Union, the United Kingdom, and the United States—established the International Military Tribunal (IMT) in order "to prosecute and punish 'the major war criminals of the European Axis'". In total, twenty-two senior political and military leaders were indicted, along with seven Nazi organizations that were deemed "criminal organizations".[12] The trial lasted eleven months, finding nineteen guilty and imposing punishments ranging from fifteen years in prison to death by hanging.

The aftermath of the Nuremberg Trials and the work of the IMT led to the ten-point Nuremberg Code of Ethics, which is still in use today. This code guides the ways in which human beings may be used in medical research, so that any experimentation that involves human subjects is "justified only if its results benefit society and it is carried out in accord with basic principles that 'satisfy moral, ethical, and legal concepts'".[13] The trials also had an effect on international criminal law, which would protect human beings from crimes against humanity, holding even a head of state criminally responsible for such crimes.[14] The

[11] "Josef Mengele", United States Holocaust Memorial Museum, April 2, 2009, https://encyclopedia.ushmm.org/content/en/article/josef-mengele.

[12] "The Nuremberg Trial and the Tokyo War Crimes Trials (1945–1948)", Office of the Historian, Department of State, United States of America, accessed June 30, 2023, https://history.state.gov/milestones/1945-1952/nuremberg.

[13] "Nuremberg Code", UNC Research, University of North Carolina at Chapel Hill, accessed June 30, 2023, https://research.unc.edu/human-research-ethics/resources/ccm3_019064.

[14] "The Influence of the Nuremberg Trial on International Criminal Law", Robert H. Jackson Center, accessed June 30, 2023, https://www.roberth jackson.org/speech-and-writing/the-influence-of-the-nuremberg-trial-on-international-criminal-law.

Nuremberg Code of Ethics arose from a recognition of the atrocities individuals and regimes are capable of when political ideologies rise to power, and we must never forget its principles.

The Tuskegee Experiment

The Tuskegee experiment is another example of the atrocities committed in the name of science when experiments fail to respect the dignity of the human person. It was formally known as the Tuskegee Study of Untreated Syphilis in the Negro Male, and it enrolled four hundred impoverished Black men in a longitudinal study on men with untreated syphilis. The experiment took place at Tuskegee University in Alabama, in collaboration with the United States Public Health Services, and lasted from 1932 to 1972. Over twenty years after it ended, President Bill Clinton apologized to all the victims, calling this experiment shameful and racist.[15]

There are four stages of syphilis. The first symptoms appear in the primary stage. If the disease is left untreated, it progresses to the second stage, with worsening symptoms. Again, if not properly treated, the disease progresses to the third phase, called the latent phase, where symptoms disappear but the disease remains in the body. Finally, if the patient still receives no treatment, the disease can progress to the fourth phase, which can damage organs, including the brain, and cause death.[16]

---

[15] The White House, Office of the Press Secretary, "Remarks by the President in Apology for the Study Done in Tuskegee", news release, May 16, 1997, https://clintonwhitehouse4.archives.gov/New/Remarks/Fri/19970516-898.html.

[16] "Syphilis—CDC Basic Fact Sheet", Centers for Disease Control and Prevention (CDC), last reviewed February 10, 2022, https://www.cdc.gov/std/syphilis/stdfact-syphilis.htm.

The men who were recruited for the study were all in the latent stage of syphilis. Many were not even told that they had the disease. They were offered a variety of incentives to participate in the study "such as a burial stipend, promises of free treatment (initially given to some men), and hot meals on clinic days".[17] At the beginning of the study in 1932, penicillin was not yet being used as a treatment for syphilis. But in 1943, when it became the treatment of choice for syphilis, the men in the study were not offered this treatment.[18]

Clearly, the ways these men were recruited and used in this study are breaches of the ethical guidelines for human participation in research experiments. The subjects in the study were the victims of coercive techniques. They received no benefit from their participation but were in fact exposed to harm when they were denied treatment. The Tuskegee study was a blatant example of government involvement in medical racial discrimination. In addition, these ethical violations have caused understandable long-standing skepticism toward science and medicine in the Black community, who witnessed this exploitation of the poor and vulnerable.

Some twenty-five years after the Nuremberg Trials, the National Research Act was passed in the United States in July of 1974. This act established the Institutional Review Board "to review biomedical and behavioral research involving human subjects".[19] The act also

[17] David M. Pressel, "Nuremberg and Tuskegee: Lessons for Contemporary American Medicine", *Journal of the National Medical Association* 95, no. 12 (2003): 1220.

[18] "The Syphilis Study at Tuskegee Timeline", Centers for Disease Control and Prevention (CDC), The U.S. Public Health Service Syphilis Study at Tuskegee, last reviewed December 5, 2022, https://www.cdc.gov/tuskegee /timeline.htm.

[19] "Institutional Review Board Overview", Fred Hutchinson Cancer Center Extranet, accessed June 30, 2023, https://extranet.fredhutch.org/en/u/irb /institutional-review-board-overview.html.

created a commission that met over a period of four years whose deliberations resulted in the Belmont Report in 1979, which "identifies basic ethical principles and guidelines that address ethical issues arising from the conduct of research with human subjects".[20] The guiding principles named in their report are respect of persons, beneficence, and justice.

The Tuskegee study is an especially important cautionary tale for us today because it is not so much a story of brute force, like the Nazi medical experiments, but of subtle coercion and especially of exploitation of the vulnerable.

The Lobotomy Experiment

A piece of history with even more striking parallels to the present situation surrounding medical treatment for gender dysphoria is the story of the use of lobotomies to treat mental illness—because like surgeries and hormone treatments used today, lobotomies were justified by the claim that they were of benefit to the patient. Another similarity is that the lobotomy was a treatment popularized and accepted without sufficient medical research to support it.

In 1949, Egas Moniz, a Portuguese neurologist, was awarded the Nobel Prize for his invention of the lobotomy. Moniz's theory was that people who suffered from obsessive-type behaviors had a problem with fixed circuits in the brain. The treatment he offered these patients involved drilling holes on either side or on the top of the

---

[20] "The Belmont Report", U.S. Department of Health & Human Services, last reviewed October 17, 2022, https://www.hhs.gov/ohrp/regulations-and -policy/belmont-report/index.html.

skull. He would then push a sharp instrument, called a leucotome, into the brain and sweep the instrument from side to side to cut the connections between the frontal lobe and the rest of the brain. After he had conducted this procedure on twenty of his patients, he reported dramatic improvements in their behavior. Walter Freeman, an American neurologist, embraced this theory and performed his first lobotomy in the United States in 1936. He is known for creating the "ice pick" method, which takes only minutes to cause damage to the prefrontal lobes of the brain by driving a pick through the bone of the eye socket. When the Nobel Prize was awarded to Moniz, it gave more credibility to the treatment, and more physicians began performing lobotomies.

Freeman alone is said to have performed thousands of these surgeries in the 1940s and 1950s. Howard Dully was only eleven years old when his father and stepmother first took him to see Freeman. According to journalist Elizabeth Day, Freeman's own notes describe him as "an average child, perhaps a little unruly but nothing that would strike one as exceptional for a boy of his age". In his memoir *My Lobotomy*, Dully recalls how his parents had him admitted to a hospital in December 1960, in San Jose, California. He was then taken into the operating room and given electrical shocks to sedate him—he does not remember much after that. The next day, when he woke up, he had a severe pain in his head. "I was in a mental fog," Dully says. "I was like a zombie; I had no awareness of what Freeman had done." Elizabeth Day comments:

What he didn't know was that he had been subjected to one of the most brutal surgical procedures in medical history. He had undergone a lobotomy and no one, not his parents, not the medical community or the state authorities, had intervened to stop it. More disturbingly, there seemed to have been no obvious necessity for the operation.[21]

With the development of new antipsychotic drugs with apparently beneficial results, the lobotomy went out of fashion. In 1967, Freeman performed his last lobotomy on a patient named Helen Mortensen, her third lobotomy from him, which resulted in her death by a cerebral hemorrhage.[22]

The recklessness with which this radical and extreme new treatment was adopted, along with the carelessness (as in Dully's case) with regard to diagnosis, should be warnings for us today.

The United States' Coerced Sterilization Policies of the Twentieth Century

Another historical lesson that we must not fail to learn from—this one with a special focus on the dignity of the human reproductive capacity—is the history of forced sterilizations in the United States in the twentieth century. Sir Francis Galton, the originator of the term "eugenics", believed that if "the best people" from "the finest families" married people with similar characteristics, they would have children who would make "a superlative species of

[21] Elizabeth Day, "He Was Bad, So They Put an Ice Pick in His Brain", *The Guardian*, January 13, 2008, https://www.theguardian.com/science/2008/jan/13/neuroscience.medicalscience. For Dully's story, see Howard Dully and Charles Fleming, *My Lobotomy: A Memoir* (New York: Three Rivers Press, 2007/2008).

[22] Emma Dibdin, "The Controversial History of the Lobotomy", Psych Central, May 6, 2022, https://psychcentral.com/blog/the-surprising-history-of-the-lobotomy. See also Clyde Haberman, "The Quest for a Psychiatric Cure", *The New York Times*, April 16, 2017, https://www.nytimes.com/2017/04/16/us/psychiatric-illnesses-lobotomy-controversial-surgery.html.

grace and quality".[23] By the early 1900s, biologist Charles Davenport, considered the father of the American eugenics movement for his widespread influence, set up the Eugenics Record Office (ERO) in Cold Spring Harbor, discussed above. Davenport and his colleague Harry Hamilton Laughlin also ran the Eugenics Research Association in affiliation with the American Association for the Advancement of Science. These organizations held powerful sway in the scientific community as well as within government bodies. Laughlin published what was seen as model legislation in 1922, which was "the bedrock of forced sterilization programs throughout the country".[24] Here is an excerpt from Laughlin's report under the heading "The Problem of the Feeble-Minded in Connecticut":

These 11,962 feeble-minded persons—the total number who came under the purview of the Survey—have been studied individually in reference to nine subjects as follows: (1) sex, (2) age, (3) recidivism, (4) diagnostic class, (5) intelligence quotient, (6) race descent, (7) nativity, (8) citizenship, (9) kin in institutions.... At the present rate every inhabitant of Connecticut is expending... five and one-third times as many dollars on the socially inadequate and the individually handicapped as the average inhabitant was spending for the same purpose twenty years ago.[25]

[23] Edwin Black, *War Against the Weak: Eugenics and America's Campaign to Create a Master Race* (New York: Four Walls Eight Windows, 2003), 15.

[24] Steven A. Farber, "U.S. Scientists' Role in the Eugenics Movement (1907–1939): A Contemporary Biologist's Perspective", *Zebrafish* 5, no. 4 (2008): 244, https://doi.org/10.1089/zeb.2008.0576.

[25] Carnegie Institution of Washington, *Year Book No. 37, July 1, 1937–June 30, 1938* (Washington, D.C.: Carnegie Institution of Washington, 1938), 61, 64. See also Farber, *Eugenics Movement*, 244, for a discussion of Laughlin's and Davenport's eugenical research.

Laughlin uses financial considerations to justify his eugenics program. The "unfit" were regarded as a financial burden on society and, as such, "undesirable", and government force was recruited to address the perceived problem, using the influence of people such as Woodrow Wilson, who as governor of New Jersey had signed into law a eugenic sterilization bill in 1911, permitting the forced sterilization of criminals or adults regarded as "feeble-minded".[26]

Wilson was not the only U.S. president to support eugenics. President Theodore Roosevelt also encouraged sterilization for criminals and individuals with cognitive disabilities, arguing that they must be "forbidden to leave offspring behind them".[27] If these policies were not enacted, he warned, the United States would be committing what he referred to as "race suicide"—meaning the "American race" would die out.[28] According to Roosevelt, stating what he says "is exactly [his] position":

> I wish very much that the wrong people could be prevented entirely from breeding; and when the evil nature of these people is sufficiently flagrant, this should be done. Criminals should be sterilized, and feeble-minded persons forbidden to leave offspring behind them. But as yet there is no way possible to devise which could prevent all undesirable people from breeding. The emphasis should be laid on getting desirable people to breed.[29]

[26] James W. Trent Jr., *Inventing the Feeble Mind: A History of Mental Retardation in the United States* (Berkeley, CA: University of California Press, 1994), 173.

[27] Theodore Roosevelt, "Twisted Eugenics", *The Outlook*, January 3, 1914: 31, quoted in Adam Cohen, *Imbeciles: The Supreme, American Eugenics, and the Sterilization of Carrie Buck* (New York: Penguin Books, 2016/2017), 3.

[28] On Roosevelt and "race suicide", see Linda Gordon, *The Moral Property of Women: A History of Birth Control Politics in America* (Urbana, IL: University of Illinois Press, 1974/2007), 86–104.

[29] Roosevelt, "Twisted Eugenics", 32. See also "Roosevelt and Race Suicide", *The Labor Journal* 18, no. 33 (September 3, 1915): 4.

It should be noted that Roosevelt appointed Justice Oliver Wendell Holmes Jr. to the Supreme Court, who wrote the opinion in the famous *Buck v. Bell* case, which upheld the Virginia law to sterilize those deemed "undesirable" or "inadequate". Carrie Buck, a young "feebleminded woman", had been committed by the state of Virginia to a mental institution. It was noted that three generations of the Buck family had suffered from Carrie's condition: Carrie's mother, Carrie herself, and Carrie's daughter, Vivian, who was conceived after Carrie had been raped (and because Carrie had been a victim of rape, she was described as "promiscuous"). Virginia law allowed for patients in state institutions to be sterilized to promote the health and well-being of the patient and, presumably, the welfare of society.

The crux of the case hinged on Carrie's due process, as she should have had a hearing to ascertain whether sterilization was to be permitted. Expert testimony was given by Dr. Arthur Estabrook, from the ERO. There was no hearing, and he did not test Carrie's IQ. When questioned, Estabrook replied, "Yes, sir. I talked to Carrie sufficiently so that with the record of mental examination—yes, I did. I gave a sufficient examination so that I consider her feebleminded."[30] The court ruling in 1927 upheld the Virginia law, with Holmes issuing his famous statement that in the court's opinion, "Three generations of imbeciles are enough"—a chilling statement to our ears today.[31] This Supreme Court decision paved the way for more than thirty states to legalize their involuntary coercive sterilization programs. California took the lead by forcibly sterilizing over twenty thousand

[30] Arthur Estabrook, quoted in Cohen, *Imbeciles*, 192.
[31] Buck v. Bell, 274 U.S. 200 (1927).

people in the twentieth century,[32] and it is estimated that nearly seventy thousand people were sterilized nationwide during this time.[33]

Have we learned anything from these dark periods of history? Many states still allow the involuntary sterilization of disabled people, although these laws are framed in terms of benefit to the subject and not eugenics.[34] However, far from rejecting eugenics as a society, we have now entered the phase of what is called the "new eugenics". Where the old eugenics stopped the "weak" from reproducing and encouraged the "fit" to procreate, the "new eugenics" seeks to design "better babies" through technological progress and enhancement, often in the name of the laudable desire of health for one's children.

Gattaca, a 1997 American dystopian science fiction movie, illustrates how the goal of building a "better race" can be presented in a way that seems innocuous on the surface. One particular scene in the movie illustrates how dangerous ideas can present themselves under the guise of simple concern for a child's health. Antonio and Marie live in a time when everyone born is genetically tested and labeled "valid" or "invalid" according to the results. Their first son, Vincent, was created the "old-fashioned way", and his genetic profile shows he has an increased chance of several kinds of diseases and has a calculated life-expectancy

[32] Lutz Kaelber, "California", Eugenics: Compulsory Sterilization in 50 American States, accessed June 30, 2023, https://www.uvm.edu/~lkaelber/eugenics/CA/CA.html.

[33] Adam Cohen, "The Supreme Court Ruling That Led to 70,000 Forced Sterilizations", interview by Terry Gross, NPR, March 7, 2016, https://www.npr.org/sections/health-shots/2016/03/07/469478098/the-supreme-court-ruling-that-led-to-70-000-forced-sterilizations.

[34] "Forced Sterilization of Disabled People in the United States", National Women's Law Center, January 24, 2022, https://nwlc.org/resource/forced-sterilization-of-disabled-people-in-the-united-states/.

of 30.2 years—thus, he has been labeled "invalid". As he gets older, he is assigned a menial job as a custodian. His parents regret their decision not to use reproductive technology that would have screened Vincent out. Now, wanting a second child, they have decided to do genetic testing prior to implantation to have a child who they hope will receive the "valid" status.

This particular scene begins with Antonio asking a geneticist, "We were just wondering if—if it is good to just leave a few things to chance?" The geneticist replies by casually framing the question in terms of the good of the child: "We want to give your child the best possible start. Believe me, we have enough imperfection built in already. Your child doesn't need any more additional burdens. Keep in mind, this child is still you. Simply, the best of you. You could conceive naturally a thousand times and never get such a result."[35] Vincent and Marie want to be good parents. Who wouldn't want to give his child "the best possible start"? They consent to genetic testing, and their son is born a perfectly healthy baby, thanks to the wonders of "progress".

Gattaca is science fiction, but the ideas it explores are historical fact. They can be seen, for example, in the "better babies" contests in the United States during the early 1900s at state fairs, where judges would rank babies according to their health—and eventually these contests expanded so that both babies and whole families were chosen for their lineage, their perfect health, their flawlessness—just as animals are judged at a county fair. These contests initially "sought to amuse and promote wellness, but from their inception, they also lent popular exposure to the study of eugenics, which, in the early part of the 20th

[35] *Gattaca*, directed by Andrew Niccol (Sony Pictures Releasing, 1997).

century, became increasingly acceptable as an enlightened science."[36]

The "positive eugenics" of the past and the imaginary future are alive and well today in technologies such as pre-implantation genetic screening, which allows parents to choose or reject embryos on the basis of their genetic profile because of factors like familial genetic diseases or even sex. Such techniques make the relationship between "positive" and "negative" eugenics clear—the desire for "better babies" ends with the destruction of embryos judged "unfit". The same thinking that drives preimplantation screening drives prenatal testing. It has been estimated that from 60 to 90 percent of children diagnosed with Down syndrome are aborted in the United States, compared to 18 percent of all pregnancies.[37] The "old" eugenics has transitioned seamlessly into the "new" eugenics, which still prefers the "strong" over the "weak", the genetically intelligent over those with intellectual disabilities, and the mentally and physically healthy over those declared "feeble-minded".

Lessons to Be Learned

What lessons should have been learned from the Nuremberg Trials, the Tuskegee experiment, the lobotomy experiment, and the forced sterilization practices in the United States? How do these scandals help us assess the claim that

---

[36] Francine Uenuma, "'Better Babies' Contests Pushed for Much-Needed Infant Health but Also Played into the Eugenics Movement", *Smithsonian*, January 17, 2019, https://www.smithsonianmag.com/history/better-babies-contests-pushed-infant-health-also-played-eugenics-movement-180971288.

[37] Jaime L. Natoli et al., "Prenatal Diagnosis of Down Syndrome: A Systematic Review of Termination Rates (1995–2011)", *Prenatal Diagnosis* 32, no. 2 (February 2012): 150, https://doi.org/10.1002/pd.2910.

we can medically and surgically alter the bodies of children who suffer from gender dysphoria as a cure for their emotional and psychological problems?

The Nuremberg Trials drew important conclusions about the experimental use of human beings as research subjects, and these conclusions were written up as the Nuremberg Code.[38] Experimentation on humans must do no harm and not produce unnecessary physical or mental suffering or disabling injury. There must be a direct benefit to the person that outweighs any risk of harm or injury, and there must be informed consent. Clearly, the principles of the Nuremberg Code were violated not only in Nazi Germany, but also in the lobotomy experiment and the Tuskegee experiment.

Are these principles also being violated today in the case of medical treatments such as puberty blockers, fertility preservation, cross-sex hormones, and surgical interventions for gender dysphoria? The first question is whether such treatments should be considered experimental.

Finland's Council for Choices in Health Care's report[39] asserts, under the section on "Risks, Benefits, and Uncertainty", that cross-sex hormone therapy did not alleviate children's problems with "functioning, progression of developmental tasks of adolescence, and psychiatric symptoms" and cites another recent study that arrived at the same conclusion. It continues:

[38] Jon F. Merz, "The Nuremberg Code and Informed Consent for Research", *JAMA (The Journal of the American Medical Association)* 319, no. 1 (2018): 85–86, https://doi.org/10.1001/jama.2017.17704.

[39] Council for Choices in Health Care, "Recommendation of the Council for Choices in Health Care in Finland (PALKO/COHERE Finland): Medical Treatment Methods for Dysphoria Related to Gender Variance in Minors", 2020, https://segm.org/sites/default/files/Finnish_Guidelines_2020_Minors _Unofficial%20Translation.pdf.

Potential risks of GnRH therapy include disruption in bone mineralization and the *as yet unknown* effects on the central nervous system. In [boys], early pubertal suppression inhibits penile growth, requiring the use of alternative sources of tissue grafts for a potential future vaginoplasty. The effect of pubertal suppression and cross-sex hormones on fertility is *not yet known*.[40]

Finally, in its conclusion, the report states:

In light of available evidence, gender reassignment of minors is an experimental practice. Based on studies examining gender identity in minors, hormonal interventions may be considered before reaching adulthood in those with firmly established transgender identities, but it must be done with a great deal of caution, and no irreversible treatment should be initiated. Information about the potential harms of hormone therapies is accumulating slowly and is not systematically reported. It is critical to obtain information on the benefits and risks of these treatments in rigorous research settings.[41]

Finland now sees the importance of giving young people good psychological therapies and of not rushing them into experimental treatments that lack information on potential short- and long-term harms.[42]

---

[40] "Medical Treatment Methods for Dysphoria", 6 (emphasis added).

[41] "Medical Treatment Methods for Dysphoria", 8.

[42] For a critique of informed consent in "gender-affirming care" for children, adolescents, and young adults, see Stephen B. Levine, E. Abbruzzese, and Julia W. Mason, "Reconsidering Informed Consent for Trans-Identified Children, Adolescents, and Young Adults", *Journal of Sex & Marital Therapy* 48, no. 7 (2022), https://doi.org/10.1080/0092623X.2022.2046221, and Stephen B. Levine and E. Abbruzzese, "Current Concerns about Gender-Affirming Therapy in Adolescents", *Current Sexual Health Reports* no. 15 (2023), https://link.springer.com/article/10.1007/s11930-023-00358-x?fbclid=IwAR100mWkC9hrLftTqDrcxhdVZZsrAcpEUBx--jaLDAeTp2hYGs1qg2bmdO4.

This first problem—the experimental nature of these medical treatments—leads to the second question: Can meaningful informed consent be given when the science and research are so unsettled? What are the criteria for full consent? First, consent must be fully voluntarily; consent out of the desire to receive money, benefits, or privileges in exchange for participation in a study does not constitute a free and voluntary form of consent. In addition, there are four criteria that must be met to ensure that the consent given is truly informed: adequate decision-making capacity, proper documentation of the consent, disclosure, and competency.

How can minor children and young adults with comorbidities such as autism (people with autism are overrepresented among those with gender dysphoria),[43] body dysmorphia, gender dysphoria, psychological trauma, and mental health issues possibly meet the requirements of informed consent regarding decision-making capacity and competency? Disclosure is impossible, because information about potential harms is incomplete. Do minor children with these sorts of comorbidities have decision-making capacity? How can they possibly be competent to make decisions around fertility preservation? Can they fully understand or imagine that they may be losing their ability to have children in the future?

Finally, the Nuremburg Code explicitly states that any experiment must not result in unnecessary physical or mental suffering or disabling injury. The regret voiced by the detransitioners in the following stories clearly shows how the bodies of these young people were unnecessarily harmed, permanently damaged, or irreparably injured.

---

[43] "Medical Treatment Methods for Dysphoria".

3

Helena

Helena says that when she was a child, nobody would have described her as gender-nonconforming or a tomboy.[1] She fit in with other little girls and liked dressing up and playing with make-up and Barbie dolls. She liked some "boy things", but overall, nobody would have pegged her as different from other girls. She doesn't recall a time when she was young that involved feeling any kind of distress at being a girl, being female, or doing stereotypically feminine things.

She describes losing her primary caretaker when she was very young and how difficult that was for her and the emotional struggles that followed. Her family wasn't comfortable talking about such matters, preferring to ignore emotional problems and brush them under the rug—but the loss upset her for many years. By the time she turned thirteen, she was depressed. She did not want to socialize, preferring to spend time alone. Her depression and isolation caused her to develop an eating disorder and to engage in self-harming behavior. All these factors led her to explore online groups, where she found other girls her age who shared her musical interests.

---

[1] Helena, interview by Jennifer Lahl, Pleasant Hill, California, February 24, 2022. All quotations from Helena in this chapter are taken from this interview.

At age fourteen, she was spending a lot of time online, especially on Tumblr. There she picked up on an underlying theme with regard to gender that she thought offered her clues about her depression and isolation: messages like "If you don't fit in, that's a sign you're trans" and "If you don't like your body, then that's a sign you're trans." The suggestion was that the solution to these feelings was to transition, and then she would fit in and like her body. Through hours of online engagement, she began to think that she was a boy—a feminine boy.

Her family noticed the resultant changes in her behavior and took her to a few therapists. She says she didn't connect with the therapists and wishes she had just received support from the people around her, who knew her. She had no respect for the therapists, who failed to understand her, which led her to rebel against them. At school, no one reached out to her even though she was clearly in distress and struggling. But, she says, when she finally came out as trans, "They all wanted to bend over backwards to help me be trans."

Helena spent most of her waking hours connecting with other adolescents on Tumblr whose belief system was heavily influenced by social justice ideology, which creates a hierarchy of oppression and privilege: the more oppressed a person is, the more her opinion counts and the more she is listened to and validated, but a privileged person has no right to an opinion. On Tumblr, she reports, "people just think it's okay to be mean" to a privileged person, and they will even "tell you to kill yourself" because you are "privileged".

Helena was torn. On the one hand she had found a community of girls who had similar interests and personalities, people she could relate to; on the other hand, she was being made to feel guilty because she was a "cis straight white girl", and she was constantly feeling as if she had to apologize for herself. At fifteen, she decided that the best way to deal with this discomfort was to change her pronouns from "she/her" to "they/them". Immediately, people started to treat her better. This acceptance reinforced the self-talk that had started with the messages she had received on Tumbler: "I don't fit in, I don't like my body, so I must be trans." This inner feedback loop kept her on the lookout for what more she could do to come across as less privileged and to provide more evidence that she was transgender.

The affirmation from her online community felt good and seemed to make sense—and she got carried away. After she changed her pronouns, she spoke of herself as "nonbinary". Then she declared herself to be a "demi-girl", which means *close to* being a girl, but *not quite* a girl—therefore "trans". It took her a year or two before she started referring to herself as a "boy". In the beginning, she didn't want to change her body to look more like that of a boy, but the feedback loop playing in her mind, along with the community support and validation, led her to cut her hair and to start dressing more like the boy she thought she really was.

There was another element to the social media she was using that stoked her growing confusion: the prevalence and normalization of pornography. She was ten years old when she was first exposed to pornography online, and she recalls how it disturbed her for days, causing her to make up her mind as a little girl never to get married and never to have sex, but instead to adopt children. Yet here she was in online communities where young people had pro-pornography conversations every day. The conversations went far beyond discussion about how to be comfortable in, and accepting of, one's own body. In fact, they constructed a new hierarchy surrounding how "kinky" one can be. One online conversation, for example, was about rape, "knife play", and "gun play". At this point in her life, she had never held a boy's hand, gone on a date, or even flirted. But she worried that if she revealed her true feelings about these violent pornographic fantasies— that they were "gross and really scary"—her community would brand her an "antifeminist". So she felt she had to play along.

She still had not told her family of her transition, confiding only in her close friend group, who were all also identifying as "trans". (Notably, she says, the members of this group also no longer consider themselves "trans".) Finally, in her senior year of high school, she told her parents that she wanted to be "trans", and they reacted negatively. They didn't like her decision and they didn't support it, and that caused even more distance between her and her family. If her decision to become trans was discussed at home, it usually ended up in a huge fight. On the other hand, her friends were very supportive, and when she finally discussed her new identity with the staff at her high school, the guidance counselor referred her to the school psychologist. Both the guidance counselor and the school psychologist encouraged her and told her that they were very sorry that her parents were not accepting of her, but that they would help her.

About two years later, Helena felt the desire to make her body look more masculine, and she decided to begin testosterone treatment. She tried to persuade her parents to take her to the children's hospital gender clinic, but they refused. At that time, without her parents' consent, she had to wait until she turned eighteen before she could access the testosterone treatment. As soon as she turned eighteen, she made an appointment with Planned Parenthood, where she knew she could receive testosterone. She had one appointment, which lasted about an hour. She spoke for about twenty minutes with a social worker, who asked her a handful of questions such as "What are you expecting to get out of it?" Helena answered that she would be much happier and would not be depressed or suicidal anymore. She was told she was the perfect candidate for testosterone. She was next sent to see the nurse practitioner, who gave her a packet of information on the basis of which she was to provide her informed consent. The information included a very short list of risks. The nurse practitioner was going to prescribe a small dose to start with, but Helena told her that she wanted a higher dose on the grounds that, as she recalls saying, "I have excess estrogen, because my thighs and breasts are big." The nurse practitioner asked Helena what dosage she wanted, and Helena asked for "the highest we can go". She received her prescription for 100 mg per week at that first Planned Parenthood visit.

After her initial dose of testosterone, and a few weeks following, she did not feel much of a change in her body. In the subsequent weeks, though, she started to notice that she was more prone to anger and that her sex drive was heightened. She noticed that small things would set her off and she didn't enjoy being around people. She began to avoid social settings because she knew she would become irritated. Before the testosterone treatment, she had felt she had an average sex drive, but the effects of the testosterone caused anything remotely sexual to overwhelm her. She describes herself as feeling "out of control" and says that her anger made her feel as though she was possessed. But she didn't understand that these changes were a side effect of the testosterone surging through her female body.

With the continued high dosage of testosterone, her anger kept getting worse. In the past, she might have cried or raised her voice in response to anger, but now she experienced explosions of extreme rage within herself that made her feel like she wanted to break things and hurt people. In order to control this strong urge to do harm, she turned her rage inward and hurt herself instead. She felt completely out of control.

Eventually, she hurt herself so badly that she needed to go to the emergency department for treatment. The staff at the hospital said that she should be checked into the psychiatric unit because she was a danger to herself. She stayed there for about a week and was diagnosed with borderline personality disorder and psychosis and prescribed four different medications.

No one connected her testosterone use to these drastic changes in her behavior. Upon discharge from the hospital, with her new antidepressant and antipsychotic medications, she still noted no improvement in her mental health. "My life just became a total disaster," she says. "I wasn't functioning at all. I wasn't holding down a job. I wasn't going to school ... I just felt like a monster."

Helena was on testosterone for a total of seventeen months. After about a year, she developed anxiety over giving herself the testosterone injection. She would sit and cry for hours before she could take the three-inch needle and jab it into her thigh muscle. She would procrastinate, telling herself, "It's too late to do it now; I'll just wait until next week." Eventually, she was only giving herself one or two shots a month instead of one a week. Then, after a couple of months, she realized that taking the hormone had been a mistake, and she quit completely.

The entire time she was on testosterone, none of the professionals caring for her connected any of the symptoms she was experiencing to the hormone treatment. It was not until she had stopped the testosterone that she noticed she wasn't having "these insane rage meltdowns anymore". All her symptoms went away, and she started feeling like herself again. Despite the high dosage, she had not experienced many physical changes from the testosterone—only that her voice became deeper and she lost the ability to make higher-pitched sounds. As for facial hair, she had only grown a small, wispy mustache, which eventually vanished.

Even before Helena started her transition, she had thought she would go on to have surgeries in order to complete her move from female to male. When she went to Planned Parenthood to get her testosterone, she told the practitioners of her plans for chest surgery and facial masculinization surgery. One of her co-workers had told her about an organization in the city where she was living that would give grants to people to cover their transition surgery costs. She began applying for a grant but kept procrastinating. As her life spun out of control from the hormones, she was unable to go through all the steps required, including arranging appointments with surgeons and dealing with her insurance provider. She was beginning to realize that what she was doing was not making her happy, that transitioning wasn't helping her. So, she continued to procrastinate—and this procrastination, she believes, is what saved her from taking the drastic step of surgery.

After being discharged from the hospital for a mental health crisis a second time, she thought, "What the hell has my life become?" Transitioning was not turning out to be what she had expected. She had thought she was going to blossom and finally become her authentic self. But instead, she had become profoundly dysfunctional.

About this time, someone close to her had made a video montage of pictures of her with a friend. The photos were in chronological order, dating from the time when she and this friend had met—which was a few days after she had started to use the testosterone—up until more recent times. On watching the video, she was suddenly struck by how unhappy and unwell she looked in the later pictures. Once she noticed that progression, she thought, "My God, this has all been a mistake—*everything*. From the first moment that I changed my pronouns on Tumblr, it has all been a mistake." She cried at the painful realization that she had been lying to herself the whole time.

She was now nineteen years old and had only one or two people to whom she was close. She confided her new attitude to one friend who also called herself trans, who became very upset with Helena—although eventually, this friend came to the same realization and also detransitioned. Helena's parents, on the other hand, were happy with her decision to detransition, but she says their reaction still didn't bring her any closer to them.

To Helena, detransitioning meant both stopping the medical treatments and no longer presenting herself as transgender. It meant understanding that she had never been and could never become a member of the opposite sex.

For the first few months after she decided to detransition, Helena thought she was one of the only people to whom this had ever happened. It didn't occur to her that others might also experience regret over their decision to transition. But then she found online forums and feminist communities where other girls were posting about similar experiences. She also discovered groups for parents of children who considered themselves to be transgender, where the parents were talking about their daughters' personalities and interests—and the girls being described seemed a lot like her.

Through these parents' groups, she learned about rapid-onset gender dysphoria (ROGD) and the research of physician and scientist Dr. Lisa Littman on gender dysphoria and detransitioners.[2] Helena could see her own patterns of behavior in Littman's interviews with parents, and she felt that Litttman's findings perfectly described her own experience.

She also came to learn that Dr. Littman and her research were being targeted by trans activists and that there was a lot of misinformation circulating in the trans community intended to discourage people from looking critically at facts that challenge the trans agenda and to encourage attacks on the kind of dissent that was expressed in Dr. Littman's work.

Helena told her story publicly on Twitter, expressing agreement with Dr. Littman's research and using her own history as an example of ROGD. The response made her realize that there were a lot of people going through this: not just a handful, but thousands. The feeling that she belonged to only a small minority of people who regretted their decision to transition dissipated as she began to talk to detransitioners with experiences similar to her own. Many of them were interesting and smart people, she discovered, who could help her understand her experience. She says, "It wasn't enough for me to just detransition and get on with my life. I really wanted to understand what had happened to me, and I wanted to understand what was going on in the world, because there are just so many people getting caught up in this."

[2] See Lisa Littman, "Parent Reports of Adolescents and Young Adults Perceived to Show Signs of a Rapid Onset of Gender Dysphoria", PLOS ONE 13, no. 8 (2018), https://doi.org/10.1371/journal.pone.0202330.

Before detransitioning, Helena had a friend who also considered herself trans. She recalls getting a text from this friend saying that she thought she was having regrets about her decision. Helena remembers feeling overcome with fear. Here was a friend who seemed very similar to her, and to whom she related closely; if this friend now regretted transitioning, what did this mean for Helena? What did she have to confront in herself? Helena desperately tried to talk her friend out of detransitioning, which she still regrets, because she feels her friend was probably correct in questioning what she was doing.

Now that Helena sees gender ideology from a different point of view, it is difficult for her to understand how anyone who has experienced what it's like to be a teenager can fail to understand how unprepared adolescents are to make such life-changing decisions. Teenagers do not have developed foresight and can't realistically picture being adults—they tend to get attached to the idea that appeals to them at the moment and think their perspective will never change. It is hard for Helena to understand how the physicians, therapists, and school personnel she spoke with lacked this common-sense understanding of adolescent experiences, and she believes it is irresponsible for people who work with adolescents not to take a look at the demographics and observe the rise of gender confusion in adolescent girls. A responsible, ethical person who thinks critically and rationally would surely know that we must not allow adolescents, who are in a state of emotional and intellectual immaturity, to make permanent life-changing decisions based on incomplete knowledge.

The bare minimum of proper care for adolescents, she reflects, must surely include recognizing the possibility that there is more to their story than appears on the surface.

She is disappointed that even these very basic professional expectations are no longer being met—that adults with authority are willing to say, "Let's carry out these permanent medical changes to your body."

4

Grace

At the time of our interview with Grace, she was twenty-eight years old.[1] She was twenty-two when she made the decision to transition and began injecting testosterone into her body. About five months later, she underwent what is called "top surgery"—a double mastectomy. A few months after her surgery, she started to realize that she had made a big mistake. She explains that leading up to her transition was a whole journey of questioning her gender and experiencing gender problems, which had been a recurring theme since she was nineteen. Her personal gender problems amounted to "a lifelong preoccupation and discomfort" with her body, although looking back now, she sees this discomfort as common among young women.

The reason she initially started identifying as "trans" was that she had always been a person oriented toward social justice issues. She was passionate about issues surrounding homosexuality and transgenderism, and, as a teenager, she had stumbled upon the website Tumblr, which had influenced her thinking. She describes herself as very idealistic and very passionate about systemic inequality, and that was the lens through which she viewed the world.

---

[1] Grace, interview by Jennifer Lahl, New York City, June 25, 2022. All quotations from Grace in this chapter are taken from this interview.

When she began college, she became engaged in "deconstructing gender"—meaning dismantling "the binary of male and female"—which involved engaging with the concepts of "nonbinary identity", "queer feminist" analysis, and breaking down the hierarchies of society. At nineteen to twenty years of age, she started to call herself nonbinary. She didn't feel that she fit into the social stereotype of a woman and was uncomfortable being seen as a woman. She recounts that at this time, she was preoccupied with—even neurotic about—how people saw her, and she restricted her eating so as to stay thin. She was uncomfortable in social settings, describing herself as "one of these intense young women who hadn't really figured out her place in the world"—and she interpreted this sense of discomfort to mean that she was "nonbinary". While still presenting herself as a woman, she began identifying as nonbinary, which confused people. Because her locus of understanding the world was her preoccupation with how people perceived her and how she was "slotted into society", their confusion made her feel oppressed and judged. In retrospect, she sees that her thinking was maladaptive.

After she graduated from college, Grace had a mental health crisis, which led to some serious consequences. She was experiencing a lack of direction from no longer being in the kind of structured environment that college had provided. She was struggling to figure out what to do with herself and felt lost and depressed. She suffered from suicidal thoughts. She began to focus on her body, especially on "fixing" it—because this was something that she felt was under her control.

During this period, she had some friends who had started to transition medically. She always felt that she fit in with the "trans" crowd, because to her they seemed artistic, cool, and quirky—"my kind of people". Medically transitioning just seemed to be something that people like Grace were doing, and, in her mind, it made sense for her to do so too. She concluded that the reason she had always been so obsessed with her body, why she had always been so restrictive in her eating and ended up being so skinny, was all because, apparently, she did not have "the right body".

She describes this realization as something like a religious experience. Finally, she thought, she had discovered something that would make her feel better. If she could "become a man", she would finally stop feeling such discomfort with herself and with her own body. The idea of "becoming a man" also appealed to her because she had idealized the experience of men in society. If she could shed the expectations that society imposes on women, she thought, she would feel comfortable, safe, and able to be herself.

Almost everyone else in her circles encouraged her in the decision to transition, but her parents were definitely not excited by her plans. They had accepted her claim to be nonbinary as an expression of her individuality, but they were unhappy with her plan to transition medically. Wanting to be supportive, however, they did not try to stop her. They thought she knew what she was doing and assumed she needed to go forward with her transition.

During her transition, Grace went to a therapist who specialized in "LGBT issues" in Indiana. In retrospect, she thinks the therapist was not very well informed about the transgender issue: she did not seem to understand the context of the current cultural discourse around what gender means to people who call themselves "trans", and she did not know the World Professional Association for Transgender Health (WPATH) Standards of Care. Looking back, Grace says it was a mistake to go to this therapist, who told her, "Well, it sounds like you've got a good idea of what you're doing." She went through a few sessions, explaining that she was having suicidal thoughts and that she believed transitioning would help her, and the therapist simply affirmed her decision to transition medically. She stopped seeing the therapist but did go back for one more visit, because she needed a letter from a therapist stating that Grace was a good candidate for "top surgery". Her informed consent process was minimal. The therapist asked Grace, "Why do you want to do this?" and Grace replied, "Being a woman is not working for me anymore." The therapist said, "All right, sounds good." That was the entirety of the assessment.

Prior to her top surgery, Grace had been taking testosterone. It made her feel like she was becoming a whole new person: "It felt like being born again," she says, as if she were making a new start and at last becoming her true self. It made her feel euphoric—it was acting like an antidepressant. Before, she had been weepy and sad, but now all her negative feelings were gone and she felt stronger, no longer lost. And she was getting physically stronger too: "I got these awesome arm muscles without even trying." The testosterone made her breasts shrink, and she started losing body fat, becoming leaner. She was growing a lot of body hair on her face, legs, and stomach. Something transformative was happening, she felt. She was finally becoming a new person.

While it was all "very exciting at first", she recalls she had a "small, underlying anxiety, beneath the excitement, that was a fear that I might be doing something wrong". She brushed these feelings aside, telling herself that this was just "internalized transphobia" and that her reaction had been shaped by our "transphobic" society, but there was always a little worry beneath the surface. One little red flag was that with the testosterone's effect on her vocal cords, she began to lose her nice soprano singing voice. She was sad to hear it go, for she had always loved to sing. She recalls saying to her mother, "I'm like the Little Mermaid. I have to give up my voice to become a real person." She adds, "My mother said, 'That's really sad.' And I said, 'Yeah, it is sad.'" At the time, though, she figured this was a sacrifice she needed to make. In spite of the sadness of losing her pretty soprano singing voice, she still thought she was on the right path. What she was doing felt right because she had been so lost and hopeless before.

Once Grace started transitioning, her path seemed to become clearer, and she began to feel a lot of hope. Soon she would look more male and be able to pass as a man. After surgery, she thought, she would be in a body that fit her better, and that would improve her ability to function in general. She even entertained the possibility of a career in gender medicine or of getting a nursing degree so that she could help people transition. She began dressing in a more masculine way and adopted an androgynous name, planning to change it again after surgery to something fully masculine when she could integrate into society as a man. But she never got to this step, because after her double mastectomy surgery, things took a dramatic turn for the worse.

In the days leading up to her surgery, Grace developed an enormous amount of anxiety about it. She was ruminating over it and spending a lot of time online looking at trans influencers who had the male body that she wanted. She read happy testimonials. She also detected a lot of fear online within the trans community at this time. With Donald Trump's presidency, people were worried that it would become illegal to transition. Grace now feels embarrassed that she let these fears push her into a life-changing decision. She says it was "such a madness-of-crowds moment, but it really affected me at the time"; specifically, it pressured her to have her surgery while it was still available to her. At the same time, though, she recognized a double mastectomy was a really serious big step, which was very scary. But many of her friends told her, "You're ready. You can do it." People were encouraging her because they had all read the "how-to-be-a-trans-ally" literature.

Grace also believed that surgery was the only way she could deal with her gender dysphoria and her obsession and discomfort with her own body—she was aware of no other options that would help her deal with her emotions. So she concluded that having the surgery was the best thing for her to do.

At the age of twenty-three, Grace underwent a double mastectomy. She expected to feel emotional improvement, just as she had when starting on testosterone. She expected to feel less depressed, more purposeful, and more hopeful for the future because she would be "finding her true self". But after surgery, still incredibly weak and on painkillers, she was immediately hit with deep regret, the sense that she had made a huge mistake. When she would look down at her body and see "weeping gashes" on her chest, she was struck by an "undeniable 'Oh no! What have I done?'" Of course, she turned to the internet to find out if there were others who had had these post-surgery feelings and found accounts from people who had experienced these intense, even suicidal, feelings of despair, but who had "overcome" them. So, she decided her reaction must be normal—that she had not made a mistake and she could expect these feelings to dissipate over time.

She continued on her path of transitioning, but her doubts remained. In pursuing next steps, while researching phalloplasty surgeries, she came across a blog that echoed her own realization that although she now had a flat chest like a man's, her hips were still wide like a woman's. How can that be addressed? There's no such thing as hip bone removal surgery. Plans started to take shape in her mind: "Okay. So now I have to work out. I need to make my shoulders as broad as possible." But these thoughts didn't give her peace.

Grace further studied the blog she had discovered. The writer said that she had started out just wanting to masculinize her face with testosterone, but then she had realized that she also wanted a flat chest—followed by a desire for phalloplasty surgery. It dawned on her that her dysphoria was simply moving from one part of her body to another. At that moment, Grace realized that the process of transitioning would never be complete for her, and that even if she did everything she could do to masculinize her body, she might very well still be miserable. This realization terrified her. She had already made irrevocable changes with testosterone and surgery, and there might not be light at the end of this tunnel after all. She realized that while testosterone may have helped, the surgery was physically awful and made her feel not like a man, but only like a woman who has had her breasts cut off.

Coming to terms with what she had done was a gradual process. She decided to stop taking testosterone, telling herself that maybe she was just "nonbinary" and not a "trans man". Next, she reclaimed her name and started to ask to be called Grace again, a solid step back toward self-acceptance. Slowly, she began to see that her interpretation of her gender dysphoria as her inner "trans" identity asserting itself was based on an artificial framework. This realization allowed her to take another important step: understanding that in trying to delete the fact that she was female, she had only maimed her body and hurt herself.

She had not changed anything for the better in doing so; she had only made herself more miserable.

Taking these steps back toward reality helped Grace move away from her obsession with her gender and her body and what she describes as her "leftist style of being really worried about how people were perceiving me and how I was affected in society". This move was a big paradigm shift away from her maladaptive approach, and it allowed her to embrace maturity and take care of herself as she really was. Becoming a man had been a fantasy, she realized. Her problems would be better addressed by first accepting that she was a woman.

Grace sees how young people can struggle with coming to terms with their body and the changes they undergo during puberty, and she acknowledges they can have doubts about their sexuality and experience discomfort with it. She believes these factors can contribute to dissatisfaction with their body and gender. During her "nonbinary" phase, she dated mostly men, but also some women. She did not consider herself a lesbian, but she thought that she was perhaps bisexual, and these thoughts made her feel even more isolated. At the time she was transitioning, she was dating a straight man who eventually became her husband. Although she has settled into a heterosexual marriage, she remains sympathetic and understanding toward people with the deep anxiety that comes from feeling abnormal, which, as she knows, can support the false conclusion that one has been "born in the wrong body".

The long-term health problems caused by surgery and hormones are still in need of further study. In the meantime, the effects of the testosterone linger for Grace—her soprano singing voice did not return. Now in her twenties and newly married, she is thinking about having children, and she is worried that the testosterone may have affected her fertility. When asked about whether she will have breast reconstructive surgery, she is unsure. Her insurance provider covered the removal of her healthy breasts but will not cover reconstructive surgery. She is unhappy with how she looks without breasts, but she knows that any surgery carries risk.

Grace is deeply grateful for her relationship with her husband, who has been with her throughout this whole ordeal. While he was not happy when Grace was attempting to transition, he supported her because he loved her and wanted her to be happy. He was also the one who supported her during her detransition, when everything fell apart for her. She says he was willing to accept her at every stage of the journey and pulled her through.

These days, Grace is doing well. It has been important for her to move on and build a life, and she has lost her obsession with social forces beyond her control that gripped her when she was younger. She finds it empowering to talk to other detransitioners and to write about her story on her Substack account. She wants to raise awareness that there is life after detransition, even after making serious physical changes to one's body, and to remind people that "humans are very resilient. Humans survive all kinds of things."

Yet Grace worries about young people who are being convinced that transitioning is the answer to problems that would actually be better solved in another way, and this drives her passion to speak out. Becoming an adult can be difficult and painful, and she has a special understanding of the anguish girls can experience. She insists that their pain must not be trivialized and that it is important to help them make sense of their discomfort with their body.

The prevailing interpretation is that gender dysphoria indicates that a person is in "the wrong body" and *must* transition or die. In reality, there are many different reasons why people experience gender dysphoria and therefore many different ways to address this distress, depending on its cause. Grace believes that what is sorely missing is more clinician competency in the different ways that gender dysphoria can be handled.

Grace also hopes for better understanding in the broader culture, since that is the source of many vulnerable people's belief that they were born in the wrong body. Broadening the discourse and learning about the many ways to treat gender dysphoria will be helpful for everyone, especially practitioners who treat children.

The safeguarding of children and adolescents today is a real concern. Grace's experience shows how misleading the messages and claims our children are hearing can be. The real possibility of informed consent is also a serious question, given the current state of gender medicine research, particularly what is called "gender-affirming care" and its uncritical model. The claim that "the science is settled" is simply false: there are no good studies on the long-term effects of this treatment, and the studies that do exist have a high dropout rate. The scientific facts should be fully established before minors are given medical and surgical treatments that can do irreparable harm.

The backlash Grace experienced after appearing on *60 Minutes* with Lesley Stahl was intense, even though the episode was remarkably balanced and the detransitioners in the segment were just talking about their own personal experiences. Grace says Stahl told her that this was "the most pushback they've gotten on any episode before it even aired". Detransitioners need to have their stories told, heard, and understood. This is a population with real needs, and the voices of the detransitioners can no longer be denied or ignored. Even with this backlash and the accusation of being a hateful person, Grace remains hopeful. She predicts it will be an ugly time with legislative fighting. And while we try to figure out how to make things better, there will be people who continue to offer hormones and carry out surgeries, so that many people will still be hurt.

5

Nick

We sat down with Nick when he was twenty-nine years old.[1] When Nick was in elementary school, he says he was creative and sensitive, with "over the top" energy. He was the leader of his group of friends, always coming up with ideas for games they could play, and he loved to draw comics. Because of his high energy, his parents and teachers had a hard time keeping him under control, but he says it's strange to think back on those days—he hasn't been like that for a long time. During puberty he started to gradually shut down.

He describes his family life during elementary school as "weird and confusing". He felt as though family members were disconnected from each other, but he didn't know why. He had nothing to compare his experience of family life to and no help to make sense of these feelings, so he concluded that his parents simply didn't have a close relationship and that they were very different from each other. For example, although his mother wouldn't have described herself as a feminist, Nick thinks she fit the description, at least partially, whereas his father was quite the opposite. His father had New England sensibilities:

[1] Nick, interview by Jennifer Lahl and Kallie Fell, Providence, Rhode Island, July 17, 2023. All quotations from Nick in this chapter are taken from this interview.

people should be polite and noncompetitive in social settings. He also had certain expectations surrounding masculinity, and he pushed Nick into sports and working with his hands. When his father would try to instill those "masculine" skills, his mother would undermine her husband, saying, "Nick doesn't need to do anything he doesn't want to do." He realizes now that teaching your children to work and help around the house is important, along with finding healthy outlets for a boy's natural competitiveness. But the tension between his parents sent him a lot of mixed messages.

Nick had a very good relationship with his older brother, who shared his sense of disconnectedness within the family. While they weren't always comfortable expressing their emotions, they saw eye to eye on many things. He looked up to his brother, who exposed him to new perspectives about the world. His brother was skeptical about the religion they were raised in ("nominally Catholic"), asking questions like, "Do I really believe in this religion, or is it just that I was born into it?" These questions made Nick wonder whether he would have different beliefs if he had been born into a different family. His brother also introduced him to LGBT issues. These conversations with his brother fueled debates with his father about socialism, Marxism, and capitalism, and he began to think more for himself and develop his own beliefs.

Around the age of four or five, Nick began to wish that he were a girl and that he could do the same things girls did. This desire would emerge even more strongly when he was older. He recalls one day when he and his brother were coming up with games to play, and Nick pretended he had heard of a new game in which one person had to play the boy, and the other had to play the girl. He said that since his brother was older, he would be the boy, and

Nick would be the girl. This was Nick's way of allowing himself to pretend to be a girl without admitting that
he wanted to be one. He remembers seeing women who
wore dresses that exposed their shoulders, and he thought
it looked beautiful. So, he would tuck in his collar and
pull his shirt down to expose his shoulders while he played
the girl.

During elementary school, the boys naturally played
with each other, while the girls played with other girls.
Nick doesn't recall having any anxiety over navigating the
differences between girls and boys, but he felt that he res-
onated more with the girls. As he got closer to puberty,
he became more withdrawn; he developed social anxiety
that made him "want to shut down". Looking at pictures
of himself now from this time in his life, he can see how
he was trying to force himself to be the goofy child he had
once been.

Once he entered puberty, he started thinking, "I need
to figure out how to talk to girls." He found the changes
in his sexuality that came with puberty "really confusing
and distressing". Although the new feelings were good,
they left him with a "mix of guilt and sort of disgust". He
felt as though he were two different people: he wanted a
sexual relationship with a girl—one of his classmates—and
he also wanted to treat girls like normal people. These
two desires seemed to him to be completely at odds with
each other. The tension kept building, especially when the
developments of puberty were in full swing. He was no
longer the cute kid who amused people with his comics
and jokes; it wasn't cool to be that way now that the boys
and girls were starting to become interested in each other.
Nick wanted to maintain his youthful innocence, which
he felt his puberty was destroying. He describes being
"grossed out" by the definition of his muscles and his jaw,

and the appearance of facial and body hair, yet wanting to be attractive to girls even though he felt "like a creep" for looking at them.

He very quickly developed a lot of social anxieties as he tried to navigate these feelings and changes in his body. He stopped making eye contact with people and limited the group of people he talked to. During middle school and high school, he had only a handful of friends who were female because he felt awkward in the presence of girls, especially if he was attracted to them. He thought they would see all the sexual thoughts going on in his head. His strategy was to play it safe and cut himself off from relationships, a sort of "mental castration".

Halfway through high school, he really gave up on the idea of trying to find a girlfriend. He was increasingly conflicted: he wanted a girlfriend, but at the same time, he felt as though he were a girl and not a guy. LGBT terminology he had absorbed from his talks with his brother crept into his analysis, and he started to think that maybe he was androgynous and didn't have a gender, that gender doesn't exist, or that he was both genders. The more he thought about it, the more he came to the conclusion that he was a mix of genders. Ostensibly, he knew "I'm just a guy", but increasingly he felt that the "girl side" of him was "all the good stuff", "the truer and freer part" of himself—but that this better part was locked inside himself.

Nick remembers that when he was seventeen, he knew about transgenderism and thought that it was great for transgender people. He thought about feminine "guys like me" and masculine girls, and concluded that it was true that some people are transgender. He figured that to go through all the steps it takes to live as a transgender person—to do what it takes to get "as close as you can to the body of the other sex"—someone must be very dissatisfied with the body he has. So this didn't seem like a possibility for him at first, but he continued to wonder: What if he had been born a girl, with a female body, and had developed his social life as a girl? Could he have felt more typical, more like the other members of his gender? Would he have been happier to accept the expectations imposed on girls than those imposed on boys? He thought that these expectations would have been much easier for him to meet than the ones he was facing. On top of the turmoil and confusion, he found himself struggling with depression and anxiety.

Nick hadn't yet settled on the idea that he was transgender, but he really wished he had been born female. When he started college at age nineteen, he began to go to therapy because his anxiety and depression were weighing heavily on him. During his first session with the therapist, he described his depression that "comes out of nowhere" and explained that he didn't understand why he had such anxiety. He also disclosed that he really wished that he had been born female and that he sometimes felt as if he were a woman. He brought these things up cautiously, hoping that these problems could be resolved and he could learn to accept that he was a man. But Nick says his therapist "latched onto" the part of him that wondered if he were a woman and said, "I think we need to be addressing that head-on." For Nick, "that kind of sealed the deal." When he heard from a mental health professional that transitioning helps people like him, he thought maybe this was his best hope for happiness. Living in a liberal and progressive town, he knew people would accept his identifying as a woman and treat him as such.

His parents, who divorced when Nick was eighteen, were very surprised when he told them that he was thinking about transitioning. His brother wasn't, though, since he already knew Nick identified as bisexual. His mother was very accepting and actually really liked the idea, but Nick knew he needed to send his father a letter because he couldn't tell him in person. Later he heard that his father felt as if he were going to have a heart attack when he received the letter and that he reached out to several of his friends for advice. His father needed time to gather himself, but after two weeks invited him to dinner so they could start to reconnect. His father wasn't happy about Nick's decision but went along with it. His mother, though, was insistent on using feminine pronouns to refer to Nick, saying, "She is a woman. That's who she really is inside." She encouraged him, telling him, "You have to do this." She was very serious and gave a bunch of pamphlets to his father, who took them but said he would not be reading "any of this stuff".

There was not much Nick's father could do about the direction Nick was headed. In the end, he "kind of just went along with it", Nick says, and began treating him like a daughter. His father hoped that this transition would be successful so that Nick could live a comfortable, happy life. During this time, Nick and his father became a little closer and were able to be a little more honest and friendly with each other, partly because his father stopped imposing expectations on Nick about what a man should do and be. He gave Nick a tool set one year for Christmas, saying, "I know that you're identifying as—I know that you're a woman, but a woman still needs to fix things sometimes instead of calling a mechanic every time something needs to be fixed." At this point in his life, Nick was living in his own apartment while attending college. He felt more comfortable with his parents and also socially, living as a woman without people giving him "a hard time".

Nick's mother continued to support him, and he thinks she wanted to be part of what she saw as the historical "social progress" that was taking place. She also had a certain discomfort with the aggressive side of masculinity, and it seemed to Nick that she was happy that her son was more on the feminine side. He thinks she was also happy to see that he was not like his father, who was a "classic hardworking" man who labored in farming and landscaping. Nick says his father is a good man but does have a male chauvinism streak. Nick had an artistic personality and wasn't receptive to the things his father found important, and he felt this disappointed his father.

There's a lot of speculation about the role parents play in transgenderism. Do parents influence their children through their attitudes toward "toxic masculinity" or through the demonization of masculinity? Nick said that his parents did play a "minor" role, but that there were larger forces at work. There are men, like his dad, who have a "sort of pushiness" that was not helpful to him because this made him think masculinity was bad. But Nick also wanted to be a part of what he saw at the time as social progress. He wanted to be on the side of tolerance, and he felt that overly masculine men were just following society's expectations for them. He saw that the tide was changing, and that guys were being encouraged to suppress their masculine qualities, to tone down their aggression, sexuality, and competitiveness, to consider all that stuff really "gross" and "distasteful". Seeing the flaws in the "old-fashioned" understanding of masculinity, which was pushed on him, legitimized the idea that it's actually "cool to be a feminine man". In his high school Gay-Straight Alliance and his college Pride group, he was exposed to the ideas of changing pronouns, fluid identity, and the endless ways that people define themselves.

In front of certain people, Nick might have been embarrassed to behave in a stereotypically feminine way.

He didn't feel it was immoral or bad, just a difficult thing to do, and he saw it as a "righteous struggle". It never occurred to him that he might just be a typical masculine guy with specific interests and a certain kind of personality. It never occurred to him that he was reacting against his own masculine qualities, and now he wonders how he could have been embarrassed about being a masculine man. The mixed messages from society and his parents added to his confusion.

At the beginning of puberty, Nick stumbled upon pornography, and he believes this had a devastating impact on him. He became "instantly addicted". He says it makes sense that pornography has such a powerful effect on boys going through puberty, when they are discovering strong sexual desires for the first time. Nick explains his state of mind at the time: "I just want to be normal and kind of get into the social world. But also, I really, really want to have sex. And those two things were just seeming increasingly incompatible. And then as I start feeling like I sympathize with girls, I start feeling really guilty about the porn addiction."

Nick tried many times, even early on in middle school and high school, to break the addiction. Nothing he did seemed to work. Whenever he watched pornographic videos, he thought about how this was not what women are really like—that this was just him "getting my urges out", that porn was "an outlet". He thought if he were to have a girlfriend, he would respect her and not treat her the way he was seeing women treated online.

It was during college, as Nick continued meeting with his therapist and also after finding a therapist specializing in gender issues, that he began socially transitioning. He bought and wore women's clothes, told people to refer to him as "she" and "her", and used a female version of his first name. People at school were very receptive to him, and he was treated with respect by his friends and a lot of the girls in the pride group. They took his transition very seriously, as his mother had. Nick says all this felt good, and he wanted to keep going. He liked the way people were treating him and had a sense of euphoria. Even though he was presenting as a woman, he says, "I'm sure people could tell that I was male 98 percent of the time."

Overall he was happy with how his life was going. So, at age twenty, six months into his social transition, his therapist referred him to an endocrinologist, who started him on estrogen and testosterone blockers. He took hormones for a little over a year. His body fat started to redistribute itself, making him look a little more feminine, along with his women's clothes and hairstyle. He didn't go on estrogen and on testosterone blockers specifically to decrease his sex drive, but he was happy that this was one of their effects.

Nick didn't think that he was going to get major surgery, because that made him squeamish, but he considered electrolysis for his facial hair, getting his prominent Adam's apple shaved down, and training his voice to be more feminine. He is thankful he never made any such permanent changes. He is also grateful that he was never involved in online transgender communities, because he feels that would have pulled him down a rabbit hole that might have been harder to get out of.

Nick's realization that transition was a mistake was very sudden, but there was a lot of thought packed into a short period of time. He was simply confronted with reality. He realized that although he was doing as much as he could to live a female social life and cultivate a female appearance, there was not a lot he could do about his bone structure. He could signal to people that he identified as a woman, which made people accept him and act accordingly, but he found, over time, that people weren't really able to think of him as a woman. He says, "There's an extreme level of minutiae in social interactions that we don't think about. I mean, it's a common idea that people point out—the vast majority of communication is nonverbal. It's expressed through the body. You cannot detach yourself from your body like that." As he became convinced that people didn't really see him as a woman, he realized that he couldn't see himself as one either. So, it came down to a choice: "Am I just a disembodied person" whose body is incapable of expressing myself? "Or, do persons express themselves through their bodies? Which is it? And I started to realize this is the body that I have. This is a male body."

One day, Nick and a female friend took acid together. He does not advocate the use of psychedelic drugs because they can do serious, even irreparable, harm, which is the reason they are illegal. However, he experienced a heightened state of self-awareness, which opened his eyes to the truth about himself. He realized that he couldn't relate to girls the way they relate to each other. Not only that, but he realized he was attracted to this friend. This triggered a cascade of thoughts: he thought about how he wanted to be a father, about the parts of his maleness he couldn't bypass, and about whether he wanted to fight against them for the rest of his life. His friend had had a traumatic childhood, and he discovered he had fatherly feelings toward her: he cared for her, but not as a mother would. Nick decided to sit in front of a mirror and ask himself, "What if I just saw myself as a man?" And he suddenly did see himself as a man.

It has been difficult for Nick to tell people that he has detransitioned. He has always prided himself on his honesty, and he began to tell his friends. But when it came to his feminist and gender studies friends, it took a while longer because he knew that they would require him to give an account of himself and he needed to be ready for that. As he detransitioned, he also "converted—reverted—to Catholicism", which, he says, made people nervous. About six months after his decision to detransition, he posted on Facebook an explanation of both his detransition and his newfound faith. In order to avoid pushback from people about his decision to detransition, he left a lot of social media groups, having witnessed how aggressive people were toward those who disagreed with them. It's hard for Nick to separate his faith from his detransition. He says they are two different matters, although they are very much intertwined. He doesn't know if people would have been more receptive to his detransition if he hadn't accepted Christianity, and Catholicism in particular, at the same time.

Nick struggled with gender dysphoria during his transition, but he's had some triumphs by reversing some of his own thinking. He knows it is hard to help someone who is struggling with his sexual identity, but he wonders if someone could have talked him out of his decision to transition. He wonders whether he would have listened if someone who was attentive to what was going on with him at that time in his life had spoken with him. He recalls that no one even suggested to him that he wasn't trans, that he wasn't really a woman.

Looking back with honesty, Nick realizes that many of his decisions on how to present himself to society were driven by fear, especially his decision to reject the idea of looking for a girlfriend. He now sees how healthy it could be for him to pursue an intimate relationship with a woman. He is also working through his feelings of disgust with himself over his body and physical appearance. To this end, he has connected with a group of other men who have detransitioned and has started going to therapy again. This type of support has been important in Nick's detransition.

Nick recalls one summer when he was away from friends and on his own and was watching a lot of fantasy movies, such as *Pan's Labyrinth*. He was drawn into the story of a girl who sees another world that other people don't see and goes there, but people don't understand her. He remembers pausing one movie where a character was laughing at fairies flying around her. The mystery and magic of this place was so distressing to Nick that he stopped the movie and fell to the floor, thinking, "I can't keep having these attacks of gender dysphoria. When is this going to stop?" He started sobbing and said to God, "I want to be like her, and I'm not. What do I do? ... I want this. What do I do? I'm like this. What do I do? I hate that I'm a man. What do I do?" Nick wasn't expecting to receive an answer. He was just expressing his exasperation to God. But then he realized it was all right to feel the way he did, and knowing this gave him "the courage to feel it all". He felt it all thoroughly, and then he stood up and danced.

At the time of this interview, Nick was just about to complete his master's degree and has hopes of becoming a high school philosophy teacher. His hormone levels are back to normal again, and he hopes to one day be married and have children.

6

Cat

Cat says she was a weird kid who loved to dress up in different costumes.[1] Sometimes she would put on her dad's work hat and shoes and walk around the house or just wear very boyish clothes. She would often become obsessed with cartoon or movie characters and emulate them. She was a very musical child, and she started singing when she was about two years old. She began performing with her parents when she was about seven years old.

As a child, Cat was interested in a lot of different things. She loved reading, especially the Harry Potter series, and playing old Nintendo games. As she got older, she became more involved in sports, but she was not particularly athletic and describes herself at that time as "kind of out of shape and chubby"—an introverted, indoorsy, bookworm, artistic type.

From around the age of five, she felt limited by being female and was afraid to grow up as a woman. She believes this might be because of some traumatic experiences she had at that age. A friend, who she thinks might have been abused by one of the adults in his life, physically bullied her. When they got to be about six or seven years old, he started making sexual advances toward her. He would ask

[1] Cat, interview by Jennifer Lahl, Grass Valley, California, April 27, 2022. All quotations from Cat in this chapter are taken from this interview.

her if she wanted to be his girlfriend and tell her to take her clothes off, which made her feel very unsafe.

When she was five years old, she asked her mother if it was possible to change sex, and her mother said that it was possible for a man to become a woman but not for a woman to become a man. She believed her mother without question. She was a bit disappointed, but she told herself, "Okay, I can't change"; and that was that—or so it seemed at the time.

But when she was thirteen years old, Cat was shocked to find a website that was specifically for females who wanted to transition to male. Her mother had said it was impossible, but here were people saying, "I used to have female genitalia and now I have functional male genitalia." Her thirteen-year-old brain "latched onto that", and the gears were set into motion: maybe this was something she could do if she wanted when she got older. She was uncomfortable in her body and thought she would have been happier as a boy, but before this she didn't have a label for what she was feeling. Now she knew what it was called: gender dysphoria.

Cat always felt older than her age. She had learned to read as a toddler, and her teachers had invited her to skip grades, although she chose not to. She was already much smaller than her classmates because of a growth disorder, which made her the target of bullying, and she thought that being with older children would be even more intimidating. People in her family told her that she was very mature for her age and very articulate for a young child.

The nineties culture around her added to her dysphoria. The way the movies and television shows portrayed female characters seemed misogynistic and limiting—they were only portrayed as love interests, while the male characters were powerful, intelligent, and interesting. The female characters were given beauty as a substitute for personality and character development, and she found them boring. These influences formed her understanding of what it means to be a woman, and she didn't like it. She wanted to be more like the intelligent and interesting male characters, which only increased her gender dysphoria. As she got older and became interested in science, she observed that people tended not to take her seriously until they found out she was getting top scores in chemistry exams—then they would ask her to help them with their homework, and this was very satisfying.

At the age of thirteen, she cut her hair for the first time, and she cut it very short. Her mother was still picking out most of her clothes, and Cat began asking for more boys' clothes. She stopped wearing dresses to her school band performances—she began wearing suits instead. At around fifteen, she started switching up her style a lot. As an artistic type, she was known for being a "shapeshifter" and dressing as different characters. Her parents saw all this as simple exploration until she came out to them as "trans".

Her mother was initially supportive. Then, after some discussion, her parents told her that they didn't think she was a good candidate for transition. They knew she was suffering from some serious mental health issues and thought these underlying factors were causing her desire to transition. They were also concerned that she would not be happy living as a man because she is very petite—just five foot two inches—with a feminine frame. The idea of their fifteen-year-old daughter injecting steroids and growing a beard was very disturbing to them, and they worried that transitioning would only make her mental health issues worse. This was all very hard for her to hear. She asked her parents if she could at least use male pronouns, but they refused. She was still going by Cat and considered the possibility of changing her name, but she couldn't think of anything that she would like better.

When she was seventeen, her gender dysphoria had not gone away, and her parents took her to see a gender therapist, the "the head honcho of gender care in Sacramento", who they thought could actually help her. At this point, she was suffering from an eating disorder and some other serious mental health illnesses. But instead of addressing her issues, the therapist affirmed her "trans identity". At that first appointment, he told her that all her issues were caused by her gender dysphoria, and at the third appointment, he recommended that Cat begin medically transitioning with testosterone.

Looking back, she says the term "gender therapist" is deceptive, because it implies that the therapist is an expert and will be able to listen to someone with gender dysphoria and find the underlying issues that need to be addressed. But she says what often happens instead, as she herself experienced, is that gender therapists see it as their role to affirm their clients' perceived identity without question. Cat believes that gender therapists tend to assume automatically that what a client with gender dysphoria needs is to present himself or herself to the world as a different gender. Cat says that uncritical affirmation, without any attempt to understand and resolve underlying issues, is a dangerous practice.

Cat was hesitant to take testosterone because she knew she would be starting college soon and would not have parental support in her new environment. Also, singing was a big part of her life, and she knew the testosterone would affect her voice. So, she decided to hold off. She reports going "back into the closet" for a few years because she knew it was impossible to "pass as a man" at school and she didn't want to have to explain her pronouns to everyone. Changing pronouns was not as accepted in 2010 as it is now. The social and political climate was changing, but transitioning was also not as accepted then as it is now (at least in California, where Cat lives).

While away at college, Cat had a couple of relationships with men, and she was afraid they would break up with her if she called herself "trans". In fact, she did not want to be trans or have gender dysphoria, so she pushed these feelings down and ignored them. But refusing to address her dysphoria only caused her eating disorder to flare up again, and she began to struggle with alcohol and drug addiction as well. These problems led to her dropping out of college. After many years of dysphoria, addiction, eating disorders, and depression, she came to the conclusion that it was just not possible for her to be happy as a woman, and she decided to try medical transitioning. She felt that she had tried everything else.

Her first step was to call Planned Parenthood because she knew that they offered transitioning services. She thought she would have to go through some sort of process to get the hormones—a certain number of therapy visits or some kind of psychological evaluation. Instead, she was told that a doctor would call her. After they talked for about thirty minutes, Cat received a prescription for testosterone, which she picked up the same day.

The conversation was not very detailed, and although the doctor had a female name, the voice on the phone sounded male. The doctor sounded captivated by gender ideology. "Obviously," Cat says, "if you [the physician] have something that you perceive to be helpful for you, I feel like you're more likely to recommend it to other people and just kind of assume that they're similar to you." The doctor asked a few questions about how old she had been when she started to consider herself trans or first started experiencing gender dysphoria. Cat explained that she had had these feelings since she was five years old, and she spoke of eating disorders and other issues. But she explained that the dysphoria was the root cause of her problems.

The doctor simply accepted her assessment, which caused Cat to have some doubts, because, as she reflects, "accepting a self-diagnosis is considered problematic in basically all other areas of psychiatry or psychology." Then the doctor asked about her medical history, and Cat downplayed the alcohol and drug abuse because she wanted to get the testosterone. The doctor could easily have learned about these factors by looking at her chart. She had a history of suicide attempts. She had been institutionalized and undergone inpatient treatment for her eating disorder, which she had had for fifteen years at this point. Her medical history was filled with red flags, but the outcome of the conversation was, "Here's your drugs."

At the drugstore, Cat was embarrassed. She had been dressing in a very masculine fashion and had a shaved head at the time, but she had no chance of passing as a man because of her petiteness. She was looking over her shoulder at the people behind her when the pharmacist called out her name and said, "Here's your testosterone." At the time she was living in a small town where the people were not very aware of transgender issues.

The pharmacist briefly described how she was to inject the medication and showed her the written instructions that come in the package. She was so nervous that the instructions just went in one ear and out the other, and she had to rely on the written instructions when she got home. It is disconcerting to Cat that patients are assumed to be competent to inject themselves. While most women are instructed to inject testosterone into a large muscle, often their thigh, Cat was instructed to take her testosterone by subcutaneous injection, which is done into fatty places like the abdomen. After about four months, she noticed that she was getting strange cysts on her lower abdomen. These were pockets of fluid that were not fully draining, causing lumps. She decided to ignore these and rationalized that the testosterone side effects were "so worth it" if they allowed her to finally become a man. She recognizes the similarity between this thought and the mindset that accepts self-harm or an eating disorder: a person ignores serious signs of harm because of the "greater good" of reaching an impossible ideal.

In the beginning, testosterone felt like a miracle cure for all her problems. Cat felt a lot better. Her depression lifted, her mood instability went away, she felt a sense of euphoria, and she had a lot more energy. Menstrual cycles make women feel different at different times during a cycle, but testosterone stops the cycles and creates an equilibrium. It had the effect of one of the better antidepressants that she had previously taken. There were some negative effects too, though: she became agitated. Before testosterone, when she felt emotional, sadness would predominate, but now her emotions were more likely to be irritation or anger, if, for example, someone upset her.

At first, this shift was a relief, because there's so much stigma around crying. The remark "You're too emotional" had long felt like an insult. But she began to regret the loss of some of her previous emotional reactions when she noticed that the testosterone was affecting her songwriting and other expressions of her creativity. It was almost as if this part of herself was shut off and she could not access it. Her personality felt distorted. She was becoming a different person, one she did not even recognize.

After about three months, the worst of the side effects started to surface. First, she developed a pain in her right side. Sometimes it was more of a pressure or a dull ache, but sometimes it was a really sharp pain that made it hard to stand up and move around. It would get worse if she ate certain things, such as fatty foods, or if she had an alcoholic drink. She started to feel nauseous all the time. She did not go back to the doctor, so she is unsure whether it was her gallbladder or liver; but something was definitely wrong, because her "body wasn't fully accepting the testosterone". She was also having palpitations, which were worse when she wore the breast binder she had been using on and off for about fifteen years. She recalls being in public when she started to have bad palpitations, which made her panic. She knew she needed to take the binder off, but she felt unsafe going into the men's bathroom and uncomfortable going into the women's bathroom. Despite these serious side effects, she wasn't ready to quit the injections, telling herself, "I know this bright future as a man is ahead of me. I know this is the right choice." She believed these medical treatments were the only way to address her gender dysphoria.

During this same time, she was looking into scheduling "top surgery"—a double mastectomy. Her insurance required a letter from her physician, so she called Planned Parenthood and was struck by how easy it was for her to obtain the letter. Planned Parenthood arranged for her to speak to a new doctor on the phone—again, there was no in-person meeting. They spoke for about forty-five minutes, and she received the letter she needed to schedule her double mastectomy. Next she had a consultation scheduled with the surgeon.

A new development caused her to rethink the surgery. The testosterone, which had been making her voice gradually deeper, sent her voice over the edge—when she opened her mouth to sing, nothing came out but air and squeaks. Even speaking was becoming painful. Her voice was raspy, and it felt as if there was a barrier in her throat whenever she talked. She struggled whenever she had to project her voice, and she had to stop performing, which had an impact on her social life. She found herself thinking, "Oh, my gosh, what have I done to myself?" A vocal coach told her that her voice would never go back to how it was. She had known that the testosterone would make her voice deepen, but she had not realized how much that would affect her musical career and even her quality of life—she had acquired what amounted to a vocal disability. She decided to try to salvage what she could of her voice and went "off everything, cold turkey". She also canceled her plans for "top surgery". When she requested to reverse her legal name change, she had to complete more paperwork to explain that she wanted to drop the whole thing.

At this time, Cat was still describing herself as "trans". She did not feel like a woman, but she also thought she would never be able to pass as a man or live as a man in any capacity. She took a step back and started calling herself "nonbinary" and using the pronouns "he/they", although people often spoke of her as a woman. This was a very difficult time for her, because the miraculous cure everyone had insisted she could achieve was now off-limits.

She was twenty-eight when she started testosterone and twenty-nine when she stopped. Shortly after her thirtieth birthday, she socially and ideologically detransitioned. Looking back, she identifies the series of events that caused her to question gender ideology and all the beliefs that had led her down this damaging path. The first was the negative impact the testosterone had had on her health. When she did some research into the health effects of cross-sex hormones, she found that there is a serious lack of quality data. Ideologues claim that medical transition is proven to alleviate gender dysphoria and improve mental health and that detransitioning is rare. Cat's background in science enabled her to examine the studies by experts in the field, and she found that there actually isn't much quality evidence supporting medical transition as the best treatment for gender dysphoria. There was almost no research at all on detransition—the few studies she could find were designed in such a way as to leave out detransitioners.

When she started her research, Cat thought, "Well, I know I'm detransitioning, but I don't want to be a 'bad' detransitioner; I don't want to be someone who's detrimental to the community. I'm probably just not going to talk about it." But when she discovered how the detransition rate was being calculated to exclude people like herself and misrepresent the outcomes of transition, she grew concerned about the scientific and medical misinformation being spread by ideologues. Gender ideology claims that being a woman or a man is a feeling in a person's head rather than a biological reality. Thus, gender activists demand that we define a man or a woman on the basis of each person's thoughts and feelings, which are intimately connected to sex-role stereotyping.

As Cat learned more about the experiences of other transitioners and how these experiences were being recounted by the activists, she began to question whether thoughts and feeling can trump biological reality. She realized she had never listened to the critical voices of those whom trans activists pejoratively call "trans-exclusionary radical feminists" (TERFs) because she had been led to believe that these people were mean and bigoted and should be ignored.

She searched the internet for the phrase "trans women aren't women", and one of the first videos that popped up was an episode of a podcast featuring Posie Parker (Kellie-Jay Keen). She credits Parker with helping her to think more critically about gender ideology. Parker gave many examples of how this ideology puts women in danger and how it's not fair to women to assert that being female is just a feeling in somebody's head. Cat realized that she held many misogynistic beliefs, and that these were part of her reluctance to think of herself as a woman. It wasn't that she was not a woman; it was that she had misperceptions about what it means to be a woman. For instance, she thought she couldn't be a woman because she was adept at math and science. Even though she knew other women with these skills, she had been influenced by stereotypes in movies and television shows. She had been thinking of her analytical and scientific tendencies as male aspects of her personality, which made her "nonbinary". She came to realize what an incredibly sexist idea this actually is.

Cat doesn't blame anyone in her life, such as friends or family members, for her original attempt to transition. Her parents had been worried from the beginning, and now she is grateful that they did not encourage her decisions—if they had, she thinks, she might now harbor some anger toward them. For a while, she was angry at the gender therapist and the doctors who had enabled her to go through with the testosterone injections. She was especially angry about losing her voice.

Cat feels that the entire transgender industry needs our attention, from the pharmaceutical companies that are profiting from people's suffering to the surgeons and the doctors who enable unproven and damaging treatments—including those who don't really believe in what they're doing but who don't speak out for fear of losing their jobs. And then there are the trans activists, some of whom Cat believes have a nefarious agenda. Modern trans ideology and the gender-affirmation movement could be part of a larger transhumanist agenda, whose endgame is not clear—but whose activists have little regard for the safety of young people their agenda affects and the long-term outcomes for their health and well-being.

Cat understands that a lot of people are struggling with dissatisfaction with their body and their sex and that they don't always receive the support they need to accept themselves. Instead, they hear a multitude of voices saying that the solution to their emotional and psychological pain is to transition, and pharmaceutical companies, surgeons, and doctors seize the opportunity for financial gain.

Reflecting on women's rights and the feminism of the eighties and nineties, Cat is struck by the fact that in many powerful circles someone cannot be considered a feminist now without supporting gender ideology. Yet, this surge in gender ideology is, to her mind, the antithesis of women's rights, and definitely not in alignment with feminist values. Gender ideology has been extremely detrimental to girls and the way that they view themselves, she says. According to the gender doctrine, if you're born female, you are designated AFAB: "assigned female at birth". But no one "assigns" the baby's sex at birth; instead, it is observed by the doctor (and everyone else present). Then, there is the pejorative term "cisgender", which is applied to women who, presumably, must conform to regressive stereotyping—the very condition women's rights activists have been fighting against for decades because it is limiting and restrictive.

Cat began to think more about the concepts that gender ideology constructs. She realized that stereotypical gender roles are coming to be regarded as the essential criteria for defining a girl or a boy, a woman or a man—not biology. She realized that trans ideology calls a biological male a woman if he fulfills a certain role—or even if he has a certain appearance. Instead of being recognized by the fact of her biology, a woman is categorized as someone with long hair, long painted nails, and makeup—a very superficial idea of what it means to be female, Cat says. She does not think there is anything wrong with wearing makeup or dressing in a "feminine" way, if that is how people, including men, want to express themselves. But deconstructing the word "woman" into an aesthetic or a role that anyone can fulfill is extremely damaging to young girls. And because gender ideology is present even in primary schools now, this understanding is instilled in them when they are very young. A false, narrow, and shallow idea of womanhood is being promoted, confusing girls from a very young age and making them think that if they don't fit this idea, they are in the wrong body: that they're not supposed to be a girl, and, later, a woman.

Cat wants girls to know that being a woman is not limited by the narrow and shallow ideas being presented to children. She wants them to understand that they can accomplish whatever they want to accomplish and that there is no need to buy into any kind of regressive sex-role stereotyping. They do not have to change their bodies in order to be themselves.

Cat is happier and healthier than she has been in a long time. Meditation, yoga, and therapy have been especially helpful to her. She says that there *are* good therapists out there, and she would never want to discourage anyone from going to one. But, for Cat, meditation has been absolutely life-changing. She has been on ten-day silent retreats and has practiced daily meditation for about five years. It has helped her navigate all her emotional ups and downs and played a very important part in her healing.

If she is having negative feelings about her body or self-destructive thoughts, she now knows how to see them as valid, though untrue, and can acknowledge that they have a reason for being there; but she also knows how to avoid getting caught up in them and ruminating on them. Meditation helps Cat to step back from her thoughts and feelings and observe them, without allowing them to take over her life and control her behaviors and actions. She has learned how to master her thoughts and feelings rather than letting them master her.

7

Chloe

Chloe is one of the people not featured in the original movie *The Detransition Diaries* who agreed to be interviewed for this book.[1] Her story is important because it shows just how easily a young girl can be offered cross-sex hormones and surgical intervention.

Chloe says she was "feminine" when she was a little girl. She was the youngest child in her family, growing up with brothers and sisters who were at least seven years older than she was, so it was almost as if she were an only child. She had some tomboy tendencies, but, for the most part she was "pretty girly". At age seven, Chloe was diagnosed with autism and attention-deficit/hyperactivity disorder (ADHD). It should be noted that people with a diagnosis of autism are more likely to experience gender dysphoria. One of the largest studies to date found that those who do not "identify with the sex they were assigned at birth are three to six times as likely to be autistic as cisgender people".[2]

[1] Chloe, interview by Jennifer Lahl, Zoom interview, October 3, 2022. All quotations from Chloe in this chapter are taken from this interview.

[2] Laura Dattaro, "Largest Study to Date Confirms Overlap Between Autism and Gender Diversity", *Spectrum*, September 14, 2020, https://www.spectrum news.org/news/largest-study-to-date-confirms-overlap-between-autism-and -gender-diversity. See also Varun Warrier et al., "Elevated Rates of Autism, Other Neurodevelopmental and Psychiatric Diagnoses, and Autistic Traits in Transgender and Gender-Diverse Individuals", *Nature Communications* 11, no. 1 (2020), https://doi.org/10.1038/s41467-020-17794-1.

This study and others like it point to the possibility that many people who experience confusion about their gender have undiagnosed autism. Chloe says that autism and ADHD are common comorbidities seen in people like herself diagnosed as gender dysphoric.

She experienced puberty at age nine, which is on the early side for girls. She started using social media and spending time on the internet around the age of eleven, and she absorbed what becoming a woman might mean from the sites she was visiting. In her own words, she was "exposed to a lot of stuff that I shouldn't have been". She saw comments from other girls that devalued being female, devalued women's experiences as a whole, and complained about how bad it was to have a monthly period or to give birth. Chloe mainly spent time on Instagram and was active in online communities that had a lot of Tumblr influencers. She consumed a lot of content focused on transgenderism.

Her parents and her older siblings, many of whom had already moved out of the home, were unaware of her internet usage, and her access to online content was "pretty much unrestricted. Nobody really checked up on me at all." She thought this was great, because she had total privacy to do whatever she wanted online and spend as much time there as she desired. She remarks that if she ever has children of her own, they will not have this sort of unrestricted access to the internet.

She does not understand why, but the algorithms on Instagram always seemed to recommend content focused on transgender issues, specifically about "female-to-male" young people, or "trans boys", as they have been called. These sites really spoke to her. She admired the "really tight" sense of community she saw in the groups. She describes her younger self as an awkward child who struggled socially and had trouble connecting with her female peers. She felt she could relate more to boys her age—eleven and twelve—than to girls. These online friends were meeting the need she had for friendship.

Around this time, she changed her appearance, wearing more masculine clothes and shorter hair. She told her sister and a handful of friends that she was transgender. At twelve, she came out to her parents in a letter telling them to start seeing her as their son and to refer to her by her new name.

Chloe's parents were supportive, but they didn't know much about the topic and didn't know how to respond. They took her to a therapist to "get this sorted out, both for me and themselves". From this point on, she experienced constant affirmation of her thinking that she was a boy and not a girl. All the doctors and therapists she saw were only affirming, and she says these professionals also "kind of coerced" her parents into affirming her as well.

Pretty soon after she turned thirteen, she was seeing a gender specialist, and she began taking Lupron to block her pubertal development. About a month later, she began testosterone injections to further the masculinization process.

When asked if anyone in her family or friends network or any of her healthcare providers said maybe she should wait or cautioned her to slow down, she said that only one of her brothers did. He expressed concern about the testosterone and how it might affect her brain development. Chloe ignored his concerns, though, as she was overwhelmingly being affirmed by others. She tolerated the injections well, but as she got leaner and developed more muscles, the shots became more difficult and painful, and she was afraid of needles. Even though she had entered puberty at around age nine, her monthly periods were not very regular, and the Lupron stopped her cycles. She remained on Lupron for about a year and a half.

The testosterone had the immediate effect of causing her voice to drop, and she noticed that she was more tired and had trouble focusing. The testosterone gave her bursts of energy and had a stimulant effect, but it also made her feel angry at times and more emotional. Because of her family's genetics, she did not grow a lot of facial or body hair, but she did develop more muscle: her shoulders got larger. The bones in her nose, forehead, and jaw got bigger too. These bodily changes have not gone away since she stopped taking testosterone.

At the time Chloe took Lupron to block puberty, she was not offered ovarian tissue cryopreservation (OTC) to attempt to preserve her fertility. Currently, girls receiving "gender-affirming care" are often offered OTC to freeze and bank their ovarian tissue for later use. Fertility preservation on minors is experimental, but it is offered because cross-sex hormones can have a negative impact on future fertility. Chloe had met with an endocrinologist who gave her some literature to inform her that testosterone might affect her ability to have children in the future, but she was thirteen at the time. "Of course, I wasn't thinking about that," she said.

When Chloe decided to detransition, she stopped taking testosterone, and her body seemed to be able to produce its own hormones naturally. About two months after she stopped the injections, her monthly periods came back, and they have been fairly regular; however, this is no guarantee of future fertility.

When Chloe was about fifteen and had been taking testosterone for two years, she started looking into having a double mastectomy. She had already been wearing a breast binder to flatten her breasts against her rib cage for a more masculine appearance, but she found it terribly uncomfortable and hot to wear during California summers. As she was dressing more "male", wearing long jeans and T-shirts and also the compression device, walking home from school in over one-hundred-degree weather was almost unbearable. That made "top surgery" seem like the solution for her. Although her breast binder was marketed as "safe to use", Chloe now knows that binding the breasts is not safe, because it pushes the breasts into the ribcage. Her ribs, she says, remain deformed from wearing the binder. Chloe was referred to another specialist to approve the double mastectomy. The time period between meeting with the specialist and "going under the knife" was about six months. The vetting process, she says, was almost nonexistent: she wasn't required to have a psychological evaluation.

Her siblings had all moved out of the home by this time, and she didn't have much contact with them. Her sisters were supportive of her decision, but one of her older brothers was concerned—she dismissed him as ignorant or transphobic. Looking back, she is thankful that he tried to speak up, even if she didn't listen to him. Her family had been told by therapists, nurses, and other medical professionals that transgender adolescents have a suicide rate above 40 percent if they are not affirmed. Of course, this makes families fearful—no one wants to cause their child distress. The mantra families and parents hear is "Would you rather have a live son or a dead daughter?"

Even though it involved a double mastectomy at the young age of fifteen, Chloe was confident about her decision to transition both medically and surgically. Unlike others who undergo this surgery, Chloe did not have a lot of pain, which was a relief because the opioids she was prescribed actually made her pain worse and gave her bad indigestion, so she stopped taking them. She describes the pain as a deep muscle soreness. She had trouble showering and had to wear a lot of big bandages, and for several months she had limited range of motion and couldn't lift her arms above her head. For a while, she couldn't go out with her friends, so she spent a lot of time at home.

Three years since having this surgery, at age eighteen, Chloe still does not feel that her body has fully recovered or healed. She still must wear bandages on the graft areas around her nipples because they still bleed and leak. Her surgeon said the grafts would heal within nine months, so she's not sure why the problem persists. She reached out to her surgeon, but instead of helping, he gave her some advice that "temporarily made my problem worse", so she felt she could not rely on her healthcare provider anymore. She says the process of mastectomy surgery on women who think they are trans is different from breast surgery on women who have breast cancer. Her surgery involved not only removing breast tissue but also an area of the chest. She says it was described to her as "like scraping the knee, but in a more controlled fashion, and then they remove the nipple and then basically paste it onto that area that has been scraped." During the last few appointments Chloe had with her surgeon, he seemed nervous, she says, and she felt he was rushing her through the appointments and not willing to spend time addressing the concerns she was raising.

She told her surgeon that she has detransitioned, and he said that, of all his patients, she is the first one he knows of who has done so. Anything medical professionals say must fit the "gender-affirming care" model in some jurisdictions or it is seen as "conversion therapy". Anything that doesn't conform to this model goes against their medical practice and professional societies' recommendations that require them to offer only gender affirmation.

During her post-op period, Chloe started developing some feelings of grief. It was hard for her to identify these feelings at the time, and because, as she says, she "was just so deep in this" and "had been affirmed so much", she was afraid of thinking she had made a mistake. There was no way of going back, she thought. She had been taking hormones for several years, had even gone so far as to have a mastectomy, and presented herself as, even "passed" as, a man. It wasn't until about eleven months later, when she was taking a high school psychology class, that she started to think about what she had done and what it would mean for her when she became an adult.

During one of her psychology classes, she was learning about the Harlow surrogate mother experiment with infant rhesus monkeys. In the 1950s, American psychologist Harry Harlow tested his theory by taking infant monkeys from their mothers and giving them the choice of two inanimate surrogate mothers. The experiment was as follows:

> One [surrogate mother] was a simple construction of wire and wood, and the second was covered in foam rubber and soft terry cloth. The infants were assigned to one of two conditions. In the first, the wire mother had a milk bottle and the cloth mother did not; in the second, the cloth mother had the food while the wire mother had none. In both conditions, Harlow found that the infant monkeys spent significantly more time with the terry cloth mother than they did with the wire mother. When only the wire mother had food, the babies came to the wire mother to feed and immediately returned to cling to the cloth surrogate.[3]

---

[3] Association for Psychological Science, "Harlow's Classic Studies Revealed the Importance of Maternal Contact", June 20, 2018, https://www.psycho logicalscience.org/publications/observer/obsonline/harlows-classic-studies -revealed-the-importance-of-maternal-contact.html.

Harlow also went on to show that when they were fright-ened or in uncertain situations, the monkeys would go back to the surrogate for comfort. Without their own bio-logical mother or a surrogate mother, the baby monkeys "were paralyzed with fear, huddled in a ball sucking their thumbs. If an alarming noise-making toy was placed in the cage, an infant with a surrogate mother present would explore and attack the toy; without a surrogate mother, the infant would cower in fear."[4]

Learning about the Harlow experiments got Chloe thinking about what it would be like to have and raise a child and about mother and child bonding—especially the role breastfeeding plays and its ability to comfort a baby. At this moment she realized that because of a decision she had made at such a young age, she would miss out on breastfeeding any children she might have in the future—if she was even able to conceive and bear children.

A few weeks after she had completed this class, Chloe broke down crying one night because she realized that she missed her breasts. She wanted to be pretty. She wanted to look like a woman. In spite of all she had taken away from herself, she had come to the realization that "no matter what I did to myself, I would always be a woman."

She was sixteen when she made the decision to detran-sition, just one year after her double mastectomy. Because of the type of mastectomy she had, she will never be able to produce milk, even with reconstructive surgery. She thinks that she will not have more surgery because it would only be for cosmetic purposes: no normal breast function would be restored.

In February 2022, Chloe created a Twitter account and started speaking out on the issue of transgenderism. She

---

[4] Association for Psychological Science, "Maternal Contact".

spoke the truth courageously, in terms of both objective fact and her own personal experience, and she paid a high price: she has been blocked and harassed, and many have attempted to bully her into silence for expressing her views and telling her personal story. The animosity shown to her by people who consider themselves trans has been, to say the least, cruel and hateful—and often threatening as well. She says that being so outspoken has cost her all of her "friends in person". At first, she had given in to the demands that she be silent. But then she wondered why so many people from the "trans community", even those who were her friends, wanted to silence her. "If they are so secure in their transition," she asks, "then why? Why do I need to submit to their demands to just shut up?"

On Twitter she also discovered that she was not alone. Others were also experiencing regret over their decision to transition, and she was meeting many other detransitioners like herself online. Hearing their stories made her realize how needed her voice was, all the more so because she had undergone hormone treatment and surgery while she was still a minor.

Chloe has since traveled all around the United States to tell her story. She has spoken at conferences, testified in state legislative hearings, done podcasts, been interviewed for print stories, and participated in briefings hosted on Capitol Hill. She traveled to Atlanta, Georgia, to speak at a conference hosted by No Left Turn in Education and was interviewed by Sara Higdon, founder of the *TRANSform to Freedom* podcast, who considers himself both "transsexual" and Catholic. The conference was aimed at combatting indoctrination and sexual grooming in K–12 schools. She testified in Sacramento, the capital of California, against the bill SB 107, the Gender-Affirming Health Care Act, which turned California into a "sanctuary state" where minor children from other states that have banned this practice will be permitted to access what is called "gender-affirming care", including hormones and surgeries. Governor Newsom signed the bill into law on September 30, 2022. Chloe attended the annual conference of the American Academy of Pediatrics in Anaheim, California, on October 8, 2022, where parents, educators, advocates, and detransitioners carried signs with slogans like "Puberty Blocking Is Not Safe" and "Stop Transing Kids".

Chloe is grateful for the support of her parents and siblings through this difficult time in her life. She admits that the publicity has required a considerable adjustment as she used to be a "pretty withdrawn person". Her family and relatives have been a rock for her, especially the brother who raised concerns about her path early on.

Because of the effects unlimited and unrestricted access to social media had on her, she cautions parents to "keep your kids off social media, keep them off technology for as long as you can, and once they are old enough to use it, keep track of what they're doing and how much time they spend [on it]." She suggests that parents get their children involved in extracurricular activities and spend time with them, letting them know that they are loved.

Chloe also has sage advice for young people themselves: she encourages them to get outside of their bubble of friends—to avoid surrounding themselves only with people who think just as they do—because she herself was surrounded by people who told her she was on the right path. She emphasizes how important it is to listen to people with different opinions, even ones you disagree with.

8

Torren

Torren grew up in northeast Ohio with his mother, father, and four siblings.[1] He describes himself as "your normal, average everyday kid" with a "normal everyday rural/ suburban Ohio upbringing" in a family of second- and third-generation immigrants. Torren recalls spending a lot of time with his extended family on both sides, but not fitting into either very well. His father's family was broken and riddled with substance abuse and addiction, which his father was able to escape. His mother's family was a crew of ironworkers and union laborers who enjoyed hunting, fishing, and cars, which did not interest young Torren. He was more drawn to his father's pursuits: sports, music, and the arts.

Torren's father ran a camera shop, but Torren rarely saw him practice photography as an art form. He knew his dad played the guitar and sang in a local band, but Torren never saw him perform. His dad was also an avid painter, but again, Torren rarely saw him painting. In fact, Torren recalls that his dad's artistic side was almost completely hidden. What Torren did see and modeled was his father's

[1] Torren, interview by Jennifer Lahl and Kallie Fell in Philadelphia, Pennsylvania, July 24, 2023. All quotations from Torren in this chapter are taken from this interview.

love for sports. Torren says that at five or six years old, he could name all the players on a given team. "By the time I was ten or eleven, I knew all the stats, had everything memorized." Despite not seeing his father demonstrate his artistic talents, Torren was drawn to them. Having the same creative streak as his father, he wanted to learn guitar and explore the arts.

As a child, Torren was very outgoing. He loved the small neighborhood where he spent his youngest years, a community with a "bunch of different kids" where he could play and hang out. He loved talking to people so much that his coach wouldn't let him play catcher on the tee-ball team because he would stand at the backstop and just carry on a conversation with the batter.

Unfortunately, as Torren grew, his family moved farther and farther away from the city and his small, beloved community, eventually landing on seventy-eight acres "out in the middle of nowhere". As a fifth-grader, Torren felt his personality fade—he was no longer that outgoing kid always talking to other people. He didn't learn to play the guitar or explore art, despite the desire to do these things. He does remember asking his dad once to teach him to play the guitar. They sat down and plucked some strings, but only once. Torren admits that his dad probably didn't realize that his son wanted to keep learning because Torren was afraid to ask. This was just one of the self-imposed fears that would keep him from stepping out of a box he had defined for himself.

Torren spent much of our interview reflecting on these limits he imposed on himself and why he did so. He says he learned that "it's not safe to step outside the box. It's not okay to take risks. It's best to be able to know what you're going to get into, have control over it, and just follow the path of least resistance." And so he came to the conclusion that he should stay stoic and analytical, and suppress the outgoing, exploratory parts of his personality.

Torren played football and baseball and found himself gifted in math. His sense of who he was began to change, even though his new identity didn't "feel right" to him: "I had myself pegged as this person who's just introverted, not very outgoing, not very creative, just mathematical, just played sports." His sisters, by contrast, were able to explore dance, enjoying the artistic and creative energy that Torren also desired to explore.

Early on, Torren became acutely aware of clear-cut gender roles, especially on his mother's side of the family, that were never violated. These gender roles weren't so much imposed as subtly encouraged by both the family and the outside world, and not fitting into them made him feel awkward within his own family. He remembers being only three or four years old when he tried to help his mother carry her purse because her hands were full. A family member laughed at him for picking it up, telling him, "Boys don't carry purses." Torren remembers the feeling as shame, shame at being involved in anything feminine. And he felt as if he were growing up to be someone who wasn't his real self, as if important elements of his personality were being suppressed. He says, "As I saw gender roles play out in my family ... that frustration over the pieces of me that I felt were missing just became stronger and stronger over time."

In high school, Torren remembers a baseball coach who would yell at his players if they showed any emotion. He laughs about that now: "It's actually funny. As a baseball fan, I've been watching the sport [change]. And there's emotion all over the field now, which I think is great." But at the time, all these voices, influences, and subtle messages had a lasting impact on young Torren.

Eventually there came a time when it was clear to him that he couldn't integrate what he thought of as the masculine and the feminine parts of his life. While his parents were working, Torren recalls, he spent time at the homes of his aunts, uncles, and grandparents, where he watched daytime television. This is where he was first introduced to the idea of "transitioning". He recalls thinking, "Oh, wait, that's a man, but [he's] feminine. Something's happening here. What is that?" Torren describes this exposure as "a little seed" that grew over time. More seeds like this were planted—he remembers reading about "sex change operations" when he was eleven or twelve. Unable to fully integrate his personality in a way that felt safe, Torren began to wonder whether he could become another person.

This tension became a war that raged within him, as he buried as much of what he thought of as his "feminine side" as he could to avoid shame among friends and family. He felt like a split personality, living two lives, unable to be whole. Despite his internal conflict, he excelled in high school and graduated from college, desiring the whole time to express the "more feminine side" of himself, but keeping up his masculine appearance. He says, "There was always a temptation to say, just screw it. I'm going to go and transition. I'm going to live my life as a woman. But I couldn't do that because of just the shame that I would feel or the fear of shame that I would feel from my family."

After college, he spent a year living overseas doing mission work in Southeast Asia. He tells us, "For some reason, being in that place where I was completely uncomfortable made me completely comfortable to just be me." All his creative energy flooded back, and he picked up photography, played the guitar, and led worship services at churches—all things he "never in a million years would have done because they didn't fit inside my box". He remembers, "During that year, I didn't struggle with gender at all because I was whole. I was still the person that liked sports. I was still good at being analytical in math, but I was tapping into my creativity. I was tapping into some of my extroversion. I was meeting people. I was exploring, and I was telling stories. It was great."

Unfortunately, this new freedom did not last, and Torren found himself being forced back into his box by a mission leader who told him, "You're not a good male missionary. You're not what we want from a man as a missionary." He didn't understand why and came to the conclusion that all the things he was doing and loved doing were somehow not acceptable for a man to do. At the same time, he fell in love with the woman who would eventually become his wife, and he felt the same disapproval with regard to this relationship from the mission leaders. He tells us, "Here I am, being fully myself, fully a man, being everything that I felt like I was called to be and wanted to be as a human and as a man. My boss is saying, 'This isn't good enough. This isn't okay. You are a detriment to the advancement of the Kingdom of God' ... And so all of that integration work that I was unknowingly doing at the time just fell apart. It broke me."

Back in the United States, from about the age of twenty-four to twenty-eight, a "poison took hold" of him, he says. "It was a secret struggle that just kept building" as he read accounts on social media sites like Reddit that portrayed transitioning as a solution to problems like his: "You see all of these people transitioning, and they just seem happy. You see them on social media, they seem like they're saying it solved all their problems. They're not depressed anymore. They're not anxious anymore. They're finally able to be themselves and who they are."

At the same time, the gender identity industry was taking off, and the taboo surrounding medical transition was beginning to disappear. Transgender people were being portrayed in movies and on television, like the character played by Laverne Cox in *Orange Is the New Black*. Suddenly, transgenderism was out in the open. "For somebody who's struggling with obsessive and even compulsive thoughts around that, it's almost like an addiction," Torren explains. "And when finally, society comes in and says, 'Okay, all of those taboos, all of those walls, all those boundary lines are gone,' like a dog diving headfirst into a food bowl, you're just going after it. I was like, I have to explore this."

After being rejected from a church community once, Torren questioned if he could feel safe within the church to disclose his struggles. He eventually concluded that there was no way he could or would talk to his church leaders about these struggles. His mental health suffered, and eventually his wife left. He found himself in "a dark spiral" and began to struggle with what he calls "transition ideation". He was obsessed with the idea that transitioning would solve all his problems. Looking back, he sees this obsession as a form of suicide ideation directed toward the "masculine" part of his personality, which he identified as the source of all his trouble. He explains, "Transition ideation really was a form of wanting to kill a part of myself in favor of another."

The therapist Torren had been seeing for a while suggested that his obsessive thoughts indicated that he was, in fact, transgender, and she didn't see any harm in trying to transition. Torren didn't feel pressured by his therapist, but she also didn't encourage him to be cautious. He found it "pretty easy to start taking steps down the path". He signed up for an appointment at the local gender clinic but then panicked so much that he changed his phone number so they couldn't contact him. He sees now that this episode shows how mentally unstable he was at the time—it should have been a red flag. But he eventually called the clinic again, and after one half-hour Zoom conversation with a physician's assistant, he was prescribed estrogen.

Torren was on estrogen for three months when he had another crisis. He compared his present self to who he was while he was a missionary, when his masculine and feminine elements felt integrated—and he wanted to be that person again. He stopped taking estrogen and canceled his follow-up appointments at the gender clinic. He told himself, "I'm going to fix myself, get healthy, and try to bury this whole transition thing again." But, he says, "That didn't work." He would go back and forth, doing well for a while, but then the anxiety and depression would reemerge and he would begin to obsess again over transitioning. He would vacillate wildly, sometimes hour to hour, between feeling ready to accept himself as he was and being convinced he needed to transition. A year after starting estrogen the first time, he found an online provider and, after a fifteen-minute appointment, was prescribed estrogen again.

Torren decided that this time he was going to try to "dive in fully". He started going by the name Audrey, and six months after he started taking estrogen the second time, he began to present himself publicly as a woman, although he was a large man. He shaved his thick beard, and he took voice lessons in an attempt to sound more feminine. But instead of feeling relief, he felt "terrified and ashamed". He knew he was trying to be someone he wasn't, "trying to escape from who I was and escape from a lot of the pain that I was in"—but he was unwilling to stop. "I just kept forcing myself forward," he says.

Eventually, in 2022, he couldn't deny his realization that none of this was helping and that he felt more shame, frustration, and alienation than ever. He had stopped talking to his parents, who didn't support his transition. His experience was not at all like those he had read about on social media. He found "each step more painful than the last". Even when he received support to run for public office as the first trans person in his community to enter an election, he was miserable. Initially, he thought the cure for his misery might be to increase his medical treatment or even to undergo surgery. But then he thought, "If I'm miserable right now, why is taking the next step going to help?" Torren realized that "all of these steps that I was taking to try to somehow be my true self, were actually taking me away from my true self. . . . I started realizing that in all of these things I was doing to try to grasp part of myself that was cut off, I was trying to cut off another part of myself in the process; and it wasn't working."

About a week after this realization, Torren experienced a sense of wholeness in which all the broken pieces of himself came back together. This illumination came to him while under the influence of mind-altering drugs, one of which was administered through a clinic. He recounts, "I almost felt like I could reach out and just put my hand on the shoulder of the Torren that was in Southeast Asia." Then he understood: "That person is still me. I'm still here." He saw that he could still be outgoing and creative. "All of these things I can still do. They didn't die. . . . They weren't inaccessible because I'm a man and I have to be stoic. No, I can actually do these things. I'm free to be myself."

Torren found he had no desire to continue his transition. He was finally able to say, "It doesn't matter what the world is telling me, what these messages are. I know who

I am as Torren. These masculine parts of me are good. They're okay. They're fine. And these more feminine aspects that were inaccessible to me growing up—they are actually accessible.... I can do these things, and I want to keep doing them." Even though the use of mind-altering drugs helped Torren to make these discoveries about himself, he says he has learned from experience that these drugs can be dangerous and "should only be used in a supervised medical/professional setting".

Torren stopped taking estrogen and stopped presenting as Audrey. But his mental and physical health have suffered from the hormonal treatment. He has had depression and anxiety that have left him barely functional at times along with brain fog that keeps him from processing information as he used to be able to.

Torren now understands that his gender dysphoria was not the cause of his mental health struggles, but a symptom of them. The cause of his gender issues was "something that was broken" in his identity that caused him to feel self-hatred, a brokenness both caused and exacerbated by the abuse he suffered in his church as well as the shame surrounding the violation of the strict gender roles of his upbringing. The pain of his broken identity, he says, presented as gender dysphoria, and the appropriate treatment is addressing its underlying cause. For him, he says, this requires confronting his self-hatred and self-rejection and learning to integrate his personality. He knows this is an ongoing project, and that the residual effects of his brokenness may last a long time.

Torren is concerned about the misdiagnosis of mental health conditions that is leading people down a potentially addictive path of altering their bodies and about the regret some people feel after transitioning. He now sees many examples of people who initially feel better after medical intervention, but then, a few years later, begin to struggle with depression again. Torren has found an integrative health physician whom he trusts and who understands his story, and he is now on the path to healing.

Torren has become more outgoing. He's learning more about himself and regaining who he is and who he wants to be. He says, "I've had myself pegged incorrectly my entire life and have been trying to force myself into some role … that just isn't me." He says he has learned a lot about himself and how he fits into the world, and he understands the root causes of his struggles better. He works to balance an accurate assessment of the influences that led him to transition, while acknowledging his own responsibility for his choices. He looks at his past mistakes not to beat himself up with shame or guilt but in order to make better decisions in the future, to move forward in loving God and his neighbor as himself. "It's hard and it's dark," he says, "and I'm carrying the weight of these decisions that I made. Every day that I wake up in this house that I bought with my wife, who's no longer here, it's hard." Yes, it is hard work to detransition, to realize that one has been heading in the wrong direction and to make a 180-degree turn, but Torren is on the road to healing.

To other people struggling with gender dysphoria, Torren recommends taking advantage of the removal of the stigma against gender identity disorders. He encourages those who are struggling to talk to their parents, their friends, their teachers, or their pastors without shame and to resist the temptation to treat their dysphoria with medicalization and surgeries. He especially decries the "insidious movement" that convinces children that any discomfort they feel with their identity is an indication that they need to transition.

9

Rachel

Rachel's story, like that of many detransitioners, is complicated: there is more than one reason why she attempted to transition medically and then decided to detransition.[1] Now, as an articulate and kind thirty-one-year-old woman, she offers her perspective and shares her harrowing story.

For Rachel, it all started with her discomfort at being seen as female, knowing how her body was perceived and treated by others. She grew up in an abusive home, and she has a long, sad history of sexual abuse, which started when she was just four years old. A close family member molested her, and she has been raped four times. The first time was when she was fourteen, by a nineteen-year-old man she had been dating. This trauma made Rachel distrust men.

Rachel also struggled with her sexual orientation and rigid stereotypes surrounding gender roles, especially in the context of her strict upbringing. In her family's religion, dating was not encouraged, her parents expected to choose her husband, and female gender roles were strictly enforced. Rachel wanted to escape from the abuse she had

---

[1] Rachel, interview by Kallie Fell, in The Center for Bioethics and Culture Network, *Venus Rising with Rachel: Why I Detransitioned*, April 25, 2022, https://youtu.be/E-dFvıu3Lpo. All quotations from Rachel in this chapter are taken from this interview.

endured as female and from her feelings of inadequacy in not being able to meet the gendered expectations according to which she had been raised.

When she was sixteen, her parents divorced, and her sister was placed in her father's custody. She wanted to protect her sister, so she also chose to live with her father. At the age of seventeen, Rachel was kicked out of that home because of her same-sex attraction, and she moved across the country to live with her mother and start over. In her early twenties, in her own words, she "tip-toed out of the closet and started dating women exclusively".

Around this time, she went on a date that would become the catalyst for her acceptance of the deception that she was "born in the wrong body". Unknowingly, Rachel had agreed to go on a date with someone she describes as "a nondisclosed transgender person" whom she had met online—a man who was masquerading as a woman. This self-proclaimed "trans woman" was aggressive and abusive. He pressured her, telling her that she could not really be attracted to women unless she was willing to be in a sexual relationship with him—even though he had not had any surgery to make his genitals mimic a woman's. The first time he met Rachel in person, he called her a "bigot" and told her, "You're not a lesbian. You're actually a man." Doubts about her own sexuality and mindset began to creep in.

Rachel was mentally and emotionally unstable, and she took all of this to heart, especially since she had already been questioning her sexuality. She began to discover transgender ideology through online videos, Reddit discussions, and private chats with other women who were presenting themselves to the world as male. Some of these women, like her, had grown up sexualized against their will, feeling as if they could not fight back against the

societal sexualization of their bodies, and they were looking for ways to escape from being touched or even seen
by men. Many of these women also had histories of eating
disorders, abuse, and mental illness. They all claimed that
transitioning had helped them. She continued to read and
listen to stories from women who were living as men,
and the more she connected with them, the more she
could relate to their feelings. Rachel started to think, "If I
don't act like a woman, and I don't feel comfortable being
seen as a woman, maybe I am not a woman."

From there, her transition "happened really fast".
This suddenness is another common experience among
detransitioners—so common, in fact, that physician-
scientist Dr. Lisa Littman coined a new term to describe
this phenomenon: *rapid-onset gender dysphoria* (ROGD).
Dr. Littman, an expert in the field, conducts research
"focused on gender dysphoria, the experiences of people
who desist (or re-identify) after identifying as transgender, and people who detransition after gender transition".[2]
ROGD is defined as "a type of adolescent-onset or late-
onset gender dysphoria where the development of gender dysphoria is observed to *begin suddenly* during or after
puberty in an adolescent or young adult who would not
have met criteria for gender dysphoria in childhood".[3]
It is still unclear how many girls or young women would
fit into this definition, as it is not yet a clinical diagnosis.
Like most topics surrounding gender dysphoria, it is a field
of study that requires further attention.

[2] "Dr. Lisa Littman", personal website, accessed July 6, 2023, https://litt
manresearch.com.
[3] Lisa Littman, quoted in "Rapid-Onset Gender Dysphoria (ROGD)",
Rapid-Onset Gender Dysphoria (ROGD), website of Parents of ROGD
Kids, accessed July 6, 2023, https://www.parentsofrogdkids.com/rapidonset
-gender-dysphoria.

At twenty-two, Rachel consulted a gender therapist. She notes that a gender therapist is very different from a general therapist or a therapist who specializes in anxiety or depression. In her experience, gender therapists tie any mental health issue their clients are experiencing to gender identity. Also, these therapists are encouraged to affirm the perceived gender identity of their clients rather than explore any connections to their trauma or mental health conditions. Not only had Rachel suffered sexual abuse as a young child, but she was diagnosed with schizophrenia and struggled with an eating disorder as a teenager. She says that while she was being seen by her gender therapist, she was mentally unstable and her schizophrenia was not well managed. Looking back, Rachel wishes she had received care from anyone other than a gender therapist, describing the care she received as "insufficient and harmful".

She saw her therapist a total of three times before the therapist signed a letter stating that she was of sound mind and could consent to cross-sex hormones (testosterone) and future medical procedures, such as a double mastectomy. According to Rachel, the therapist also stated that Rachel had been with her for longer than she actually had. The therapist was perfectly aware of Rachel's mental health history and her vulnerable state, but these were not addressed. The same week as that third visit, she saw a primary care physician "experimenting" (Rachel's word) with diagnosing people with "gender identity disorder" (the term used at the time). It was only a month and a half from the time Rachel first met her gender therapist to her first prescription of testosterone—and only three months since she had learned what "transgender" identity was. Rachel considers herself fortunate that she never underwent any surgery.

Taking testosterone, Rachel at first felt elated and euphoric. She had been struggling with so many mental health issues, and, like the people she had met online, she convinced herself that this drug would fix everything. She says, "When you're desperate, you'll reach for anything." She was urgently searching for the root cause of her pain and suffering, and she was confident that medically transitioning with testosterone would finally make her feel like she was who she was supposed to be. But the resolution she anticipated never came.

After a few weeks, Rachel started to notice changes in her body. First the testosterone affected her voice, making her sound like a teenage boy with all the goofy sounds and cracking that accompany puberty—a voice she has still to this day. Rachel remembers having a lot of acne and noticing changes to her genitals. These were all changes she could deal with, she says; but two or three months into taking the testosterone, she was "shaken" by a changing hairline. She recalls becoming "wildly depressed", even attempting to end her life. She talked with her gender therapist about this depression, telling her, "I am having a lot of doubts. This does not feel right. I don't recognize myself anymore. What I see in the mirror doesn't look like it's supposed to look. This doesn't feel good." Even though she was suicidal, the gender therapist simply assured her that her doubts were normal and urged her to push through, promising it would get better.

Not only was Rachel receiving reassuring words from her gender therapist, she was also hearing encouragement from her circle of friends who called themselves trans. These relationships were laden with peer pressure, toxicity, and coercion. Rachel was not free to be honest about the effects of testosterone on her body or the way that she felt. It was taboo to speak about any negative experience related to transition; that was labeled "internalized transphobia". "We were encouraging each other to do surgery that could cause us harm, or go on hormones that could cause us harm," she says. "The motto was 'Go for it.' Instead of being brutally honest with one another, we encouraged delusion and ignorance of real problems."

This peer pressure, even though she was a young adult, affected her deeply, and despite her doubts, she stayed on testosterone for five and a half years. Interestingly, at one point, her prescribing doctor refused to allow her to refill the testosterone prescription until she had consulted with a surgeon for a double mastectomy. Rachel was already flat-chested, and she was unable to afford surgery, so she had no desire for the procedure. She recalls a lot of pressure to raise funds or take out loans for a surgery she didn't really want. She went to a surgical consultation to appease the prescribing doctor and was rewarded with the renewal of her testosterone prescription. Rachel's story is one of ongoing neglect, lies, and manipulation.

While on testosterone, Rachel became underweight and lost muscle mass. She battled chronic skin issues, such as severe acne. At age twenty-five, her whole body was in protest: she was tired and frail and hurt all over. Her kidneys and liver had begun to fail, and she became jaundiced and started urinating and vomiting blood. She had three mini-strokes. She recalls not being able even to stand up most days. She slowly stopped taking testosterone, weaning herself off the injectable to the gel form, which helped, and she began to feel better quickly. It wasn't until she was twenty-seven years old that she decided to stop the testosterone altogether, which launched her into the detransition process without the support of her friends or even her physician.

For Rachel, "detransition" means doing your best to reverse your transition process. She explains that people in the detransitioned community describe themselves as "having done some sort of medical thing in order to transition" and as now attempting to reverse that process. For her, the medical attempt consisted of taking testosterone. Rachel decided she could not be silent any longer, and she began sharing her own health experiences to warn others of the possible detrimental side effects of testosterone. She was immediately met with a backlash from the "trans community", from people she had once considered friends. She was called a "transphobe" and a "traitor". She even received death threats.

Betrayed by her friends, humiliated by the decision she had made to transition, and intimidated by the work ahead of her to undo the damage, Rachel began to read about and talk to other women who "had come into trans identity" much like herself, "with histories of pain, looking for family and truth". These women "made a point that should have been obvious from the start—changing your body doesn't change the damage you hold."

Rachel has found the stability she had so desperately needed. She lives in a thriving city she enjoys, working in a job she loves, surrounded by supportive friends. She has found a community where she is able to talk freely about her experiences as a detransitioner and as a woman. She has also found help through therapy where she is able to address her mental health issues. Unfortunately, though, because she has been labeled a TERF and as transphobic for talking about her transition experience to health professionals, she refuses to disclose it to her therapist, which makes her unable to grieve properly over what she was encouraged to do to her body.

Despite the positive changes to Rachel's life since detransitioning, her health has been severely compromised by her attempt to transition medically. She has developed endometriosis, even though there is no family history of the disease or indications of it in her younger years. Since our interview, Rachel has spoken to four other women who were suddenly diagnosed with endometriosis after stopping synthetic testosterone, and she has heard of other transitioners with the same diagnosis. Rachel has vaginal atrophy—her vagina continues to tear and bleed. Her estrogen levels are lower than that of a woman going through menopause, and she will be on supplemental estrogen for the rest of her life.

The Mayo Clinic offers warnings about these possible side effects of testosterone on the female body: acne, male-pattern baldness, sleep apnea, abnormal levels of cholesterol and other lipids (which may increase cardiovascular disease), high blood pressure, type 2 diabetes, infertility, deep vein thrombosis, pulmonary embolism, atrophic vaginitis, pelvic pain, and clitoral discomfort.[4] Studies suggest that women taking what is known as "gender-affirming hormone therapy" have increased risks of myocardial infarction (heart attack), ischemic stroke, venous thromboembolism, and lower bone mineral density.[5] Many of these side effects or complications, like Rachel's receding hairline, are permanent, even though she was reassured that all changes would be reversible. Rachel is now at high risk for having strokes and heart attacks. There is also the risk of other kinds of damage that research has not

[4] "Masculinizing Hormone Therapy", Mayo Clinic, February 21, 2023, https://www.mayoclinic.org/tests-procedures/masculinizing-hormone-therapy/about/pac-20385099.

[5] Nyein Chan Swe et al., "The Effects of Gender-Affirming Hormone Therapy on Cardiovascular and Skeletal Health: A Literature Review", *Metabolism Open* 13 (March 2022), https://doi.org/10.1016/j.metop.2022.100173; Rafael Delgado-Ruiz, "Systematic Review of the Long-Term Effects of Transgender Hormone Therapy on Bone Markers and Bone Mineral Density and Their Potential Effects in Implant Therapy", *Journal of Clinical Medicine* 8, no. 6 (2019), https://doi.org/10.3390/jcm8060784.

yet discovered. Despite all these lingering effects, though, Rachel has found peace. She has learned to advocate for herself and her health.

Now, Rachel advises women with problems accepting their bodies that "gender dysphoria is not the cause; it's a symptom. Your discomfort is coming from trauma, abuse, depression, sexual orientation issues, circumstantial issues, the sexism in our culture." She believes that the doctors and therapists treating gender dysphoria are failing to treat the real underlying issues plaguing young women. Even worse, Rachel thinks that there are gender therapists and medical providers who know they are causing harm but refuse to stop. They are pressured and encouraged to believe in transgender ideology to the degree that they repress their conscience.

Further, Rachel believes that the voices of detransitioners are being silenced. Through online communities, Rachel has met hundreds of men and women who have detransitioned or desisted hormonal treatments for their dysphoria. Despite the growing numbers of detransitioners, Rachel describes how hard it is to speak out as a detransitioner. "There is so much pressure from the [trans] community and so much encouragement to step into the spotlight to say that this [transitioning] is the best thing you've ever done. Even if there are issues and doubts and problems, you're not going to talk about that because you'll get booted." So, when a woman like Rachel decides to detransition, she leaves or is ostracized by the sole community that had previously provided a type of refuge, leaving her lonely and isolated. Yet, Rachel says, detransitioning is worth it.

Rachel believes that healthcare providers are unethically pushing people to transition and are abusing their power. In her own story, during a period of self-destruction, she sought help, but instead of receiving the care she needed, she was encouraged to alter her body permanently. She knows that the practitioners she saw could have "helped her in a less drastic, non-medicalized way", but those less-medicalized methods of therapy were never approached. Instead, she was pushed to start testosterone and, even though she was mentally ill, encouraged to cut up her body. She stresses that no one who is mentally ill should be pushed in this way—vulnerable patients like herself should be protected.

Rachel is concerned that people who are transitioning aren't getting the facts they urgently need to make healthy choices. To her mind, people who are curious about transitioning are better served by going to more holistic therapy for much longer and avoiding gender therapists altogether. She urges those who are uncomfortable in their own skin to "be patient and don't go for the quick fix that is offered", and she encourages everyone, despite the pressure, to "go to detransition message boards and websites to learn from those who have lived through it".

Rachel has found that many women, including those who have not transitioned, struggle with their bodies, because walking through this world as a woman comes with great challenges—including male violence, unequal treatment in the workplace, the stigma and costs related to periods and women's health, and underrepresentation as leaders or in areas such as technology, medicine, and science in general. Or how about the challenge of simply walking down the street in safety?

When asked what she would say to other detransitioners, she begins to cry. Clearly, Rachel is heartbroken over what has been done to her and to others. Recognizing the trauma that transitioning has caused and the permanent changes it has made to her body, she says: "You want someone to be angry at, you want justice, and you wish you could go back, but the truth is you can't, you can't go back, you can only go forward; and going forward means advocating for yourself, learning to love yourself ... Your journey through transition into detransitioning will ultimately teach you about how to take care of yourself."

Rachel has now been living as a detransitioner for the past five years, "moving on from a place of bitterness and short-sightedness" and no longer feeling "with as much fervor the anger and pain" as she once did. She plans "to continue doing work for detransitioners, while backing away from the social identity of *being* a detransitioner. There are so many genuine, intelligent, victorious detransitioners."

10

Why Is the Trend Higher among Adolescent Girls?

Popping up all over the United States are clinics that claim to offer "medical services for gender nonconforming youths and their families in one central location".[1] Who are these "youths" they serve? Interestingly, in recent years, it appears that most patients are teenage girls—more specifically, girls with no history of childhood gender identity issues. Data presented by Jack Turban, assistant professor of child and adolescent psychiatry at the University of California San Francisco, seems to refute this claim, and he concludes that the proportion of natal females who have come out as transgender has not increased.[2] However, other studies, as well as overwhelming anecdotal evidence, seem to contradict his data. For example, a review commissioned by the United Kingdom's National Health Service found that two-thirds of the five thousand adolescents referred to a large gender clinic in 2021 were girls.[3] And according to Abigail Shrier in the *New York Post*:

[1] "Pediatric and Adolescent Gender Clinic", Stanford Medicine, accessed July 6, 2023, https://www.stanfordchildrens.org/en/service/gender.

[2] Jack L. Turban et al., "Sex Assigned at Birth Ratio among Transgender and Gender Diverse Adolescents in the United States", *Pediatrics* 150, no. 3 (August 2022), https://doi.org/10.1542/peds.2022-056567.

[3] Amelia Gentleman, "'An explosion': What Is behind the Rise in Girls Questioning Their Gender Identity?", *The Guardian*, November 24, 2022, https://www.theguardian.com/society/2022/nov/24/an-explosion-what-is-behind-the-rise-in-girls-questioning-their-gender-identity.

Between 2016 and 2017, the number of gender surgeries for natal females in the US quadrupled; in the UK, the rates of gender dysphoria for teenage girls are up 4,400 percent over the previous decade. An ailment that typically began in early childhood, and overwhelmingly afflicted males, suddenly has a new dominant demographic: teenage girls.[4]

In an interview with Shrier, Dr. Erica Anderson, a clinical psychologist who specializes in gender identity, stated, "At our clinic at UCSF, for two years now running, we're running two to one natal females to natal males. Two to one."[5] In another article published in *Quillette*, Dr. Anderson is quoted as saying, "The data are very clear that adolescent girls are coming to gender clinics in greater proportion than adolescent boys. And this is a change in the last couple of years. And it's an open question: What do we make of that? We don't really know what's going on. And we should be concerned about it."[6] It is certainly concerning. Despite Turban's study, there is data to show that girls are more likely than ever to believe they were born in the wrong body.[7] This chapter seeks to answer

[4] Abigail Shrier, "How 'Peer Contagion' May Play into the Rise of Teen Girls Transitioning", *New York Post*, June 27, 2020, https://nypost.com/2020 /06/27/how-peer-contagion-plays-into-the-rise-of-teens-transitioning.

[5] Abigail Shrier, "Top Trans Doctors Blow the Whistle on 'Sloppy' Care", *The Free Press* (blog), *Substack*, October 4, 2021, https://www.thefp.com/top -trans-doctors-blow-the-whistle.

[6] Erica Anderson, interview by Lisa Selin Davis, "A Trans Pioneer Explains Her Resignation from the US Professional Association for Transgender Health", *Quillette*, January 6, 2022, https://quillette.com/2022/01/06/a-trans gender-pioneer-explains-why-she-stepped-down-from-uspath-and-wpath.

[7] Thomas D. Steensma, Peggy T. Cohen-Kettenis, and Kenneth J. Zucker, "Evidence for a Change in the Sex Ratio of Children Referred for Gender Dysphoria: Data from the Center of Expertise on Gender Dysphoria in Amsterdam (1988–2016)", *Journal of Sex & Marital Therapy* 44, no. 7 (2018), https:// doi.org/10.1080/0092623X.2018.1437580; Madison Aitken et al., "Evidence

these questions: Why are our adolescent girls believing that they were born in the wrong body? Why is this trending higher among adolescent girls? And why does it seem these girls are being rushed into medical transition?

These questions cannot be answered without looking first at what female detransitioners and desisters (those who transitioned socially, but not medically, and then reverted) are saying. In the film and in the stories shared in this book from women, we see three interwoven yet distinct themes: untreated mental health concerns and related trauma (including sexual abuse), peer or social contagion, and fear of being female (or at least a dissatisfaction with the perceived limits of being female).

Grace reports that when she graduated from college, she had a very serious mental health crisis that ultimately led to her desire to transition medically. Feeling lost and depressed and besieged by suicidal ideation, she had come to believe that if she could become a man, she would finally stop feeling such discomfort with herself and with her body. Also, she had idealized the experience of men in society to the degree that she thought that if she could be a man, she would finally feel comfortable and safe.

When Helena was young, she lost her primary caretaker—an unresolved trauma that ultimately led to depression, isolation, and the development of an eating disorder. At a young age, online engagement introduced her to a new belief system and she began to believe that she was a boy, and exposure to pornography made her reject the ideas of marriage and sex. The effect of pornography on young girls cannot be overstated, and it is clearly woven through each of the three themes we are exploring in this chapter.[8] It is readily and easily available online and promoted in online communities, and it affects, as in Helena's case, how a young girl views herself and her role in this world.

Cat, who also experienced trauma at a young age, admits to feeling both limited and afraid to live life as a girl or a woman. Chloe, who was diagnosed with ADHD and autism at a young age, was also captured by an online community that devalued being female and minimized women's experiences as a whole. Rachel's gender dysphoria began with a lasting discomfort with being seen as female and with knowing how her body was perceived and treated by men—an awareness that stemmed from her early sexual abuse and trauma.

Dr. Lisa Littman's 2021 study included one hundred detransitioners who gave a variety of reasons for detransitioning but expressed themes similar to the ones we will highlight and unpack in this chapter.[9] The participants said they detransitioned because they became more comfortable identifying as their natal sex (60%), they had concerns about potential medical complications from transitioning (49%), or they realized that their gender dysphoria was caused by something specific, such as trauma, abuse, or mental health issues (38%).

Stage of development or age might influence the reason for a person's decision to transition. Our focus in this chapter will be on adolescent-onset gender dysphoria in females

---

[8] See Melinda Tankard Reist, ed., *Getting Real: Challenging the Sexualisation of Girls* (Melbourne, Australia: Spinifex Press, 2009). See also Melinda Tankard Reist and Abigail Bray, eds., *Big Porn Inc: Exposing the Harms of the Global Pornography Industry* (Melbourne, Australia: Spinifex Press, 2011).

[9] Lisa Littman, "Individuals Treated for Gender Dysphoria with Medical and/or Surgical Transition Who Subsequently Detransitioned: A Survey of 100 Detransitioners", *Archives of Sexual Behavior* 50, no. 8 (2021), https://doi.org/10.1007/s10508-021-02163-w.

more broadly, but will include girls with rapid-onset gender dysphoria—a group Dr. Littman has also focused on, with preliminary data that suggest that comorbidities are a significant risk factor with this population and that social contagion can also play a role.[10] To prevent more children from being harmed, we must try to understand why so many young girls believe that they are transgender.

Trauma and Unresolved Mental Health Diagnosis

Trauma, including sexual abuse, and mental health conditions such as depression often go hand in hand. Trauma, especially unresolved trauma, can make a person more vulnerable to mental illness.[11] According to the American Psychological Association, trauma is "an emotional response to a terrible event like an accident, rape, or natural disaster".[12] Thirty-three of the sixty-nine female detransitioners in Dr. Littman's study experienced a traumatic event less than one year before the onset of their gender dysphoria.[13] Studies show that comorbidities such as autism spectrum disorder, attention and hyperactivity disorders, social anxiety, depression, suicidality, and eating disorders (Grace, Helena, and Cat each struggled with eating disorders) commonly occur along with gender dysphoria.[14] Using data that are representative of the population in the United States, one

[10] Lisa Littman, "Parent Reports of Adolescents and Young Adults Perceived to Show Signs of a Rapid Onset of Gender Dysphoria", *PLoS ONE* 13, no. 8 (2018), https://doi.org/10.1371/journal.pone.0202330.

[11] "Trauma", Mental Health Foundation, updated November 11, 2021, https://www.mentalhealth.org.uk/explore-mental-health/a-z-topics/trauma.

[12] "Trauma", American Psychological Association (APA), updated August 2022, https://www.apa.org/topics/trauma.

[13] Littman, "Gender Dysphoria".

[14] Stella O'Malley, "Brief Guidance for Pediatricians and PCPs", Genspect, accessed July 6, 2023, https://genspect.org/guidance-for-pediatricians-and-pcps.

study reported "a high prevalence and significantly higher odds of mental disorder diagnoses in the transgender population" when compared with the "cisgender population".[15] Both trauma (including sexual trauma and the influence of pornography on the developing brain) and mental health conditions such as depression, eating disorders, and alcohol or drug abuse contributed to the transgender identification and decision to transition of the women in this book, and it was not until *after* detransitioning that they understood these complex relationships.

Pediatric endocrinologist Dr. Van Meter says, "In my experience, not one single patient that I have treated, that has come to me with transgender issues, has come from a mentally healthy state."[16] He tells us that children come to him after having what are called "adverse childhood events" (ACEs), defined as potentially traumatic events during childhood that can be linked to problematic outcomes over the life course. Also known as "adverse childhood experiences", ACEs include divorce of one's parents, death in the family, familial drug abuse, incarceration of a parent, and sexual abuse. Of course, ACEs and traumatic events happen to both boys and girls, but studies have shown that girls experience more ACEs than boys,[17] and 29 percent of female youths had six or more ACEs, which

[15] Bishoy Hanna, "Psychiatric Disorders in the U.S. Transgender Population", *Annals of Epidemiology* 39 (2019), https://doi.org/10.1016/j.annepidem.2019.09.009.

[16] Quentin Van Meter, interview by Jennifer Lahl, Atlanta, Georgia, January 13, 2021.

[17] Vincent J. Felitti et al., "Relationship of Childhood Abuse and Household Dysfunction to Many of the Leading Causes of Death in Adults: The Adverse Childhood Experiences (ACE) Study", *American Journal of Preventive Medicine* 14, no. 4 (1998), https://doi.org/10.1016/S0749-3797(98)00017-8; Michael T. Baglivio et al., "The Prevalence of Adverse Childhood Experiences (ACE) in the Lives of Juvenile Offenders", *Journal of Juvenile Justice* 3, no. 2 (2014), https://www.prisonpolicy.org/scans/Prevalence_of_ACE.pdf.

was more than twice the proportion for male youths.[18] Further, girls report different types of ACEs than boys do. For example, sexual abuse is more common among girls,[19] while boys are more likely to experience physical abuse.[20] According to the Center for Disease Control, ACEs are linked to chronic health problems, mental illness, and substance misuse in adulthood, and preventing ACEs could reduce the number of adults with depression by as much as 44 percent.[21]

In 2019, Schnarrs and colleagues found in their study population that "transgender participants reported emotional abuse, physical neglect, and emotional neglect more frequently"[22] than non-transgender lesbian, gay, and bisexual participants and "demonstrated that transgender youth had higher ACE scores" when compared to non-transgender lesbian, gay, and bisexual youths.[23] Even after

---

[18] Michael T. Baglivio and Nathan Epps, "The Interrelatedness of Adverse Childhood Experiences among High-Risk Juvenile Offenders", *Youth Violence and Juvenile Justice* 14, no. 3, https://doi.org/10.1177/1541204014566286.

[19] Baglivio et al., "The Prevalence of Adverse Childhood Experiences"; Carly B. Dierkhising et al., "Developmental Timing of Polyvictimization: Continuity, Change, and Association with Adverse Outcomes in Adolescence", *Child Abuse & Neglect* 87 (2019), https://doi.org/10.1016/j.chiabu.2018.07.022.

[20] Baglivio et al., "The Prevalence of Adverse Childhood Experiences"; Carly B. Dierkhising et al., "Trauma Histories among Justice-Involved Youth: Findings from the National Child Traumatic Stress Network", *European Journal of Psychotraumatology* 4 (2013), https://doi.org/10.3402/ejpt.v4i0.20274.

[21] Centers for Disease Control and Prevention (CDC), "Adverse Childhood Experiences (ACEs): Preventing Early Trauma to Improve Adult Health", *Vital Signs*, updated August 23, 2021, https://www.cdc.gov/vitalsigns/aces/index.html.

[22] Phillip W. Schnarrs et al., "Differences in Adverse Childhood Experiences (ACEs) and Quality of Physical and Mental Health between Transgender and Cisgender Sexual Minorities", *Journal of Psychiatric Research* 119 (2019), https://doi.org/10.1016/j.jpsychires.2019.09.001.

[23] Christopher Kroppman et al., "Transgender and Gender-Nonconforming Youth Deserve Further Study in Relation to Adverse Childhood Experiences", *Journal of Gay & Lesbian Mental Health* 25, no. 1 (2021), https://doi.org/10.1080/19359705.2020.1837706.

adjusting for ACE scores, Schnarrs and colleagues found a significant association between transgender identification and psychiatric impairment.[24] This association may not be the reason for the recent uptick in the number of adolescent girls seeking to transition medically, but it does seem to be an area that needs more research and exploration— especially because, in a survey of one hundred detransitioners, "the majority (55%) felt that they did not receive an adequate evaluation from a doctor or mental health professional before starting transition."[25] Considering the mental health comorbidities that adolescents with gender dysphoria have and the abuse they have experienced, this is a substantial finding. More research in this area is warranted, but at the very least, people suffering from gender dysphoria deserve healthcare providers who will uphold their duty to care for them in a way that seeks to heal them of past trauma and treat any underlying mental health diagnosis.

Peer or Social Contagion

The suggestion that peer or social contagion is a contributing factor in the increasing number of youth with gender dysphoria and the desire to transition meets with strong resistance from transgender activists. According to the American Psychological Association, social contagion is "the spread of behaviors, attitudes, and affect through crowds and other types of social aggregates from one member to another."[26] Peer contagion is the process by which peers mutually

[24] Schnarrs et al., "Differences in Adverse Childhood Experiences".

[25] Littman, "Gender Dysphoria", 3353.

[26] American Psychological Association (APA), "Social Contagion", APA Dictionary of Psychology, accessed July 7, 2023, https://dictionary.apa.org /social-contagion.

influence each other in a way that promotes emotions and behaviors that can have negative effects on their development.[27] Examples of disorders spread through peer contagion include eating disorders and drug use. In the case of transgenderism, peer contagion happens when peers, social media, and online communities influence the development of transgender identification and desire to transition.

One of the first to recognize and study this phenomenon was Dr. Lisa Littman of Brown University. In 2016 she was "scrolling through social media when she noticed that a group of teen girls from her small town in Rhode Island—all from the same friend group—had come out as transgender".[28] Intrigued, Dr. Littman began her own research, hypothesizing that transgender identification, like cutting or anorexia, was being driven by peer contagion among adolescent females. The adolescents or young adults in her study "were predominantly natal females (82.8%) with a mean age of 16.4 years at the time of survey completion and a mean age of 15.2 when they announced a transgender-identification".[29] Nearly 87 percent of the parents in Dr. Littman's study reported that "along with the sudden or rapid onset of gender dysphoria, their child either had an increase in their social media/internet use, belonged to a friend group in which one or multiple friends became transgender-identified during a similar timeframe, or both."[30]

Abigail Shrier, best-selling author of *Irreversible Damage: The Transgender Craze Seducing Our Daughters*, has

---

[27] Thomas J. Dishion and Jessica M. Tipsord, "Peer Contagion in Child and Adolescent Social and Emotional Development", *Annual Review of Psychology* 62 (2011), https://doi.org/10.1146/annurev.psych.093008.100412.

[28] Shrier, "Peer Contagion".

[29] Littman, "Parent Reports", 2.

[30] Littman, "Parent Reports", 2.

interviewed over four dozen families whose teen girls became swept up in transgender identification. Their stories all follow a pattern,[31] one also observed by Dr. Van Meter. It goes something like this: an adolescent girl who has never expressed any discomfort with her sex hits puberty, and, with its onset, anxiety and depression develop. According to Van Meter:

> Someone she looks up to at school, or perhaps a friend, or someone in an online forum puts the idea in her head that she might be transgender and that is the issue. She then begins to see that as a possibility, becoming more and more affirmed by peers online. She goes onto the internet, types in the word "transgender" and finds that everything in her life is caused by her gender incongruence. She buys into this cult belief system of ideology that everything can be cured by "transitioning" from female to male.[32]

With her online community and school cheering her on, she tries out a new name and pronouns. She has boarded the transgender bus, and her parents are none the wiser. In fact, in some schools across the United States, parents are deliberately kept in the dark about their child's social transition (changing their name or pronouns) by school staff.

An anonymous teacher was given an opportunity to write about his experience using author and critic Wesley Yang's Substack. The anonymous teacher writes:

> I had six classes last year, and I didn't have a single one without multiple students who identified as transgender.... Most of these students were just nonbinary, but I

---

[31] Shrier, "Peer Contagion". See also Abigail Shrier, *Irreversible Damage: The Transgender Craze Seducing Our Daughters* (Washington, D.C.: Regnery Publishing, 2020/2021).

[32] Van Meter, interview by Lahl.

had at least five in the midst of actual medical transition, along with quite a few more who spent their days planning how to get the process started. I'd estimate that 70% or so of these students are female, and talk about breast binding and "top surgery" are common conversation topics at lunch time. It's hard to not step in when you hear an obviously depressed, dysfunctional teenage girl working out how she can convince her parents to approve a double mastectomy, but what can you do? If I said anything at all, I'd be fired in a heartbeat.... I can count a total of nineteen pronoun changes requested by twelve students over just the last semester, along with six for changing names. It's relatively common for students to transition, detransition, and transition again, especially in response to the identity shifts in their classmates. At one point, a single student's decision to go with they/them pronouns set off a chain reaction that resulted in four more of her friends doing the same.[33]

Of course, this account may be dismissed as anecdotal, as just one teacher's experience, but accounts like it from educators have become all too common.

In the 2021 Littman study referenced in the introduction to this chapter, participants identified the sources that had originally encouraged their child to believe transitioning would help them. Social media and online communities were the most frequently reported sources, including YouTube and Tumblr. "A subset of participants experienced the friendship group dynamics" identified in previous work by Littman, "including having one or more friend from the pre-existing friend group transition before

---

[33] Anonymous ("Moonlit Piglet"), "Gender Theory in Schools—Two Things the TERFs Get Right (Plus Two Things They Get Wrong)", *Year Zero* (blog), *Substack*, August 25, 2022, https://wesleyyang.substack.com/gender-theory-in -schools-two-things.

the participant decided to transition (36.4%)."[34] Littman found that girls felt significantly more pressure than boys to transition.

What about girls who don't have a large social circle at school? Are they at risk for being influenced by social contagion? Dr. Van Mol warns in *Trans Mission: What's the Rush to Reassign Gender?* that trans ideology is "catching on because it's the hot topic and it's inescapable. It's all over the media, social media in particular, it's on the web, it's in the entertainment industry. And now, of course, it's made its way into education."[35] There is no doubt that young children and teens today, especially given the recent global pandemic, are spending far less time with their friends in person than any previous generation and are instead spending hours online on social media or other internet platforms that only increase their exposure to transgender influencers and activists.

Van Mol expands on the theories about peer influence by speaking of "semantic contagion", which refers to the spread of words. When words such as "trans" or "transgender" become common parlance, as they have in the last decade, then this language "becomes part of people's reasoning, and they start to automatically interpret their life situation, their problems through that lens."[36] As young girls and teenagers spend more time online and are indoctrinated in trans ideology both online and in school, they begin to associate the words they hear with the problems they have. This was the case for Helena

[34] Littman, "Gender Dysphoria", 3360.

[35] André Van Mol, in *Trans Mission: What's the Rush to Reassign Gender?*, directed by Kallie Fell and Jennifer Lahl (Pleasant Hill, CA: Center for Bioethics and Culture Network [CBC], 2021), https://www.youtube.com/watch?v=rUeqEoARKOA.

[36] André Van Mol, interview by Jennifer Lahl, Redding, California, November 22, 2020.

and Grace: for them, becoming "trans" was a way to deal with discomfort with their bodies.

For those teens and young adults like Helena or Chloe struggling to find friends who look or sound like them or who are interested in the same types of things, going online becomes an escape, which can lead directly to the absorption of transgender ideology. J. K. Rowling recently wrote, "If I'd found community and sympathy online that I couldn't find in my immediate environment [as a teen], I believe I could have been persuaded to turn myself into the son my father had openly said he'd have preferred."[37] Dr. Erica Anderson, the gender clinician referred to above, says:

> I'm worried that gender minority identities have become a bit trendy, with the weird circumstances of the last two years of pandemic, adolescents who are notoriously susceptible to peer influence have found it necessary to have their communication and their social relationships online. They've gotten more information, and more social support online than ever before, and they're reliant on it. I'm worried there's a new group of adolescents who have preexisting mental-health problems, and they're looking for solutions, and they're looking for an explanation for who they are.... And there's a bit of, I would say, fantasy about seizing upon an identity that to them may explain their distress. They may believe and verbalize that: "Okay, the solution to my problem is to transition. And then I won't have these other issues—eating disorders, depression, anxiety, social problems." That is misguided.[38]

Youth struggling with self-acceptance might see transgender identification as a way of doing an end-run around

[37] J. K. Rowling, "J. K. Rowling Writes about Her Reasons for Speaking Out on Sex and Gender Issues", *J. K. Rowling* (blog), June 10, 2020, https://www.jkrowling.com/opinions/j-k-rowling-writes-about-her-reasons-for-speaking-out-on-sex-and-gender-issues. See also Shrier, "Peer Contagion".

[38] Anderson, interview by Davis.

this painful time in their life. Indeed, on account of its high social status in Western culture today, a number of adolescents may perceive transgender identification as an attractive option, especially those with autism or low self-esteem. Adopting this new identity as a member of a high-status, highly celebrated "oppressed" minority is likely to boost peer standing and garner attention from peers and adults alike. Often, these young people are bullied because they are different (for example, neurodivergent or homosexual), and presenting themselves as transgender makes them more welcome at school and by their peers.

Helena's story illustrates this effect. Until she decided to "transition", she felt ignored by school officials and other adults. In addition, the other adolescents in Helena's online community seemed to favor the oppressed. Those who were "marginalized"—in this case, because they presented themselves as transgender—were given more attention and more power in these circles. Those who were perceived as more "privileged" were denied the right to an opinion, the simple chance to be heard, especially anybody designated a "cis straight white girl". This desire for status has even been visible among lesbian youth, apart from their straight counterparts. One source, an anonymous ex-clinician at the Tavistock Clinic in England, reports having observed a similar desire for improved social status that seemed obtainable to lesbian adolescents by identifying as trans. This ex-clinician stated, in the *Times*, "Young lesbians considered at the bottom of the heap suddenly found they were really popular when they said they were trans."[39] It does seem plausible that young people might be subconsciously motivated to

[39] Anonymous, in Lucy Bannerman, "It Feels Like Conversion Therapy for Gay Children, Say Clinicians", *The Times*, April 8, 2019, https://www.thetimes.co.uk/article/it-feels-like-conversion-therapy-for-gay-children-say-clinicians-pvsckdvq2.

present themselves as transgender out of a desire to fit in and improve their social status at school and within their peer groups, online or otherwise.

Afraid to Be Female

In Littman's research, some detransitioners reported that their dysphoria was, at least in part, rooted in others' misogyny or their own hatred of being female.[40] Misogyny is a hatred of, aversion to, or prejudice against women. Like the women in this book, girls might conclude that they were "born in the wrong body" because of how they are perceived as female. They may be afraid of being female, or they may not fit the traditional or stereotypical gender roles expected of them by their family, school, society, or culture.

Colin Wright, an evolutionary biologist, writer, and editor, an academic advisor to the Society for Evidence-Based Gender Medicine (SEGM), and a fellow with the Manhattan Institute, explains how "gender-affirming care" has been persistently—and horrifically—pushed onto girls once known as "tomboys". It offers to "fix" a "perceived misalignment between 'gender identity' (i.e., social roles and stereotypes) and the child's biological sex"; that is, the term "transgender" is used more broadly to encompass "mere nonconformity with rigid traditional sex roles". Not only is this dangerous for young girls, but it also "repudiates decades of work by women's-rights activists who rightfully gauged such notions as sexist and oppressive and fought to free nonconformists from social stigma".[41]

---

[40] Littman, "Gender Dysphoria".

[41] Colin Wright, "Every Tomboy Is Tagged 'Transgender'", *The Wall Street Journal*, September 22, 2022, https://www.wsj.com/articles/every-tomboy-is -tagged-transgender-transsexual-gender-dysphoria-children-hormones-clinic -terminology-expectations-11663872092.

All the women whose stories are told in this book were strongly influenced by this misogyny. Chloe witnessed other girls online posting comments that devalued being female and the experiences of women and complained about menstruation. Dr. Van Mol explains, "For a lot of young girls, the stress of the tween years, the whole idea of 'What do you mean I'm going to have periods? What's this menstruation stuff?'—it just looks like too big of a hurdle."[42] These concerns can feel overwhelming. Options that offer the hope of escaping the pain, awkwardness, and inconvenience of puberty and the negative associations with being female—options such as transgender identification—are presented as effective solutions without regard for their consequences.

Cat grew up in the nineties, and the culture at that time encouraged her dysphoria. She says the movies and television programs she watched were misogynistic in their portrayal of women characters and presented very restricted options for what little girls could do and be when they grew up. Cat observed that the males in these shows were portrayed as powerful, intelligent, and interesting, while the female characters lacked depth—they were portrayed as beautiful love interests and nothing more; if that was what being a woman was, then Cat wanted nothing to do with any of it. The role she wanted was more like those of the intelligent, interesting male characters, and this fed her gender dysphoria.

For Rachel, it was unsafe to be female. From a young age, her body had been objectified and violated, particularly by men who had sexually abused her on multiple occasions. She lived in a world where being female put her in grave danger. In addition to the abuse, she grew

---

[42] Van Mol, interview by Lahl.

up with rigid sex-role stereotypes that she did not fit into or approve of, including an arranged marriage. Medically transitioning was a way to escape the scary female world in which she had found herself trapped.

Helena spent hours engaged in online conversations that normalized and even celebrated pornography, which made her resolve as a little girl never to get married or have sex. She worried that if she revealed her revulsion to her community, they would have branded her "anti-feminist". So, like other girls, she felt she had to "play along" with the game, which shaped the way she would view herself as female.

Here we have four separate accounts of how transgenderism can be, at least in part, rooted in a fear of being female. It is evident from these personal accounts how scary and overwhelming it can be for young girls to face a puberty coupled with abuse, stereotypes, and tremendous amounts of pressure from society and culture. As Libby Emmons, editor-in-chief of the *Post Millennial*, explains: "We've all been there, right? I loathed it, loathed my periods, which were long and miserable. It comes with being ogled and needing to buy tampons. It comes with words like 'budding breasts' and 'Aunt Flo' and people telling you to try not to get raped."[43]

Some readers might doubt the influence of traditional male and female stereotypes in a modern world where, at least in the West, girls can grow up to do or be whatever they want. We've been taught for decades how harmful gender stereotypes are, and it is true that women and men today have roles that break historical norms. But transgender ideology is nevertheless rigidly stereotypical.

[43] Libby Emmons, interview by Jennifer Lahl, New York City, March 16, 2022.

An anonymous teacher writes, as reported by Wesley Yang, that the gender stereotypes with which girls such as Cat and Rachel struggle are still in full force within America's schools:

> Every one of my colleagues, if asked, would immediately say that gender stereotypes were harmful bullshit—yet they've created (or at least encouraged) a sorting system where "girl" is the category for feminine children, "boy" is the category for masculine children, and anyone who even comes close to the edges of either gets plucked out and relabeled non-binary. It breaks my heart to think these students are growing up in such a rigid, self-policing culture, where the gendered expectations I thought we'd put behind us now structure their basic sense of self. When I was their age, my school had a fair share of bullies who would taunt girls with short hair by saying they must really be boys—but at least the school administrators back then didn't agree![44]

The prevailing culture in schools today looks for the girls who cut their hair short and don't conform to gender stereotypes. It encourages these children to change their pronouns and ushers them into a world where they can medically change their body to adhere better to sex stereotypes. Instead of changing the stereotypes that imprison them, the culture pressures them to change their bodies to fit the stereotypes better.

Natasha Chart, a woman with autism featured in our film, describes herself as a lonely girl with unusual interests. She loved dinosaurs, archaeology, and science fiction. She had been teased by her peers and remembers hating being a girl because she was forever being told she couldn't

[44] Anonymous ("Moonlit Piglet"), "Gender Theory in Schools".

do things. Like Cat, she felt limited. Like Chloe, she hated puberty and the changes that came with it. Fortunately, unlike them, she continued to grow without seeking or being offered the option to transition medically. Natasha passionately and solemnly states her essential concerns:

> Every year we don't stop this, how many hundreds or thousands of young girls like me, like some of you—all the other girls who hate their bodies getting lumpy and sore— how many of them are going to leap at the chance to have their newly-lumpy chest flattened out again by mastectomies before they stop being sore? How many of them are going to leap at the chance to have their annoying periods magicked away by hysterectomy, without realizing what it means to go on menopause in your teens and the huge impact that has on cardiovascular health? It can take decades off your life to go into early menopause.[45]

How do we stop this internalized misogyny? How do we learn to let children live outside the boundaries of gender stereotypes without labeling them "nonbinary" and ushering them to the closest gender clinic? How do we make this world safe for girls to grow up female? Rushing to offer cross-sex hormones and surgeries to remove healthy breasts and other reproductive organs cannot be the way to encourage adolescent girls to "embrace those aspects of femininity that are unique to women alone" so that they have the opportunity to "live as their authentic female selves".[46] As Libby Emmons says, "We do our girls a disservice when we lie to them and tell them they don't have to be women."[47]

[45] Natasha Chart, in *Detransition Diaries: Saving Our Sisters.*
[46] Emmons, interview by Lahl.
[47] Libby Emmons, in *Detransition Diaries: Saving Our Sisters.*

A Word on Same-Sex Attraction

In Littman's survey of one hundred detransitioners, "Homophobia or difficulty accepting themselves as lesbian, gay, or bisexual was expressed by 23 percent as a reason for transition and subsequent detransition."[48] That is, these participants felt that part of their dysphoria and transition was due to "homophobia and difficulty accepting themselves as homosexual", or they said they "assumed they were transgender because they did not yet understand themselves to be lesbian, gay or bisexual".[49] Another, more recent, study of detransitioners from 2021 by Elie Vandenbussche found that 52 percent of respondents cited "learning to cope with internalized homophobia" as a psychological need after detransitioning.[50] In another study, published in 2019, adolescents and young adults who described themselves as trans, aged sixteen to twenty-five, reported experiencing bullying, particularly "homophobic bullying, before later identifying as transgender".[51] Within the study group, females reported having experienced bullying more often than did males.[52]

There are very few studies evaluating the influence of societal perceptions of homosexuality on adolescent girls who transition. However, some believe that children and teens are adopting a transgender identification to avoid the stigma and bullying associated with being same-sex

---

[48] Littman, "Gender Dysphoria", 3353, 3357.

[49] Littman, "Gender Dysphoria", 3353, 3357.

[50] Elie Vandenbussche, "Detransition-Related Needs and Support: A Cross-Sectional Online Survey", *Journal of Homosexuality* 69, no. 9 (2022): 1608, https://doi.org/10.1080/00918369.2021.1919479.

[51] Gemma L. Witcomb et al., "Experiences and Psychological Wellbeing Outcomes Associated with Bullying in Treatment-Seeking Transgender and Gender-Diverse Youth", *LGBT Health* 6, no. 5 (2019): 224, https://doi.org/10.1089/lgbt.2018.0179.

[52] Witcomb et al., "Bullying", 219.

attracted; that is, transitioning creates the illusion that their same-sex orientation is actually a heterosexual one. So, for example, an adolescent girl who is sexually attracted to other adolescent girls can avoid the stigma of homosexuality and the associated bullying by claiming to be a boy in a girl's body. One clinician adds, "I frequently had cases where people started identifying as trans after months of horrendous bullying for being gay."[53] Another clinician shares a similar reflection: "A lot of the girls would come in and say, 'I'm not a lesbian. I fell in love with my best girl friend but then I went online and realized I'm not a lesbian, I'm a boy. Phew.'"[54]

Transgender Trend, a U.K. organization of parents and professionals challenging the gender-affirmation movement, also believes that "gender-affirming care" for minors is often rooted more in a revulsion for homosexuality than in a concern for the good of the children.[55] In the words of Van Mol, it is "radical feminist, lesbian-identified, adult women" who "look at themselves and say, 'If I were growing up now, in the modern Western culture, they wouldn't allow me to grow up to be lesbian-identified. I'd be trans. That would be the answer coming to me from the schools, from the teachers, from the administration, from the counselors, from the pediatricians.'"[56]

In addition to needing help with dealing with strong, conflicting emotions, adolescents with gender dysphoria, or those who claim to be "transgender", often have several comorbidities such as autism, body dysmorphia, and depression, making it difficult to ascertain the root cause of their bodily discomfort. As Rachel says in her story,

[53] Anonymous, in Bannerman, "Conversion Therapy".

[54] Anonymous, in Bannerman, "Conversion Therapy".

[55] "About Us", Transgender Trend, accessed July 7, 2023, https://www.transgendertrend.com/about_us.

[56] Van Mol, interview by Lahl.

"Gender dysphoria is not the cause; it's a symptom. Your discomfort is coming from trauma, abuse, depression, sexual orientation issues, circumstantial issues, the sexism in our culture."[57] In this chapter we have examined each of these themes that are common in the lives of adolescent girls. If not recognized for what they are, they can lead a sister, a daughter, a niece, a granddaughter—any young woman—to believe that she must alter her body medically to be her "true self".

What's the Rush—and *Who* Is Driving It?

Dr. Erica Anderson's reminder that "we don't really know what's going on"[58] raises important questions. If this is a trend that healthcare providers recognize, but still do not clearly understand, then why do we continue to see a rush to transition medically so many adolescent girls? Why are children, both male and female, prescribed puberty blockers when the risks of these drugs are not fully understood and the circumstances surrounding the subjects' gender dysphoria have not been fully investigated? Why have girls been prescribed testosterone on their first visit with a provider—with no attempt to obtain a meaningful understanding of these girls' internal and external worlds? Why have social factors and pre-existing mental health conditions, among other comorbidities, been dismissed or ignored altogether when an adolescent girl seeks "gender-affirming care"?

Despite the paucity of evidence, the "born in the wrong body" narrative has been—and still is—successfully spread

[57] Rachel, interview by Kallie Fell, in The Center for Bioethics and Culture Network, *Venus Rising with Rachel: Why I Detransitioned*, April 25, 2022, https://youtu.be/E-dFvIu3Lpo.

[58] Anderson, interview by Davis.

by lobby groups to the general public and even to clinical practice and the educational system.[59] When the Tavistock GIDS Clinic in the United Kingdom opened in 1989, it received only two referrals over the course of the year. Specializing as a gender therapist was considered a limiting career move, as there were not even enough patients to be treated.[60] Fast forward to 2018, and the same clinic received 2,590 referrals.[61] This is a very large increase over a fairly short time for a form of medical care. After much critique and the intervention of a number of courageous whistleblowers,[62] the Tavistock Clinic was ordered to close its doors in 2022. However, the skyrocketing of gender clinic referrals has not been isolated to the United Kingdom. Ten years ago, there were just a handful of gender clinics for children in North America. Now, thanks to the Gender Mapping Project, we know that there are already over four hundred.[63] Again, we ask: Why has there been such a sharp rise in the number of young patients claiming to be "born in the wrong body"? What—or who—has been driving the gender-affirmation movement?

[59] Jo Bartosch, "Mermaids: Leading Children up the Trans Path", *sp!ked*, July 3, 2020, https://www.spiked-online.com/2020/07/03/mermaids-leading -children-up-the-trans-path.

[60] Tim Adams, "Transgender Children: The Parents and Doctors on the Frontline", *The Guardian*, November 13, 2016, https://www.theguardian .com/society/2016/nov/13/transgender-children-the-parents-and-doctors -on-the-frontline.

[61] "Referrals to the Gender Identity Development Service (GIDS) Level Off in 2018–19", The Tavistock and Portman NHS Foundation Trust, June 28, 2019, https://tavistockandportman.nhs.uk/about-us/news/stories/referrals -gender-identity-development-service-gids-level-2018-19.

[62] Sue Evans, "How Tavistock Came Tumbling Down", *The Free Press* (blog), *Substack*, August 4, 2022, https://www.thefp.com/p/how-tavistock-came -tumbling-down.

[63] The Gender Mapping Project, accessed July 7, 2023, https://www .gendermapper.org.

It is currently estimated that 1.4 percent of thirteen- to seventeen-year-olds and 1.3 percent of eighteen- to twenty-four-year-olds describe themselves as transgender. Five years ago, both of these numbers were half of that: 0.7 percent.[64] Now transgenderism appears promoted through elementary schools, universities, media, the law, social work, and other fields, and its promotion has "influence upon virtually every aspect of society".[65] In *The Corrosive Impact of Transgender Ideology*, Joanna Williams writes that it is "clear that the transgender rights movement has been able to wield influence far in excess of the number of transgender-identifying people".[66] How did this seizure of power happen?

Transgenderism, riding on the coattails of the gains of the lesbian, gay, and bisexual community in a very focused and determined way, has been driven by ideology, politics, and economics. Trans-activist groups, such as Mermaids, the U.K. "trans kid" charity formerly helmed by Susie Green, have spent a great deal of time, energy, and money to promote transgenderism. They have done so to the extent that many troubled young people may come to regard "trans" identity as a cure-all to their unhappiness, alienation, and conflicted psyches. As Dr. Van Mol says, "Transgenderism has become the catch-all diagnosis for every problem, every maladjustment, every inconvenience that a child has."[67] More importantly, too many of our young people have bought into the falsehood that it is, in fact, the magical cure.

---

[64] Azeen Ghorayshi, "Report Reveals Sharp Rise in Transgender Young People in the U.S.", *The New York Times*, June 10, 2022, https://www.nytimes.com/2022/06/10/science/transgender-teenagers-national-survey.html.

[65] Joanna Williams, *The Corrosive Impact of Transgender Ideology* (London: Civitas, 2020), 64.

[66] Williams, *Transgender Ideology*, 64.

[67] Van Mol, interview by Lahl.

Groups like Mermaids advertise themselves as support services for children, young people, and families. Yet the potential impact of this ideology on the minds of troubled young people makes groups like Mermaids vulnerable to the accusation of pushing a political and harmful agenda at the expense of those they claim to help medically. Politically, these activists advocate for laws that would allow children to take legal action, without parental consent, against schools that do not refer to them by their chosen names and pronouns. This activism demands that children be allowed access to puberty blockers and cross-sex hormones, and teenage girls be given access to physical and surgical interventions such as breast binders and double mastectomies.[68] Interestingly, most recently, Mermaids has come under investigation by the Charities Commission because of safeguarding concerns.[69] However, Mermaids is not the only trans activist group, and there are certainly other organizations that have been captured by this ideology, such as BBC, the U.K.'s national television channel.[70] Countless organizations across the globe celebrate "Pride", which as Charlie Walsham writes, promotes a "trans agenda that undermines longstanding concepts of sex and gender".[71]

As a result of surreptitious trans activism, providers around the globe have accepted irresponsible "activist-driven medicine".[72] One brave whistleblower, Sue Evans,

[68] Bartosch, "Mermaids".

[69] Hayley Dixon, "Exclusive: Trans Charity Mermaids to Be Investigated by Charity Commission", *The Telegraph*, September 29, 2022, https://www.telegraph.co.uk/news/2022/09/29/exclusive-trans-charity-mermaids-investigated-charity-commission.

[70] Charlie Walsham, "How the BBC Was Captured by Trans Ideology", *The Spectator*, July 2, 2022, https://www.spectator.co.uk/article/how-the-bbc-was-captured-by-trans-ideology.

[71] Walsham, "BBC".

[72] Evans, "Tavistock".

a nurse, wrote about her experience at the Tavistock Clinic
with trans-activist groups and their influence on the clinic:

> At the time, various patient-advocacy groups were spring-
> ing up alongside mental-health services so that patients
> would have a voice in the examination room. At first,
> I viewed all of this as an overdue development. But as
> time progressed, it seemed clear that groups like Mermaids
> were exerting influence over doctors and clinicians in the
> service—sometimes dictating the expectations of care for
> our patients.[73]

According to Evans, the external influence of advocacy
groups has only increased from there. She says:

> Instead of being a clinical, research-focused service where
> we were learning and developing ideas, it felt like it was a
> fait accompli that we had to go along with what Mermaids
> and patients wanted—even if we, the mental-health-care
> professionals, had legitimate questions about the appropri-
> ateness of the treatments that patients and patient advo-
> cates were demanding.[74]

She reminds readers that this was all occurring *before* the
internet captivated children and teens around the globe.
Trans ideologues had already long had the ears of providers, well before "gender-affirming" message boards and
online communities invaded the homes of our children via
laptops, tablets, and smartphones.

The topic of laptops, tablets, and smartphones deserves
special consideration. Now that these devices are in almost
every home and in the hands of our children, the gender

---

[73] Evans, "Tavistock".
[74] Evans, "Tavistock".

industry has made use of them to become a "well-oiled marketing machine, filled with hyped-up TikTok adverts, SEO marketing strategies, and even Google Adwords".[75] With a click of a button, young children and adolescents can be exposed to transgender ideology via videos, applications, social media influencers, celebrities, message boards, and chat groups. After a quick internet search, children and young adults everywhere can access "gender-affirming" videos, games, and online communities that try to convince young minds that medically transitioning will fix all their problems. For example, one app, free on Google Play, is called "Crossdresser—Transform from Male to Female", and it gives tips on how to present oneself as a "woman"—*rated for ages three and up*.[76] Online communities encourage "treatment" and provide coaching to help a child or young adult to access "care" quickly and quietly. This facilitation coincides with a cultural narrative that promotes suicidal ideation with the false mantra that so-called "trans kids" will die by suicide if their new identities are not affirmed by others.

When philanthropic and political groups driving the transgender agenda began actively to promote specific unproven medical treatments for people with gender dysphoria, some realized the potential for economic gains: especially pharmaceutical and biotech firms. Dr. Van Mol explains, "If you're a pharmaceutical firm that is producing some manner of sex hormone or gonadotropin-releasing agonist, what we're going to call puberty blockers, you've

[75] "'Transgender' Propaganda Marketing is Escalating, and Young People Are Buying It", The Gender Mapping Project, February 25, 2022, https://www.gendermapper.org/post/the-outrageous-scandal-of-non-binary-surgeries.

[76] Genevieve Gluck, "App Fetishizing Forcible Transitioning of Kids Available on Google Play", *4W*, October 19, 2021, https://4w.pub/fetishizing-forcible-transitioning-kids-app.

just increased your market share tremendously."[77] Concerning biotech companies, he continues, "If you've got a company that's producing some little widget that has a stake in the game of making a biological male look more 'female,' or vice versa, there's money for you in this."[78] Once children are medicalized, they become medicalized for the rest of their lives. Studies show well over 90 percent of children who start puberty blockers will progress to cross-sex hormones,[79] and that number has been reported to be as high as 98 percent.[80] Once a girl has her body depleted of estrogen and her female reproductive organs removed, she will need hormone treatment forever—even if she comes to regret her decision and later detransitions. Because children and youth have their future fertility damaged or lost due to cross-sex hormones and surgeries, it is now suggested that they be offered fertility preservation techniques, even though they are experimental for minors with limited data on success.

It would be naïve to think that pharmaceutical firms, the fertility industry, and healthcare providers have not been using "gender-affirming care" to make a profit from the disoriented minds of young people with gender dysphoria. "That's a big market," Van Mol says. "It's a big profit; it's the dark side of capitalism." He notes, "Any company that has a stake in the game of making a biological male look more feminized, or a biological female more masculinized, knows that there is money to be made."[81]

[77] Van Mol, in *Trans Mission*.

[78] Van Mol, in *Trans Mission*.

[79] Antony Latham, "Puberty Blockers for Children: Can They Consent?", *The New Bioethics* 28, no. 3 (2022), https://doi.org/10.1080/20502877.2022.2088048.

[80] "Puberty Blockers", StatsForGender.org, accessed July 7, 2023, https://statsforgender.org/puberty-blockers.

[81] Van Mol, interview by Lahl.

Put simply, there are professionals who now profit from our children's trauma and suffering.

Recently, as noted earlier in this book, WPATH has revised its Standards of Care. Despite concerns raised by whistleblowers, physicians, parents, and others, rather than slow the rush to medicalize gender dysphoria, and rather than take time to understand why so many young people believe they need to alter their healthy bodies permanently, WPATH has removed the recommended age limits for puberty blockers, hormones, and surgery, as long as a child has reached Tanner stage II (which can be as young as age nine).[82] Organizations such as WPATH, Mermaids, GLAAD, and the Human Rights Campaign continue not only to promote the gender identity industry but also to rush it all the more. Why? Again, we must underscore the fact that money, as Jennifer Bilek has noted, can be a strong motivational factor.[83] Filmmaker and conservative political commentator Matt Walsh tweeted: "WPATH is now run by people in the gender ideology industry, meaning they all have an enormous financial stake in making transition guidelines as relaxed as possible.... And what

[82] Mary Margaret Olohan, "Top Trans Medical Group Quietly Removes Age Recommendations for Minors Seeking Transgender Surgeries, Hormones, Puberty Blockers", *The Daily Signal*, September 16, 2022, https://www.daily signal.com/2022/09/16/top-transgender-medical-group-removes-age -recomendations-for-minors; Genevieve Gluck, "Beyond WPATH: Leading Transgender Medical Organization 'Fatally Undermined'", *Women's Voices* (blog), *Substack*, October 19, 2022, https://genevievegluck.substack.com /beyond-wpath-leading-transgender; https://www.tandfonline.com/doi/pdf /10.1080/26895269.2022.2100644.

[83] Jennifer Bilek, "Who Are the Rich, White Men Institutionaliz- ing Transgender Ideology?", *The Federalist*, February 20, 2018, https://the federalist.com/2018/02/20/rich-white-men-institutionalizing-transgender -ideology. See also Jennifer Bilek, "Transgenderism Is Just Big Business Dressed Up in Pretend Civil Rights Clothes", *The Federalist*, July 5, 2018, https://thefederalist.com/2018/07/05/transgenderism-just-big-business -dressed-pretend-civil-rights-clothes.

do you know, each new set of guidelines becomes more relaxed and they all get personally richer."[84]

Of course, there is no way to prove that *everyone* at WPATH is indeed getting "personally richer", but the point remains: there is profiteering in this industry. In another tweet, on the day WPATH released its newest guidelines, James Esses, barrister and cofounder of Thoughtful Therapists, called the guidelines "one of the most shocking indictments of ideology infecting medicine that I have ever come across".[85]

Regardless of the motivation of those peddling trans ideology and profitable "gender-affirming care" to our youth, we must maintain the stance that rushing this harmful ideology is morally wrong and dangerous. We agree with Kellie-Jay Keen, who states, "This is about saving the life of your children," because, in the end, "there is only misery.... You will never become male if you're female, and you will never become female if you're male; but you may have a lifetime of unhappiness and medical surgeries and procedures."[86]

---

[84] Matt Walsh (@MattWalshBlog), "WPATH is now run by people in the gender ideology industry, meaning they all have an enormous financial stake in making transition guidelines as relaxed as possible. And what do you know, each new set of guidelines becomes more relaxed and they all get personally richer", Twitter, September 16, 2022, 1:52 P.M., https://twitter.com/MattWalshBlog/status/1570848186155302914.

[85] James Esses (@JamesEsses), "THREAD WARNING—The World Professional Association for Transgender Health (WPATH) Standards of Care. I have just read Version 8 of these standards, released last week. It is one of the most shocking indictments of ideology infecting medicine that I have ever come across", Twitter, September 16, 2022, 5:30 A.M., https://twitter.com/JamesEsses/status/1570721724332937216. See also Esses, quoted in Genevieve Gluck, "Trans Authority Cites Pedophilic Forum, Reduces Age Restrictions for 'Puberty Blockers' and Genital Surgeries", *Reduxx*, September 18, 2022, https://reduxx.info/trans-authority-cites-pedophilic-forum-reduces-age-restrictions-for-puberty-blockers-and-genital-surgeries.

[86] Kellie-Jay Keen, interview by Jennifer Lahl, New York City, March 16, 2022.

11

Lasting and Irreversible Damage

The number of people, including adolescents, requesting medical treatment to transition has been skyrocketing. As we have seen, recent data show that 1.8 percent of adolescents under eighteen describe themselves as transgender[1] and nearly 2 percent of adolescents believe that they were "born in the wrong body". This number, 2 percent, may not seem alarming, but in just five years, the number of young people claiming to be "trans" has more than doubled, with no sign of slowing.

With the rising numbers of youth who consider themselves trans, there is a rapidly increasing demand for medical treatment that goes by the name "gender-affirming care". With this "flood of referrals to mental health providers and gender medical clinics". Drs. Laura Edwards-Leeper and Erica Anderson, both psychologists, are concerned that practitioners have been providing "sloppy, dangerous care".[2] Both Edwards-Leeper and Anderson have the credentials and clinical experience needed to blow the whistle on the treatment kids are receiving.

[1] "Data on Transgender Youth", The Trevor Project, February 22, 2019, https://www.thetrevorproject.org/research-briefs/data-on-transgender-youth.
[2] Laura Edwards-Leeper and Erica Anderson, "The Mental Health Establishment Is Failing Trans Kids", *The Washington Post*, November 24, 2021, https://www.washingtonpost.com/outlook/2021/11/24/trans-kids-therapy-psychologist.

Edwards-Leeper is the founding psychologist of the first pediatric transgender clinic in the United States and the chair of the Child and Adolescent Committee for the World Professional Association for Transgender Health (WPATH). Anderson, former president of the U.S. Professional Association for Transgender Health (USPATH), is a member of the American Psychological Association committee writing the guidelines for working with patients who describe themselves as trans. They state:

> Often from a place of genuine concern, they are hastily dispensing medicine or recommending medical doctors prescribe it—without following the strict guidelines that govern this treatment. Canada, too, is following our lead: A study of 10 pediatric gender clinics there[3] found that *half do not require psychological assessment before initiating puberty blockers or hormones.*[4]

Dr. Paul W. Hruz, featured in the documentary *Trans Mission: What's the Rush to Reassign Gender?*, explains in an interview the pressures on doctors to take shortcuts:

> The practice of medicine has become very challenging, and the economic models have forced physicians to have higher patient volumes. Being focused on revenue, many of the trainees are not able to delve into the actual literature. They look at the CliffsNotes version, and they really rely heavily on these practice guidelines or recommendations.[5]

[3] Margaret L. Lawson et al., "Pathways to Care for Trans Youth Accessing Gender-Affirming Medical Care in Canada: New Research from Trans Youth CAN!", Trans Youth CAN!, November 7, 2020, https://transyouthcan.ca /results/wpath-2020-5.

[4] Edwards-Leeper and Anderson, "Failing Trans Kids" (emphasis added).

[5] Paul W. Hruz, interview by Jennifer Lahl, St. Louis, Missouri, January 21, 2021.

But what if there is a psychological assessment and care is not sloppy? Are there still risks? Who is going to take care of all these people receiving "sloppy" care? Who is going to be held responsible for harm done to these young people who have been told this care will help them? Finally, who is going to take care of each of the detransitioners who find out, like Rachel, that while being chauffeured down the medical transition superhighway, they have been misinformed by practitioners who haven't fully researched transgender medicine and who have made permanent, unhealthy, life-altering changes to their bodies?

People who consider themselves transgender aren't the only group with growing numbers: the number of detransitioners is growing as well. The detrans group on Reddit, at the time of this writing, has more than 48,000 members, up from 13,000 in June 2020.[6] Helena, Grace, Cat, Chloe, and Rachel are among those numbers. The reasons people are choosing to detransition should concern us all, especially medical providers. In a recent study of detransitioners, 49 percent of the subjects chose to detransition, in part, out of concerns about potential medical complications from transitioning.[7]

In this chapter we will explore those medical complications. Are such concerns warranted? What does research tell us about puberty blockers and cross-sex hormones? Are these drugs really safe and, as has been claimed, reversible? What can experts such as pediatric endocrinologists Drs. Hruz

[6] Abigail Shrier, "How 'Peer Contagion' May Play into the Rise of Teen Girls Transitioning", *The New York Post*, June 27, 2020, https://nypost.com /2020/06/27/how-peer-contagion-plays-into-the-rise-of-teens-transitioning.

[7] Lisa Littman, "Individuals Treated for Gender Dysphoria with Medical and/or Surgical Transition Who Subsequently Detransitioned: A Survey of 100 Detransitioners", *Archives of Sexual Behavior* 50, no. 8 (2021): 3353, https://doi .org/10.1007/s10508-021-02163-w.

and Quentin Van Meter and family practitioner Dr. André Van Mol teach us—and what can we learn from the experience of detransitioners like the ones featured in this book?

Social Transitioning

In order to understand the risks associated with medical transition, we must be familiar with the steps involved, especially for younger patients. According to Van Mol:

> The first thing that's done is social transitioning, which is simple enough, you change your appearance, your clothing, makeup, and perhaps your name.... But we know from the medical literature that social transitioning is associated with greater persistence of gender dysphoria. You've already made a decision here.[8]

Medically speaking, the first step in medical intervention involves the participation of medical professionals to affirm socially patients who think they were born in the wrong body. The risk here is not a physical one, but rather the risk that a child or a young person is now on the transition superhighway with very few exits.

Puberty Blockers

Van Mol, a family physician, explains that for a patient who has not yet begun or completed puberty but has socially transitioned, "next would come puberty blocking, which, if one is following the Endocrine Society guidelines, that's supposed to happen at Tanner stage II."[9] Introducing

[8] André Van Mol, interview by Jennifer Lahl, Redding, California, November 22, 2020.

[9] Van Mol, interview by Lahl.

puberty blockers, more correctly called gonadotropin-releasing hormone agonists (GnRHa), at Tanner stage II means that the child will not go through puberty—at least, not while on the treatment.

GnRHa halts the progression of puberty by blocking the activity of the GnRH receptor in the pituitary gland to decrease the release of gonadotropins (LH and FSH). Ultimately, hindering the gonads from releasing appropriate sex hormones results in low, prepubertal levels of estrogen in girls and androgens (testosterone) in boys. Put simply, these powerful drugs shut down the signals from the brain that tell the gonads to work. This treatment leads to the regression of any developed sex characteristics. For example, in girls, breast tissue growth is limited or stopped, and in boys, the growth of the penis, scrotum, and testicles is limited.[10] Puberty blockers can also be given to adolescents in later phases of pubertal development. In these cases, "in contrast to patients in early puberty, the various physical changes of pubertal development, such as a late stage breast development in girls and a lowering of the voice and facial hair in boys, will not regress completely, although any further progression will be stopped."[11]

These drugs, Dr. Hruz tells us, "have been used for decades in treating children who undergo puberty at an abnormally early age, or have what we call 'precocious puberty'. They're also used in adults in treating various

[10] "Puberty Blockers for Transgender and Gender-Diverse Youth", Mayo Clinic Staff, Mayo Clinic, updated June 14, 2023, https://www.mayoclinic.org/diseases-conditions/gender-dysphoria/in-depth/pubertal-blockers/art-20459075.

[11] Henriette A. Delemarre-van de Waal and Peggy T. Cohen-Kettenis, "Clinical Management of Gender Identity Disorder in Adolescents: A Protocol on Psychological and Paediatric Endocrinology Aspects", *European Journal of Endocrinology* 155, no. S1 (November 1, 2006): S133, https://doi.org/10.1530/eje.1.02231.

cancers where you want to suppress the normal function of the gonads to protect them during chemotherapy and other interventions."[12] Now these drugs are being administered to children going through normally timed puberty. "Transgender-affirming" physicians like Dr. Michelle Forcier, along with transgender activists, explains that this treatment gives children more time to be able to understand the changes that are going on in their bodies. Parents and children are told that these drugs allow a brief pause and that they can restart puberty at any point in time if they choose to do so. Hruz disagrees: "It's put forward that this is a fully safe and fully reversible intervention at that point in time. The reality is that each of those statements, as far as reasons for using that very first step of medical intervention for gender dysphoria [are concerned], should be challenged."[13]

The claim that puberty blockers are a pause button and that they merely provide a window for investigating one's gender identity, "really flies in the face of the existing information that we have, that the vast majority of individuals who begin with puberty blockers will go on to have cross-sex hormone interventions."[14] Yet, according to Hruz, the majority of prepubertal children who are uncomfortable with their gender and biological sex, if simply left alone, would eventually experience a spontaneous realignment of their "gender identity" with their sex.[15] The concern is that, rather than being a pause button, puberty blockers actually lock a child into a discordant gender identity, pushing him or her right on to the next intervention. In other words, once medicalized

[12] Hruz, interview by Lahl.
[13] Hruz, interview by Lahl.
[14] Hruz, interview by Lahl.
[15] Hruz, interview by Lahl.

via puberty blockers, almost no children turn back: they continue to take cross-sex hormones, and some even have surgery. The claim that it is only a "pause" is simply false.

Even if puberty blockers could be thought of simply as a pause button, they disrupt a child's normal developmental process. Puberty is not merely a biochemical development; it is also "a psycho-social event that occurs in concert with one's peers", according to Dr. William Malone, an endocrinologist and member of the Society for Evidence-Based Gender Medicine (SEGM).[16] That is, children of the same age tend to go through puberty more or less together. Those who choose to delay puberty are separated from their peers in this regard. So, at the very least, delaying puberty is a social disruption, just as it is in some cases of untreated precocious puberty. The difference here is that transgender medicine is a purposeful tampering with the normal biological system. It is worth noting that sometimes precocious puberty is even left untreated, depending on the cause, a child's age, and how rapidly it is progressing.

Treating a child with puberty blockers, even in the case of a disorder like precocious puberty, has such far-reaching effects that such treatment demands careful professional consideration before it is employed. But the same caution does not seem to be exercised in gender medicine at present. The science surrounding the health of and psychological risks to a child who is put on puberty blockers long-term is still unsettled. "Puberty is the time of the greatest increase in bone density in someone's life," notes Van Mol. "Well, that's been blocked now. How old will

---

[16] William Malone, quoted in Abigail Shrier, "Top Trans Doctors Blow the Whistle on 'Sloppy' Care", *The Free Press* (blog), *Substack*, October 4, 2021, https://www.thefp.com/top-trans-doctors-blow-the-whistle.

they be before osteopenia and even osteoporosis sets in? Is that going to be a problem they would face in their thirties? We don't know. There's no long-term data on this. What about brain development, psychological development? We don't know."[17]

Van Meter adds, "Gonadotropin-releasing hormone agonists are used in patients with precocious puberty sparingly and for short periods of time to hold off the progression of early puberty."[18] These drugs are given to children to (1) preserve height, because "early puberty will cause that child to become much shorter than they would have been if puberty had happened on time"[19] and (2) "to prevent any of the social controversies that would pop up in that child's life, particularly with girls, who might be menstruating in the first or second grade and not be able to socially handle that".[20] Those children with precocious puberty are monitored very closely, and puberty blockers are removed in time for them to advance through normal puberty at the appropriate age, because "puberty is a critical part of changing a non-fertile person into a fertile adult. There's so many things in the human body and the brain and the physical structures in the bone and all of the organelles that depend on that transition."[21]

The entire body, made up of cells already designated with XX or XY chromosomes, is primed to respond to this critical transition. It is not clear how blocking this transition affects each of these cells, organs, or bodily systems long-term. It is also not fully understood how pubertal

[17] Van Mol, interview by Lahl.

[18] Quentin Van Meter, interview by Jennifer Lahl, Atlanta, Georgia, January 13, 2021.

[19] Hruz, interview by Lahl.

[20] Van Meter, interview by Lahl.

[21] Van Meter, interview by Lahl.

suppression influences brain development. Hormones do not merely stimulate sex organs during puberty; they also have a major influence on the brain. To block puberty at the age when puberty should be happening stops all these processes from occurring normally, and the long-term effects of this disruption are unknown.

"Pausing puberty" not only denies children normal physiological and social processes but also comes with grave mental health warnings. The package insert that comes with puberty blockers lists the following side effects: changes in mood, depression, and suicide risk.[22] Oxford professor Michael Biggs has reported that puberty blockers exacerbate symptoms of gender dysphoria, with children reporting greater self-harm and more behavioral problems and emotional turmoil a year after use.[23] We have been told that medically transitioning is supposed to decrease suicide risk, not increase it. How can researchers even begin to differentiate one suicide risk cause from another? It seems the biggest risk associated with puberty blockers is the risk of unknown harms. Giving puberty blockers to a child going through puberty at the developmentally appropriate time seems to be a poorly regulated medical experiment with uncertain and possibly deleterious outcomes. Questions arise as to whether children being given puberty blockers will achieve normal brain and skeletal development, as well as normal development of the metabolic and other systems. To reiterate: *long-term data on these*

[22] Hruz, interview by Lahl.

[23] Michael Biggs, "The Tavistock's Experiment with Puberty Blockers", July 29, 2019, https://users.ox.ac.uk/~sfos0060/Biggs_ExperimentPubertyBlockers .pdf. See also Michael Biggs, "Britain's Experiment with Puberty Blockers", in Michele Moore and Heather Brunskell-Evans, *Inventing Transgender Children and Young People* (Newcastle upon Tyne, U.K.: Cambridge Scholars Publishing, 2019).

bodily systems in children who were prescribed puberty blockers is nonexistent. "The ultimate effect of this manipulation on pubertal development should be investigated in a long-term follow-up."[24] Until then, "to portray them as being entirely safe and entirely reversible is an injustice to these children that are being given these medications."[25]

Cross-Sex Hormones

Following puberty blockers, or in those young adults who have already completed puberty before deciding to transition medically, "What comes next is the cross-sex hormones," explains Dr. Van Mol, clarifying, "the wrong-sex hormones."[26] Estrogen is given to males and testosterone to females with the goal of inducing physical changes in line with the desired sexual identity. For example, females taking testosterone will develop a low voice, facial and body hair growth, and a more masculine body shape. According to one study, androgen (testosterone) treatment will cause "clitoral enlargement, although the final size will never reach the size of a normal male penis".[27] Most trans activists focus on these results; fewer, as Rachel discovered when she began expressing concerns about her health after starting testosterone, talk about the more uncomfortable or harmful side effects, such as vaginal atrophy. Dr. Juno Obedin-Maliver at Stanford, who specializes in the health of sexual and gender minorities, says, "Your entire body changes on testosterone. I think oftentimes people focus

[24] Delemarre-van de Waal and Cohen-Kettenis, "Gender Identity Disorder", S137.

[25] Hruz, interview by Lahl.

[26] Van Mol, interview by Lahl.

[27] Delemarre-van de Waal and Cohen-Kettenis, "Gender Identity Disorder", S133.

on their facial hair, or muscle structure, or their voice deepening. But the vagina will change too." She explains:

> Testosterone decreases the resilience of the vaginal tissues and the amount of natural lubrication, which can make the tissue more prone to tearing or micro abrasions. This—what we call "vaginal atrophy"—can make it more uncomfortable for people just walking around, and certainly during sexual activity.[28]

It is important to understand that both men and women naturally have both testosterone and estrogen—the difference is in the relative levels of these hormones circulating in the body. Young women who want to transition to male, such as those whose stories are told in this book, are given large amounts of testosterone, in excess of the amount produced by the female body. According to Van Mol:

> The advocates [of transgender medicine] would say, "No, it's not large at all. This is the usual level of testosterone for a biological male." That may be true, but for a biological female body, it's enormously more testosterone than she would ever see. Conservatively, it's thirty to fifty times the load of testosterone a female body would ever have in it—short of some manner of endocrine tumor.[29]

Little research has been done on the effects of testosterone on a female body, but as Hruz says, "We can take

[28] Juno Obedin-Maliver, interview by Emily Land, "Q&A: Gynecologic and Vaginal Care for Trans Men", San Francisco AIDS Foundation, July 23, 2019, https://www.sfaf.org/collections/beta/qa-gynecologic-and-vaginal-care-for-trans-men.

[29] Van Mol, interview by Lahl. See also André Van Mol, in *Trans Mission: What's the Rush to Reassign Gender?*, directed by Kallie Fell and Jennifer Lahl (Pleasant Hill, CA: Center for Bioethics and Culture Network [CBC], 2021), https://www.youtube.com/watch?v=rUeqEoARKOA. See, in particular, 41:51–42:13 in *Trans Mission* for this explanation.

information that we already know from other conditions, where people have endogenous hormones of the opposite sex."[30] One example is polycystic ovary syndrome (PCOS), a condition in which the ovaries produce an abnormally high level of androgens. According to Hruz, "We have long-standing data about the adverse effects of that excess male hormone that is present, increasing the risk of heart disease and cardiovascular disease later in life."[31] With PCOS, for example, it is well known that high testosterone levels increase the risk of fatty liver disease significantly and double the risk of liver disease in women.[32]

There are other known risks to women from exposure to high levels of testosterone. Those risks include the following: polycythemia (too many red blood cells); weight gain; severe acne; male-pattern baldness; sleep apnea; abnormal levels of cholesterol and other lipids, which may increase cardiovascular risk (dyslipidemia); hypertension; type 2 diabetes; deep vein thrombosis; pulmonary embolism; infertility; atrophic vaginitis; pelvic pain; menstrual irregularities; and clitoral discomfort.[33] Length of exposure is an important factor, especially with regard to cardiovascular health and the risk of pulmonary embolism. "The longer a person is on the cross-sex hormones, the higher the risk," Van Mol says.[34] Further, the vagina,

---

[30] Hruz, interview by Lahl.

[31] Hruz, interview by Lahl.

[32] "Excessive Male Hormones Leave Women with Polycystic Ovary Syndrome at Double the Risk of Liver Disease, Study Finds", University of Birmingham, March 28, 2018, https://www.birmingham.ac.uk/news-archive/2018/excessive-male-hormones-leave-women-with-polycystic-ovary-syndrome-at-double-the-risk-of-liver-disease-study-finds-1.

[33] "Masculinizing Hormone Therapy", Mayo Clinic, February 21, 2023, https://www.mayoclinic.org/tests-procedures/masculinizing-hormone-therapy/about/pac-20385099.

[34] Van Mol, interview by Lahl.

being an "estrogen-responsive organ", will become atrophied over time; it could be "months or years after being on testosterone".[35]

There are unknown risks as well. For example, conclusions cannot yet be drawn about whether masculinizing hormone therapy increases the risk of ovarian and uterine cancer,[36] or how a woman's fertility might be affected in the long term by cross-sex hormones. Obedin-Maliver says, "We don't know all of the impacts that testosterone has on the uterus and pelvic muscles."[37] The bottom line is that high doses of testosterone have wide-ranging effects on a woman's body—and further research is warranted, at the very least.

The list of risks to men who take estrogen is also long, including blood clots, heart trouble, high triglycerides, nipple discharge, weight gain, high blood pressure, diabetes, stroke, and even breast cancer. The Mayo Clinic cautions men that even if they stop taking estrogen, the changes to their testicles might not be reversible, and their fertility might be impaired.[38]

Van Meter worries especially about the combination of drugs taken by those who started with puberty blockers and went on to take cross-sex hormones. "You're taking the brain, stopping the hormones that would normally make it develop, and putting in hormones that are at odds with the biologic cells," he says.[39] Looking at the medical literature, we can see that this interference results in a diseased state of the body. By studying the effects of diseases in which opposite-sex hormones are overproduced by the

[35] Obedin-Maliver, interview by Land.
[36] Mayo Clinic, "Masculinizing Hormone Therapy."
[37] Obedin-Maliver, interview by Land.
[38] "Puberty Blockers for Transgender and Gender-Diverse Youth".
[39] Van Meter, interview by Lahl.

body, we find that the body responds adversely to these hormones with increased cancers, increased stroke risk, depletion of calcium in the bones, emotional disorders, and more. To Van Meter:

> It is unconscionable that we would take a normal, healthy human body [and] block the progression of puberty, which is incredibly critical for that body to make it to the adult side of the spectrum. Then, on top of that, confuse it with giant levels of hormones that are not designed for the physical body to tolerate, and which create disease states. This is taking a healthy body and turning it into a diseased body, all based on the ideology that that's okay.[40]

"Top Surgery" and "Bottom Surgery"

Although some stop with cross-sex hormones, others go on to what used to be called "gender-affirmation surgery" but which is now mostly called "sex-reassignment surgery", echoing the assertion that gender is not discovered at the birth of a baby, but assigned to him by society. Whatever one calls it, surgery is apparently being offered at younger and younger ages.[41] The first surgery offered to young women has been euphemistically called "top surgery", but it is medically known as a bilateral mastectomy. Bilateral mastectomies, often also called "masculinizing chest surgery", are performed in gender medicine to remove healthy breast tissue. The goal is "to sculpt a natural appearing masculine chest matched to the patient's

---

[40] Van Meter, interview by Lahl.
[41] Brandon Showalter, "Yes, Trans Surgeries Are Being Done on Minors. Here's Proof.", *The Christian Post*, August 29, 2022, https://www.christianpost.com/voices/yes-trans-surgeries-are-being-done-on-minors-heres-proof.html.

body habitus with pectoral definition".[42] The surgical technique is dependent on the plastic surgeon's individual experience, patient-specific preferences, and physical evaluation of the patient's preoperative body.

Complications of "masculinizing chest surgery" are rarely life-threatening but can include hematoma; infection; wound complications (for example, wound separation, delayed wound healing, or skin flap necrosis); contour irregularities caused by fat necrosis and oil cysts; complications with nipple healing (or loss of the nipple entirely) sometimes requiring nipple reconstruction and revision; nipple sensitivity or numbness; nipple hypopigmentation; and chest wall contour deformities or asymmetry. Hematoma, seroma, and nipple complications can all cause lasting aesthetic deformities. Early reoperation, often due to hematoma formation, infection, or wound dehiscence, occurs in 4 to 9 percent of patients, but the operative revision rate for aesthetic improvement has been reported to be as high as 32 percent.[43]

A smaller percentage of young women will go on to have "bottom surgery" to change the appearance of their external genitalia irreversibly. These women may "choose to have a neoscrotum with a testis prosthesis with or without a metaidoioplasty [sic] (transforming the hypertrophic

[42] Eric D. Wang and Esther A. Kim, "Postoperative Care and Common Issues after Masculinizing Chest Surgery", University of California, San Francisco (UCSF) Transgender Care, June 17, 2016, https://transcare.ucsf.edu /guidelines/chest-surgery-masculinizing.

[43] Stan Monstrey et al., "Chest-Wall Contouring Surgery in Female-to-Male Transsexuals: A New Algorithm", *Plastic and Reconstructive Surgery* 121, no. 3 (March 2008), https://doi.org/10.1097/01.prs.0000299921.15447.b2; A. Wolter, "Sexual Reassignment Surgery in Female-to-Male Transsexuals: An Algorithm for Subcutaneous Mastectomy", *Journal of Plastic, Reconstructive, & Aesthetic Surgery* 68, no. 2 (February 2015), https://doi.org/10.1016/j.bjps .2014.10.016.

clitoris into a microphallus) or a phalloplasty".[44] According to Johns Hopkins, "Phalloplasty is a multi-staged process that may include a variety of procedures" such as "creating the penis", "the tip (glans) of the penis", and "the scrotum" by skin grafting from a donor site (for example, the arm or the thigh).[45] There is the lengthening of the urethra, to allow standing while urinating, and the placing of erectile and testicular implants. Other "bottom surgery" procedures include the removal of the uterus (hysterectomy) and ovaries (oophorectomy).

It is undisputed that "bottom surgery" is fraught with complications that cause permanent disruption of the normal function of a significant part of the patient's anatomy. The Cleveland Clinic, one of the top hospitals in the country, explains on its website that phalloplasty "is a complex penis surgery" and that "many people experience complications."[46] Common complications of phalloplasty include infection of the incision, urethra, or donor site (cellulitis, fungal infections, or both are common); wound breakdown, including "partial phallic loss if the neopenis does not maintain adequate blood flow";[47] blockage of the urethra from scar tissue or hair growth slowing or completely blocking the release of urine from the body (which, if not addressed, will require repeated dilation); loss of sensation; pelvic or groin hematomas (pooling of blood, sometimes requiring draining); pelvic bleeding or pelvic

[44] Delemarre-van de Waal and Cohen-Kettenis, "Gender Identity Disorder", S137.

[45] Fan Liang, "Phalloplasty for Gender Affirmation", Johns Hopkins Medicine, accessed July 10, 2023, https://www.hopkinsmedicine.org/health/treatment-tests-and-therapies/phalloplasty-for-gender-affirmation.

[46] "Phalloplasty", Cleveland Clinic, last reviewed June 10, 2021, https://my.clevelandclinic.org/health/treatments/21585-phalloplasty.

[47] "Phalloplasty", Cleveland Clinic.

pain; and bladder or rectal injury, including urinary fistula (where the urinary tract abnormally forms with a nearby organ).[48] The most common complications for urethral lengthening procedures include urethral strictures, fistula, and diverticula (formation of a pouch in the urethra), which may require an additional surgical procedure to fix.[49] Radial forearm phalloplasty (a method that involves taking the skin, fat, nerves, arteries, and veins from the wrist to about halfway up the forearm to create the imitation penis) has reported fistula rates ranging from 22 to 68 percent.[50] Post-void incontinence or dribbling occurs in about 79 percent of phalloplasty patients.[51] If testicular implants are placed, then explantation rates range from 0.6 to 30 percent and increase the risk of the urethral complications already mentioned.[52]

The donor site is also not free from complications. Wound breakdown, decreased mobility around the site, hematoma, pain, decreased sensation, excessive scarring, and hypergranulation (slowing down wound healing and raising risk of infection) can all occur.[53] Sexual function

---

[48] "Phalloplasty", Cleveland Clinic; Curtis Crane, "Phalloplasty and Metoidioplasty—Overview and Postoperative Considerations", University of California, San Francisco (UCSF) Transgender Care, June 17, 2016, https://transcare.ucsf.edu/guidelines/phalloplasty; "Phalloplasty Risks and Complications", Phallo.net, last updated November 16, 2021, https://www.phallo.net/risks-complications.

[49] Liang, "Phalloplasty".

[50] "Phalloplasty Risks and Complications".

[51] Piet Hoebeke et al., "Impact of Sex Reassignment Surgery on Lower Urinary Tract Function", *European Urology* 47, no. 3 (March 2005), https://doi.org/10.1016/j.eururo.2004.10.008.

[52] Catherin Legemate et al., "Surgical Outcomes of Testicular Prostheses Implantation in Transgender Men with a History of Prosthesis Extrusion or Infection", *International Journal of Transgender Health* 22, no. 3 (2020), 10.1080/26895269.2020.1840476.

[53] "Phalloplasty Risks and Complications".

should also not be ignored. Surgery that tries to create a male phallus out of what should be a vagina and vulva does not result in a functional organ, "so implants are required in order to try to create some semblance of functionality."[54] Those with implants face more risks, such as erosion (where the implant breaks through the skin and must be removed surgically).[55] Whether patients can have sexual intercourse using their "neopenis" depends on the technique and quality of the phalloplasty. Although some patients who had a metoidioplasty report that they are able to have intercourse, the hypertrophic clitoris is usually too small for coitus.[56]

Removal of the uterus is associated with cognitive impairment and early menopause, both of which can take years off a young person's life. One study reports that "the risk of cognitive impairment or dementia was increased in women who had hysterectomy alone, further increased in women who had hysterectomy with unilateral oophorectomy (surgical removal of the ovaries), and further increased in women who had hysterectomy with bilateral oophorectomy."[57] These risks *are higher in patients who are younger* at the time of the surgery. In all cases, these surgeries are performed under general anesthesia, which has its own risks and complications, as any major surgery does.

"Bottom surgery" for men can include the removal of the penis and testicles and the creation of a "vaginal vault" and requires lifelong adherence to a dilation

[54] Van Mol, interview by Lahl.

[55] Crane, "Phalloplasty and Metoidioplasty".

[56] Amir Khorrami et al., "The Sexual Goals of Metoidioplasty Patients and Their Attitudes toward Using PDE5 Inhibitors and Intracavernosal Injections as Erectile Aids", *Sexual Medicine* 10, no. 3 (June 2022), https://doi.org//10.1016/j.esxm.2022.100505.

[57] Walter A. Rocca et al., "Hysterectomy, Oophorectomy, Estrogen, and the Risk of Dementia", *Neurodegenerative Diseases* 10, nos. 1–4 (2012): 175, https://doi.org/10.1159/000334764.

regimen.[58] This surgery, like the surgeries described above, is also fraught with long-term risks, such as tissue necrosis, incontinence, and the development of fistulas.[59]

Infertility and Reproductive Regret

One of the most serious and well-recognized effects of transgender medicine is infertility. Children who take puberty blockers almost invariably end up taking cross-sex hormones, a combination that leaves children infertile and even sexually dysfunctional.[60] Puberty blocking is "chemically castrating at the level of the brain," says Dr. Van Mol, and obviously, surgeries such as the removal of the ovaries or testicles guarantee infertility.[61] Many clinics recognize the harm that could result from causing infertility, and Hruz says that they discuss with their young patients the ways they could try to preserve their fertility through egg freezing and the like.

> Yet the number of children that actually accept that offer for fertility preservation is exceedingly small. It reflects potentially their inability to grasp what they're giving up at that stage of their life, particularly when they figure out that it didn't even solve their problems. And, then, here they're left infertile and sterilized because of these interventions.[62]

[58] "Vaginoplasty Procedures, Complications, and Aftercare", Toby Meltzer, MD, "UCSF Transgender care, June 17, 2016, https://transcare.ucsf.edu /guidelines/vaginoplasty.

[59] "Feminizing Surgery", November 4, 2022, Mayo Clinic, https://www .mayoclinic.org/tests-procedures/feminizing-surgery/about/pac-20385102.

[60] Mauro E. Kerckhof et al., "Prevalence of Sexual Dysfunctions in Transgender Persons: Results from the ENIGI Follow-Up Study", *The Journal of Sexual Medicine* 16, no. 12 (December 2019), https://doi.org/10.1016/j.jsxm .2019.09.003.

[61] Van Mol, interview by Lahl.

[62] Hruz, interview by Lahl.

Hruz's impressions are backed up by the statistics. One study evaluated fertility preservation in 102 boys and girls seeking puberty blockers and cross-sex hormones.[63] All the children involved received fertility counseling from their pediatrician prior to commencing hormones (either GnRHa or cross-sex hormones). Of the 102 study participants, 49 were girls. The average age at the time of counseling was 15.6 years, with a range of 10.8 to 18.3 years. Of the 49 girls, all declined fertility preservation; 16 gave no reason, and the remaining 33 gave a variety of responses.[64] The most common reasons given (in order of higher to lower frequency) were the following: will consider intervention in the future; did not wish to be pregnant; did not want biological children and would rather foster or adopt; or did not want children at all.[65] Is it possible for a child to consent to an irreversible intervention at an age where he or she cannot really understand what the consequences are going to be? Who among the readers of this book knew, with certainty, at the age of eleven or twelve how many children they might want, if any? Who among the readers would have been able thoughtfully to consider and grasp their own fertility and familial desires at such a young age? Our hearts break for those who wanted to "consider intervention in the future" only to find themselves infertile, unable to reproduce even if they want to. Even if these children are presented with clear information about fertility preservation, the ability of a child to understand the consequences of that decision will still be very limited. We know this. It is why we require parents to give consent to most medical procedures.

[63] Kenneth C. Pang et al., "Rates of Fertility Preservation Use Among Transgender Adolescents", *JAMA Pediatrics* 174, no. 9 (2020), https://doi.org /10.1001/jamapediatrics.2020.0264.

[64] Pang et al., "Fertility Preservation".

[65] Pang et al., "Fertility Preservation".

Grace never took puberty blockers but still wonders about her own fertility after being on high doses of testosterone for so long. She states in the film:

> I'm concerned that the testosterone may have affected my fertility and potentially will cause me some infertility issues, but I really don't know. So that's something that I'll have to find out in the future. I feel, I think, more than anything else, regret over that, because I just hadn't been thinking about having children at that time. I didn't think I really wanted them. And that's something that I began to really want in my mid-twenties. So that is something that I feel very worried about.[66]

Grace is not alone in her feelings. Recently, Dr. Daniel Metzger, one of WPATH's own physicians, acknowledged concerns for young adults who had transitioned and were now experiencing "reproductive regret". He admits that it doesn't surprise him and says, "We try to talk about it, but most of the kids are nowhere in any kind of brain space to really talk about it in a serious way." He goes on to say, "That's always bothered me, but you know, we still want the kids to be happy. Happier in the moment, right?"[67] Children are being allowed to give up their ability to reproduce before they ever even go through puberty, just for their perceived—and temporary—happiness.

Van Meter is clear that these children are incapable of making informed decisions about their fertility: "These

---

[66] Grace, in *The Detransition Diaries: Saving Our Sisters*, directed by Jennifer Lahl (Pleasant Hill, CA: Center for Bioethics and Culture Network [CBC], 2022).

[67] Miriam Grossman (@Miriam_Grossman), "BREAKING: @WPATH Doctor Acknowledges Regret About Sterilization Following Transition 'Reproductive regret … it's there, and I don't think any of that surprises us'", Twitter, October 6, 2022, 6:28 P.M., https://twitter.com/miriam_grossman/status/1578165282362703872.

children have no concept of what it is to be infertile." He describes the "magical thinking" of one child who was interviewed, who declared, "Oh, well, I don't care if I don't have my own children. I'll adopt all of the children that are unwanted, and, you see, I'm going to be there for taking care of the world." Van Meter expresses deep concern about this kind of disconnection from reality among children who describe themselves as trans:

> They're applauded as being the most wonderful, beautiful, kind-hearted individuals that are very forward-thinking, when they have no idea what the concept of parenting or raising a child or conceiving a child is. It's just beyond the scope of their ability to wrap their head around it and being infertile, not having an orgasm, not having the organs that are supposed to work in sexual function be there or work at all, putting on costume pieces that don't work.[68]

Mental Health

It remains unclear whether attempting to transition actually relieves any psychiatric distress or decreases suicide risk in adults or children, given contradictions and unknowns in the research. In fact, the case could be made that medically transitioning can even exacerbate these issues. In the case of children, parents are often held hostage by the emotional argument that if they do not agree to transition their child medically, the child will die by suicide: "Do you want a live son or a dead daughter?" They fear a tragic outcome. But there is no science to support these coercive statements. According to Van Mol, "There is no

[68] Van Meter, interview by Lahl.

long-term evidence showing gender affirmation therapy reduces suicides. It's not there."[69]

The best data we have are studies on adults who, after going through such surgeries, have been followed long-term, but even most of those studies are flawed. Hacsi, a detransitioned man who worked as an epidemiologist at the University of California, San Francisco, and who is also featured in *Trans Mission: What's the Rush to Reassign Gender?*, explains:

> We don't know what happens to people after they go down the trans road because all the studies that follow them—in fact, all but one or two studies that have followed them—lose track of as much as two-thirds of the study population within a few years. And the investigators typically say, "Well, they just wanted to get on with their lives and not be part of the study." You can't say that. If we lost 20 percent of the patients in an HIV study, that'd be a scandal.[70]

Fortunately, there are exceptions, like the study by Cecelia Dhejne and colleagues from 2011,[71] which, Hacsi says, "found [a] 19 times higher rate of completed suicide among the study population, which was all people who had received transing operations in Sweden between 1973 and 2003".[72] To reiterate, some of the largest studies with the longest follow-ups have shown that suicide rates remain markedly elevated after a person undergoes

[69] André Van Mol, in *Trans Mission*. See 17:52–17:59.

[70] Hacsi, interview by Jennifer Lahl, Zoom, December 10, 2020.

[71] See Cecilia Dhejne et al., "Long-Term Follow-Up of Transsexual Persons Undergoing Sex Reassignment Surgery: Cohort Study in Sweden", *PLoS ONE* 6, no. 2 (February 2011), https://doi.org/10.1371/journal.pone.0016885.

[72] Dhejne et al., "Sex Reassignment Surgery". See 20:27–21:04 in *Trans Mission* for Hacsi's discussion of the Dhejne et al. study.

medical interventions in an attempt to transition. Going beyond suicide to look at mental health more broadly, a large study on gender procedures (hormones or surgery) published in *The American Journal of Psychiatry* initially reported that hormonal measures did not improve mental health, while surgery did.[73] However, in 2020, the editors of the journal that had published the study issued a correction that expressly stated, "The results demonstrated no advantage of surgery in relation to subsequent mood or anxiety disorder-related health care."[74]

Concerning children, the short-term data show that suicidal ideation, as well as hospitalization for suicide, is elevated in those patients who received pubertal blockade the prior year. A study published in 2020 found that those adolescents who had "psychiatric treatment needs or problems in school, [or with] peer relationships and managing everyday matters outside of home" continued to have problems even after starting hormone therapy.[75] Authors of the study concluded that "medical gender reassignment was not enough to improve functioning and relieve psychiatric comorbidities among adolescents with gender dysphoria."[76] Van Mol agrees: "There's the overwhelming probability of underlying mental health problems, adverse childhood events, traumas, underlying causes, underlying contributors, none of which go away."

[73] Richard Bränström and John E. Pachankis, "Reduction in Mental Health Treatment Utilization among Transgender Individuals after Gender-Affirming Surgeries: A Total Population Study", *The American Journal of Psychiatry* 177, no. 8, https://doi.org/10.1176/appi.ajp.2019.19010080.

[74] Society for Evidence-Based Gender Medicine (SEGM), "Correction of a Key Study: No Evidence of 'Gender-Affirming' Surgeries Improving Mental Health", August 30, 2020, https://segm.org/ajp_correction_2020.

[75] Riittakerttu Kaltiala et al., "Adolescent Development and Psychosocial Functioning after Starting Cross-Sex Hormones for Gender Dysphoria", *Nordic Journal of Psychiatry* 74, no. 3 (2020), https://doi.org/10.1080/08039488.2019.1691260.

[76] Kaltiala et al., "Cross-Sex Hormones".

He adds: "Because the person engaged in gender-affirming hormones, gender-affirming surgery, again, transition-affirming therapy, doesn't touch those underlying issues. They're still there. They're still demanding to be dealt with. Those are often what are the seeds of regret."[77]

Bad Medicine and Faulty Science

We would like to start this section with a lengthy, yet important, quote from Hruz:

> The people that are most being affected by this are the children themselves. They are caught in the middle of this, and they are going to suffer the consequences of whatever interventions are provided for them to address their underlying problems. And I would say that there are many ways to look at them as victims of an ideology—of putting forward one particular approach to a very real problem that they're experiencing. I think most physicians that are participating in this affirmative care believe that they're doing good. They believe that they are accomplishing a good outcome of alleviating the suffering. That doesn't mean that they are correct in their assumptions, but I think they're being motivated by that. There's a group of physicians that are silently participating or ... are participating by their silence. In fact, they are even allowing this to move forward because they're unwilling to raise the questions that we should be doing as physicians and as scientists when we are looking at any new area of medical practice. And, then, there's a small group that I would characterize as the ideologists, those that have lost all focus on evidence-based medicine and have a desired outcome and are willing to go to any length possible to have that outcome.... That's not the way we do science. And that's an injustice.[78]

[77] Van Mol, interview by Lahl.
[78] Hruz, interview by Lahl.

What about all the studies proving that medical transitioning is helpful? According to Van Meter, "the quality of these studies is abysmal."[79] Ideology is masquerading as science. According to Van Mol, "The science supporting gender affirmation therapy is poor, very poor."[80]

Medicine relies on sound scientific data to inform best practices for patients and their families. In gender medicine, we continue to ask, What did the studies show? First, as Van Mol points out, "There's a lot wrong with the modern peer review process. That's been written about a lot. There's a lot of deficiencies. It's not doing what it's supposed to do."[81] The peer review process is simply a system according to which other researchers in the same field assess the quality of a manuscript before it is published.

Second, the medical literature on transgenderism is problematic and a cause for serious concern. There are, in the words of Van Mol, "a great deal of problems" with the literature. "The best studies generally have the worst results."[82] Some of these bad outcomes we have outlined previously in the chapter. There are quite a few short-term studies, of both adults and children, but long-term studies, especially of children, are lacking. Further, in many studies, we consistently see a lack of follow-up—that is, large portions of the study population are missing after time, rendering the results useless.

"There is a lot of information on the internet that is totally bogus and not based on science and which is very harmful," Van Meter says.[83] One study, by Dr. Jack Turban and colleagues, which was lauded on the morning

---

[79] Van Meter, interview by Lahl.
[80] Van Mol, interview by Lahl.
[81] Van Mol, interview by Lahl.
[82] Van Mol, interview by Lahl.
[83] Van Meter, interview by Lahl.

talk shows and online news sources, claims to have sur-
veyed over twenty-five thousand transgender individuals, asserting that puberty blockers had improved their
mental health. If they didn't have puberty blockers and
wanted them, the study maintained, their mental health
was damaged irreparably. This study was used as evidence
that puberty blockers should be considered the acceptable
standard of care. It turned out to be the case, however,
that the data set had serious deficiencies.[84] Looking more
critically, it was found that the study was not of twenty-
five thousand individuals; indeed, it was of twenty-five
thousand answered surveys of only a few hundred people; that is, *the same people answered the same survey multiple times*. Further, those answering the survey were more
particularly selected from trans activist groups and forums.
Therefore, the survey was not representative of the wider
trans-identifying population, also excluding individuals
who no longer identified as "trans", a group most likely
to be harmed by cross-sex hormones.[85]

Finally, with increasing numbers of people seeking
puberty blockers, cross-sex hormones, and surgeries to

[84] Jack L. Turban et al., "Access to Gender-Affirming Hormones During
Adolescence and Mental Health Outcomes among Transgender Adults",
PLoS ONE 17, no. 1 (January 12, 2022), https://doi.org/10.1371/journal.
pone.0261039; Michael Biggs, "Puberty Blockers and Suicidality in Adolescents Suffering from Gender Dysphoria", *Archives of Sexual Behavior* 49, no. 7
(June 2020), https://doi.org/10.1007/s10508-020-01743-6; Roberto D'An-
gelo et al., "One Size Does Not Fit All: In Support of Psychotherapy for Gender Dysphoria", *Archives of Sexual Behavior* 50 (2021), https://doi.org/10.1007
/s10508-020-01844-2.

[85] Lisa Littman, "Individuals Treated for Gender Dysphoria with Medical
and/or Surgical Transition Who Subsequently Detransitioned: A Survey of
100 Detransitioners", *Archives of Sexual Behavior* 50, no. 8 (2021), https://doi
.org/10.1007/s10508-021-02163-w; Elie Vandenbussche, "Detransition-Related
Needs and Support: A Cross-Sectional Online Survey", *Journal of Homosexuality*
69, no. 9 (2022), https://doi.org/10.1080/00918369.2021.1919479.

make their body resemble that of the opposite sex, how are these busy providers keeping their medical practices up-to-date with current literature? Van Mol says that for a professional to stay on top of the medical literature in his field, he would have to read nineteen studies a day. Busy medical providers certainly cannot do that. So, instead, they get the bullet points or "the take-home message on the study". The same studies are referenced online repeatedly—which is known as "citation bias"—and this phenomenon may be yet another source of careless medical practice. Are providers really following best practices based on sound data?

All hope is not lost, however. There are providers such as Hruz who are focusing their efforts on "putting forward best medical practices, looking at the scientific evidence".[86] We must return to evidence-based medicine in transgender healthcare. It is crucial that we take the time to evaluate all evidence from a medical standpoint, from the perspective of risk and benefit, and that we call the "transing" of children what it is: *an experiment with irreversible consequences.*

Returning to Informed Consent

As we saw previously, informed consent has four central components: decision-making capacity, proper documentation of the consent, disclosure, and competency. With so little known and so much at stake, the questions still arise: Can young boys and girls really give informed consent? Can anyone, when it comes to transgender health? Can parents really consent on behalf of their children without a full understanding of the long-term consequences?

---

[86] Hruz, interview by Lahl.

Where children are concerned, according to Dr. Hruz, "this area of consent is a very, very contentious area. And we're starting to see ... finally some discussion about the limits of a child's ability to give that consent." The ability of the parents themselves to give informed consent must also be examined. It is very difficult for parents to challenge what they are told by a medical professional, "especially if they don't have the medical background to recognize that what's being done is not established as far as long-term consequences [are concerned]".[87] In this sense, these interventions can truly be considered experimental. As Van Mol says, "The reason we consider this so experimental, particularly as it applies to children, is there are no long-term studies that show us the safety of what's going on. And there's a great deal of risk."[88] We have outlined certain risks in this chapter, alongside the risks we have witnessed through the stories of the detransitioners featured in this book.

As we have seen from many different angles, medicalization without caution has consequences. The Society for Evidence-Based Gender Medicine (SEGM) recognizes, critically, that "the history of medicine has many examples in which the well-meaning pursuit of short-term relief of symptoms has led to devastating long-term results"[89]—as we have seen in the example of lobotomies. In 2020, the Council for Choices in Health Care in Finland (CCHC) reported that what is known as gender reassignment does not alleviate comorbid mental health issues; that autistic youth are overrepresented among those suffering from gender dysphoria; and that minors should have their mental

[87] Hruz, interview by Lahl.
[88] Van Mol, interview by Lahl.
[89] "Need for Caution and Better Research", Society for Evidence-Based Gender Medicine (SEGM), accessed July 10, 2023, https://segm.org/sites/default/files/Finnish_Guidelines_2020_Minors_Unofficial%2520Translation.pdf.

and behavioral health issues resolved before determination of their stable gender identity. The CCHC asserted that no medical treatment for gender dysphoria is evidence-based; that "gender reassignment" on minors is experimental; and finally, that "no decisions should be made that can permanently alter a still-maturing minor's mental and physical development."[90] In a recent study, it was reported that 45% of detransitioners felt that they were "insufficiently informed about health risks before starting medical transition or other interventions."[91] The bottom line is that the "gender affirmative" model is leading to risky and detrimental lifelong medical treatment, and informed consent is nonexistent.

Medicalized for Life

When speaking about medical treatments used for people who attempt to transition, a phrase we often hear is "medicalized for life"—that is, once people have begun these medical treatments, they will be patients for the rest of their lives, even if they choose later to detransition. As we have seen in this chapter and from the testimonies of detransitioners, it can no longer be denied that medicalizing gender has short- and long-term detrimental effects on the body, creating a situation where transitioners and detransitioners alike become bound to a healthcare system of medications, hormones, and surgeries—for life. We

---

[90] Recommendation of the Council for Choices in Health Care in Finland (PALKO/COHERE Finland), "Medical Treatment Methods for Dysphoria Related to Gender Variance in Minors", 2020, Society for Evidence-Based Gender Medicine (SEGM), 7, https://segm.org/sites/default/files/Finnish _Guidelines_2020_Minors_Unofficial%20Translation.pdf.

[91] Vandenbussche, "Detransition-Related Needs and Support".

need to remember those children who will become infertile during their "transition"; they will later be at the mercy of the ever-growing fertility industry, needing access to fertility "treatment" and third-party reproduction.

The only way forward—the only way to minimize or reduce harm—is to provide proper care for struggling children and adults. The first step is for healthcare providers to act on their oath to "do no harm". Van Meter speaks directly to those who are seeking treatment:

> My journey with you is going to be to teach you everything I know and make sure that you are cared for and not hurt. I will not do anything to harm you. That is my job as a physician. I took an oath and that is how I practice.... We are so overwhelmed with compassion to take care of these transgender individuals with truth. I mean, come here. Come.... You belong in the sphere of people who care for you and [who] don't want to do any harm.[92]

[92] Van Meter, interview by Lahl.

CONCLUSION

How Does This Dark Moment in Medical History End?

While we cannot see into the future of the gender-affirmation movement and how its ideology will play out, perhaps we can draw some conclusions by looking at the four examples in chapter 2, "Lessons Not Learned from Medical Abuses of the Past". Using some examples from history to guide us, we can imagine how this chapter of medical abuse and experimentation might come to its conclusion.

Prior to the ending of World War II, a young Jewish man, Emanuel Ringelblum, was successful in escaping from the death camp Chelmno, the first Nazi extermination camp to be established after Nazi Germany's invasion of Poland. Ringelblum was forced to bury bodies of people who had been gassed. Upon his escape, he was able to recount his experiences at Chelmno, which were published in the Polish Socialist newspaper *Liberty Brigade*.[1] For the first time, the world got a glimpse of the horrific treatment of people who had been rounded up and taken to the Nazi death camps.

[1] "News of Holocaust Death Camp Killings Becomes Public for First Time", History, November 16, 2009, https://www.history.com/this-day-in-history/news-of-death-camp-killings-becomes-public-for-first-time. See also Paul G. Pierpaoli Jr., "Ringelblum, Emanuel", in *Modern Genocide: The Definitive Resource and Document Collection*, ed. Paul R. Bartrop and Steven Leonard Jacobs, vol. 3, *The Holocaust and the Kurdish Genocide* (Santa Barbara, CA: ABC-Clio, 2015), 1365.

However, it was not until World War II ended, in 1945, that the world discovered the depth and breadth of the German "ethnic cleansing" program. The Nuremberg Trials, the first of their kind in history, began in 1945 and ended in 1946, with defendants facing charges of crimes against peace, war crimes, crimes against humanity, and conspiracy to commit these crimes.[2] These trials gave us the Nuremberg Code, still in place today, which guides ethical research and protects human subjects being used in various studies.

How did the Tuskegee experiment end? Recall that the study began in 1932 and ended in 1972, when whistleblower Jean Heller of the Associated Press broke the story. Heller reported how the federal government had allowed hundreds of Black men to go untreated for syphilis for forty years for research purposes.[3] When Heller's story appeared, an ad hoc advisory committee was formed to find out what had happened. The panel determined that the study was "ethically unjustified" and that the "results [were] disproportionately meager compared with known risks to human subjects involved."[4] The panel also recommended that the United States Public Health Department set up the Tuskegee Health Benefit Program to provide for the medical care of the men who had survived the

[2] See "The Nuremberg Trials", Holocaust Encyclopedia, United States Holocaust Memorial Museum, last modified January 5, 2018, https://www.ushmm.org/collections/bibliography/the-nuremberg-trials.

[3] Jean Heller, "Syphilis Victims in U.S. Study Went Untreated for 40 Years", *The New York Times*, July 26, 1972, https://www.nytimes.com/1972/07/26/archives/syphilis-victims-in-us-study-went-untreated-for-40-years-syphilis.html.

[4] Centers for Disease Control and Prevention (CDC), "The Syphilis Study at Tuskegee Timeline", The U.S. Public Health Service Syphilis Study at Tuskegee, last reviewed December 5, 2022, https://www.cdc.gov/tuskegee/timeline.htm.

study. By 1975, benefits were extended to provide for the men's wives, widows, and children. In January 2004, the last subject died, and in 2009, the last widow to receive these benefits died. The final dark chapter of the Tuskegee experiment was closed when a class action lawsuit awarded $10 million to participants in the study and their families. President Bill Clinton issued a public apology in 1997.

The first lobotomy was performed in 1935 by Portuguese neurologist Egas Moniz, and the last one performed in the United States was in 1967. Moniz was awarded the Nobel Prize in 1949 for his discovery of the lobotomy procedure. It has been estimated that forty to fifty thousand patients underwent lobotomies during the mid-1900s, with about ten thousand being transorbital or "ice pick" lobotomies.[5] The lobotomy was finally discredited with the growth of awareness of its ineffectiveness—many patients saw their condition fail to improve or worsen, and some even died. Families of patients who had undergone lobotomies even called upon the Nobel Prize committee to revoke Moniz's award.

Jack El-Hai, author of *The Lobotomist*, wrote that Moniz should not have his prize revoked: "When you revoke an award, you're saying that the recipient did something wrong. I don't believe that Egas Moniz did something wrong. He proposed a treatment which, in the march of time, has turned out not to be effective, especially compared with modern treatments."[6] Others disagree, such as Christine Johnson, whose grandmother was lobotomized in 1953.

[5] A. Chris Gajilan, "Survivor Recounts Lobotomy at Age 12", CNN, November 30, 2005, https://www.cnn.com/2005/HEALTH/conditions/11/30/pdg.lobotomy/index.html.

[6] Jack El-Hai, in "Nobel Panel Urged to Rescind Prize for Lobotomies", NPR, August 10, 2005, https://www.npr.org/templates/story/story.php?storyId=4794007.

She said that had Moniz not received the award in 1949, her grandmother "would have been spared the operation". After her grandmother was lobotomized, she would just "rock in place"; she became incoherent and childlike.[7] But with the development of better drugs to help patients and the dismal outcomes of the procedure, along with calls from family members for the revocation of the Nobel Prize, the use of lobotomies came to an end.

We see a similar trajectory with regard to forced sterilizations. In 2001, at the age of twenty-four, Kelli Dillon "became one of the most recent victims in a history of forced sterilizations in California that stretches back to 1909 and served as an inspiration for Nazi Germany's eugenics program".[8] While incarcerated in the California state prison system, Dillon had sought medical care for an abnormal pap smear.[9] During a biopsy, the medical team stripped away Dillon's reproductive capacity by removing her ovaries without her consent or even knowledge. Her case sparked a statewide investigation and was featured in the PBS documentary *Belly of the Beast*.[10] From 2006 to 2010, an estimated 150 incarcerated women in the state were sterilized "without required state approval".[11]

[7] Christine Johnson, in "Nobel Panel".

[8] Erin McCormick, "Survivors of California's Forced Sterilizations: 'It's Like My Life Wasn't Worth Anything'", *The Guardian*, July 19, 2021, https://www.theguardian.com/us-news/2021/jul/19/california-forced-sterilization-prison-survivors-reparations.

[9] Toni Fitzgerald, "New Documentary *Belly of the Beast* Explores a Sadly Timely Issue", *Forbes*, October 26, 2020, https://www.forbes.com/sites/toni fitzgerald/2020/10/26/new-documentary-belly-of-the-beast-explores-a-sadly-timely-issue.

[10] *Belly of the Beast*, directed by Erika Cohn, aired November 23, 2020, on PBS, https://www.pbs.org/independentlens/documentaries/belly-of-the-beast.

[11] Ailsa Chang, Alejandra Marquez Janse, and Christopher Intagliata, "A Survivor Reacts to California's Reparations Program for Forced Sterilizations", NPR, July 21, 2021, https://www.npr.org/2021/07/21/1018924484/a-survivor-reacts-to-californias-reparations-program-for-forced-sterilizations.

While involuntary sterilization was legal and occurred in many U.S. states, California led the way in opposing this human rights violation. It is estimated that "in all, more than 20,000 people were sterilized in California, including the historic cases prior to 1979 and hundreds of additional cases in the prisons documented until 2010."[12] Now, through the Forced or Involuntary Sterilization Compensation Program, the state will offer reparations to the survivors who were sterilized at a California state hospital or institution without adequate consent, often between 1909 and 1979, because they were deemed "criminal", "feeble-minded", or "deviant"; and to survivors, like Dillon, "who were sterilized without consent while under the custody of the California Department of Corrections and Rehabilitation after 1979".[13] The California State Legislature approved a bill establishing a $4.5 million reparations fund for survivors of forced or involuntary sterilization,[14] signed into law by Governor Gavin Newsom. The monies will be used for reparations for surviving victims, for the location and notification of victims, and for memorials where these sterilization programs were established. This bill marked the end of an era of an unconscionable medical practice.

We can find encouragement in the way individuals and small groups of people played a large role in bringing these atrocities to an end. In some cases, victims spoke out, told their stories, and sought legal redress, while investigative journalists dug up the facts. Similar efforts underway

---

[12] McCormick, "California's Forced Sterilizations".

[13] "California Now Accepting Applications to Compensate Sterilization Survivors", Disability Rights Education & Defense Fund, February 15, 2022, https://dredf.org/2022/02/15/california-now-accepting-applications-to-compensate-sterilization-survivors.

[14] "Recovery from Forced Sterilization", California Victim Compensation Board (VCB), accessed July 11, 2023, https://victims.ca.gov/fiscp.

today can end the harms being done by "gender-affirming care". As Dr. Van Mol says during our interview for *Trans Mission*, this "whole transgender tsunami" will begin to recede.[15] Like him, we "don't think it'll be easy", and we agree with his assessment that "we have made so much headway just in the past two to three years."[16]

That momentum will continue as victims seek redress for the harms done to them. If there's one thing that the medical community responds to, it's the *l*-word: lawsuits. Dr. Van Meter had an opportunity for a lengthy conversation with Dr. Paul McHugh, former chief psychiatrist at Johns Hopkins Hospital, who says:

> I will tell you what is going to happen to change the tide; it's going to be major lawsuits by families or individuals who have been through this, gone down that pathway and come back out the other side—and they are going to take down not only the physicians, but the drug companies and the hospital, healthcare systems, and the insurance companies that allowed this to happen, and that's when this will all end.[17]

This is indeed a likely scenario. Massive lawsuits directed at physicians, clinical psychologists, and big pharmaceutical companies, such as the ones that manufacture and promote puberty blockers and cross-sex hormones, will put pressure on medical professional societies, universities, and the healthcare system at large. These lawsuits could come in the form of class action suits, in which a group of

[15] André Van Mol, interview by Jennifer Lahl, Redding, California, November 22, 2020.

[16] Van Mol, interview by Lahl.

[17] Paul R. McHugh, quoted by Quentin Van Meter in *Trans Mission: What's the Rush to Reassign Gender?*, directed by Kallie Fell and Jennifer Lahl (Pleasant Hill, CA: Center for Bioethics and Culture Network [CBC], 2021), https://www.youtube.com/watch?v=rUeqEoARKOA. See 48:05–48:41.

people who medically transitioned take legal action against a particular physician or hospital organization for the harm caused to them. One source remarks, "Class action lawyers are sharks. But sharks play an important role in the ecosystem. They devour the rotting carcasses of whales, whose bones drift to the murky depths of the ocean floor."[18] Whether brought by one person or several, lawsuits are having an impact.

Jay Langadinos, a thirty-one-year-old, autistic Australian woman is suing her former psychiatrist for professional negligence following her gender transition.[19] After hormonal therapy, a double mastectomy, and the removal of her ovaries and uterus between the ages of nineteen and twenty-two, Langadinos is concerned about the "on-demand" service of "gender-affirming care". Four years after her hysterectomy, Langadinos was receiving psychiatric treatment from another doctor when she "came to the realization that she should not have undergone the hormone therapy or the first and second surgeries".[20] In her court documents, Langadinos argues that her psychiatrist should have recognized her autism and referred her for further treatment. Jay, like others, now grieves the loss of her ability to have children in the future.

A U.K. suit involving several plaintiffs deserves mention. Keira Bell brought a request for judicial review against the

[18] Michael Cook, "Class Action Suits against Gender Doctors Cloud the Future of Transgender Medicine", *MercatorNet*, August 26, 2022, https://mercatornet.com/class-action-suits-against-gender-doctors-cloud-the-future-of-transgender-medicine/80512.

[19] Debra Soh, "Detransitioner's Lawsuit Will Be the First of Many", *Washington Examiner*, August 31, 2022, https://www.washingtonexaminer.com/restoring-america/community-family/detransitioners-lawsuit-will-be-the-first-of-many.

[20] Snejana Farberov, "Woman Sues Psychiatrist for Approving Gender Transition after Just One Meeting", *New York Post*, August 24, 2022, https://nypost.com/2022/08/24/woman-sues-psychiatrist-for-approving-gender-transition.

U.K.'s National Health Service (NHS) and its policy of providing puberty blockers to teenagers. She joined "Mrs. A.", the mother of a fifteen-year-old patient on the NHS Gender Identity Development Service (GIDS) waiting list, and Sue Evans, a former nurse at a GIDS satellite campus, who began their legal action in 2019.[21] Initially, the court found that children under sixteen are not able to give informed consent to puberty blockers—a decision that was subsequently overturned on appeal. But, for a brief period, the healthcare system did change its policies, and the influence of the case has had a global impact. "The case woke the world up to the reality of the medical transition of children, the dangers of the 'gender-affirmative' model and the scandal of treating children according to ideology rather than clinical evidence. Keira Bell kick-started a global conversation that has not abated."[22]

Another case from Britain involves the detransitioner Ritchie Herron, who was diagnosed with "transsexualism" after just two thirty-minute appointments with NHS's transgender health services. He shed his cloak of anonymity to share his story with the *Daily Mail*.[23] Despite being

[21] Jamie Doward, "High Court to Decide If Children Can Consent to Gender Reassignment", *The Guardian*, January 5, 2020, https://www.theguardian .com/society/2020/jan/05/high-court-to-decide-if-children-can-consent-to -gender-reassignment; Greg Hurst, "Mother Sues Tavistock Child Gender Clinic over Treatments", *The Times*, October 12, 2019, https://www.thetimes.co.uk /article/mother-sues-tavistock-child-gender-clinic-over-treatments-r9df8m987.

[22] "The Supreme Court Decision in the Keira Bell Case Is Not a Loss", Transgender Trend, May 6, 2022, https://www.transgendertrend.com /supreme-court-decision-keira-bell-case-is-not-a-loss.

[23] Sanchez Manning, "Man Suing the NHS over Trans Surgery He Regrets Shares His Ordeal", *Daily Mail*, June 25, 2022, https://www.dailymail.co.uk /news/article-10953157/Man-suing-NHS-trans-surgery-regrets-bravely -waived-anonymity-share-ordeal.html. See also "Man Who Had Sex Change Paid for by NHS Says Medics 'Betrayed' Him", *Daily Mail*, October 22, 2022, https://www.dailymail.co.uk/news/article-11343887/Man-sex-change -operation-paid-NHS-says-medics-betrayed-him.html.

a twenty-six-year-old man who could in principle give informed consent, Herron admitted that, at the time of his "care", he was vulnerable. He claims that his healthcare providers failed to consider his escalating mental health crisis and that the NHS clinic misled him about the risks and irreversible effects of gender surgery and transitioning.[24] He recounts that the four years after his attempt to medically transition from male to female were unbearable, stating that "his crotch became numb and emptying his bladder became slow and painful."[25] He is now taking legal action against Cumbria, Northumberland, Tyne & Wear NHS Foundation Trust, forecasting that "in a few years, I'm sure we'll have law firms asking people if they transitioned and would they like to claim compensation."[26]

Herron's story came out in June 2022, and in July it was announced that the NHS had ordered the Tavistock Clinic to close its doors over concerns for the safety of its patients. Not only that, but approximately a thousand families of former patients are expected to join a class action suit against Tavistock for "recklessly prescribing puberty blockers and unquestioningly launching children on a 'gender affirmation' path".[27]

Also in 2022 the interim report of the *The Cass Review* was released. Dr. Hilary Cass, a U.K. pediatrician, was commissioned in 2020 by the NHS and National Health Improvement of England to make an independent review of "gender identity services" for children and young people using these principles:

---

[24] Hayley Dixon, "I've Been Betrayed by Medics Who Left Me in Pain Because I Didn't Want to Be Gay, Says Detransitioner", *The Telegraph*, October 22, 2022, https://www.telegraph.co.uk/news/2022/10/22/betrayed-medics-who-left-pain-didnt-want-gay-says-detransitioner.

[25] Manning, "Man Suing the NHS".

[26] Manning, "Man Suing the NHS".

[27] Cook, "Class Action Suits".

- The welfare of the child and young person will be paramount in all considerations.
- Children and young people must receive a high standard of care that meets their needs.
- There will be extensive and purposeful stakeholder engagement, including ensuring that children and young people can express their own views through a supportive process.
- The Review will be underpinned by research and evidence, including international models of good practice where available.
- There will be transparency in how the Review is conducted and how recommendations are made.[28]

There are to be no predetermined outcomes with regard to the recommendations the Review will make.

The interim report has been influential in several ways. It proves that the current standard of care young people are receiving puts them "at considerable risk" and that there are "major gaps in the research base underpinning the clinical management of children and young people with gender incongruence and gender dysphoria, including the appropriate approaches to assessment and treatment". It states that "the evidence base for the affirmation-only model is severely lacking", confirming what critics of the "affirmation only" approach have been saying for years. Probably the most damning finding in the report, as it relates to children, is the assertion that "puberty blockers, rather than acting as a 'pause button' allowing children time to explore their identity, seem to lock them into a medicalised treatment pathway." This is supported by data from the Netherlands and

---

[28] *Independent Review of Gender Identity Services for Children and Young People (The Cass Review): Interim Report*, February 2022, https://cass.independent-review.uk/wp-content/uploads/2022/03/Cass-Review-Interim-Report-Final-Web-Accessible.pdf.

the U.K. study carried out by GIDS, which both showed that "almost all children and young people who are put on puberty blockers go on to sex hormone treatment (96.5% and 98%)." The *Interim Cass Report* also states that there is "too little" evidence to justify putting children on hormone therapy.[29] Things are looking up in the United Kingdom. Now England limits the use of puberty blockers to children in clinical trials.

Prior to the release of the *Interim Cass Report*, in February of 2022, Sweden's National Board of Health and Welfare (NBHW) revised their guidelines for treatment and care of children under eighteen who suffer from gender dysphoria. The NBHW explained that previous recommendations had been based on poor data and insufficient evidence. It noted an increase in the number of those who have expressed regret about their decision to transition and those who have detransitioned:

> The eligibility for pediatric gender transition with puberty blockers and cross-sex hormones in Sweden will be sharply curtailed. Only a minority of gender dysphoric youth—those with the "classic" childhood onset of cross-sex identification and distress, which persist and cause clear suffering in adolescence—will be considered as potentially eligible for hormonal interventions, pending additional, extensive multidisciplinary evaluation. For all others, including the now-prevalent cohort of youth whose transgender identities emerged for the first time during or after puberty, psychiatric care and gender-exploratory psychotherapy will be offered instead.[30]

[29] "The Cass Review's Interim Report Is Out", Sex Matters, March 12, 2022, https://sex-matters.org/posts/updates/the-cass-reviews-interim-report-is-out.

[30] "Summary of Key Recommendations from the Swedish National Board of Health and Welfare", Society for Evidence-Based Gender Medicine (SEGM), February 27, 2022, https://segm.org/segm-summary-sweden-prioritizes-therapy-curbs-hormones-for-gender-dysphoric-youth.

Finland, too, has turned away from the WPATH Standards of Care, establishing that "psychotherapy, rather than puberty blockers and cross-sex hormones, should be the first-line treatment for gender-dysphoric youth. This change occurred following a systematic evidence review, which found the body of evidence for pediatric transition inconclusive."[31]

France now urges caution in the treatment of children with gender dysphoria. The French National Academy of Medicine says that children should receive extensive psychological support and that puberty blockers or cross-sex hormones should be used very cautiously, adding that the research available in France is insufficient.

In country after country, medical authorities are saying the same thing: The data behind medical transitioning for children are of poor quality. There are gaps. The evidence is paltry or weak, at best. The way to help young people experiencing gender dysphoria or distress is clearly not by putting them on the medical superhighway of synthetic hormones and sexual surgery.

And what about in the United States? In June 2022, the Protecting Minors from Medical Malpractice Act was introduced by Senators Tom Cotton and Jim Banks. This bill would make medical practitioners who perform gender-transition procedures on a minor liable for any physical, psychological, emotional, or physiological harms from the procedure for thirty years after the individual turns eighteen.[32] Cotton understands what we are trying

[31] "One Year Since Finland Broke with WPATH 'Standards of Care'", Society for Evidence-Based Gender Medicine (SEGM), July 2, 2021, https://segm.org/Finland_deviates_from_WPATH_prioritizing_psychotherapy_no_surgery_for_minors.

[32] Protecting Minors from Medical Malpractice Act of 2022, S.4457, 117th Cong. (2021–2022), https://www.congress.gov/bill/117th-congress/senate-bill/4457.

to emphasize in this book: that doctors in the United States are performing "dangerous, experimental, and even sterilizing gender-transition procedures on young kids" who cannot provide informed consent. His solution is that "any doctor who performs these irresponsible procedures on kids should pay."[33] Cotton and Banks' bill has been endorsed by nearly a dozen groups including the Family Policy Alliance, which says that "children should be protected from politicized medicine and should have the right to recover for the damages done to them."[34]

As Sam Ashworth-Hayes writes, "Lawsuits (and the associated costs) are one of the few feedback mechanisms a state-owned health service has, beyond raw political pressure. If the greatest medical experiment of our time turns out to be deeply harmful, then it will be cases like Herron's which bring it to an end."[35] We could not agree more. But until federal laws such as that proposed by Cotton and Banks are passed, the landscape in the United States is a patchwork of legal battles.

In 2001, Arkansas became the first state to ban "gender-affirming care" for minors. Texas enacted a similar law in 2002. As of March 2023, according to the UCLA School of Law's Williams Institute, a total of thirty states had "restricted access to gender-affirming care or are currently considering laws that would do so".[36] Federal judges have

[33] *Decision* magazine staff, "New Bill Holds Doctors Accountable for Gender-Transition Procedures on Minors", *Decision: The Evangelical Voice for Today*, June 28, 2022, https://decisionmagazine.com/new-bill-holds-doctors -accountable-for-gender-transition-procedures-on-minors.

[34] *Decision* magazine staff, "New Bill".

[35] Sam Ashworth-Hayes, "Detransitioners Should Sue the NHS", *The Critic*, June 30, 2022, https://thecritic.co.uk/detransitioners-should-sue-the-nhs.

[36] Elana Redfield et al., "Prohibiting Gender-Affirming Medical Care for Youth" (highlights), UCLA School of Law Williams Institute, March 2023, accessed July 11, 2023, https://williamsinstitute.law.ucla.edu/publications/bans -trans-youth-health-care.

blocked some of these laws, and the states that passed them are appealing those decisions. In the meanwhile, some states are making it easier to file malpractice lawsuits against practitioners who prescribed hormones for or performed surgery on minors with gender dysphoria.[37]

In response to this trend, California and New York declared themselves "safe havens" for youth seeking to alter their gender medically, and President Biden issued a statement encouraging adults to help young people transition, implying support for the use of medical means: "Affirming a transgender child's identity is one of the best things a parent, teacher, or doctor can do to help keep children from harm, and parents who love and affirm their children should be applauded and supported, not threatened, investigated, or stigmatized."[38]

Despite the political support being given to trans medicine, the harms will continue and so will lawsuits. Chloe Cole, a California resident whose story is included in this book, filed a lawsuit against Kaiser Permanente on February 22, 2023, for performing what her lawyers describe as a "mutilating sex change experiment" and neglecting her mental health.[39] Chloe hopes that her efforts ensure that what was done to her doesn't happen to anyone else.

Layla Jane (Kayla Lovdahl) is suing the same hospital, along with several doctors, for "ideological and

[37] Andrew DeMillo, "Sanders Signs Arkansas Trans Care Malpractice Bill into Law", AP, March 14, 2023, https://apnews.com/article/huckabee-sanders -transgender-malpractice-lgbtq-arkansas-41b7cd39b167b3bf2f3796d8be37ecf6.

[38] Joe Biden, "Statement by President Biden on Texas' Attacks on Transgender Youth", The White House, March 2, 2022, https://www.whitehouse .gov/briefing-room/statements-releases/2022/03/02/statement-by-president -biden-on-texas-attacks-on-transgender-youth.

[39] Pete Suratos, "Kaiser Permanente Sued over Hormone Therapy", NBC Bay Area, February 23, 2023, updated February 24, 2023, https://www.nbcbayarea .com/news/local/kaiser-permanente-sued-over-hormone-therapy/3164935/.

profit-driven medical abuse". She says she was given puberty blockers and cross-sex hormones after a single session with a psychologist, and her breasts were removed when she was thirteen after one consultation with the surgeon. Like the other young women in this book, she was not assessed or treated for her comorbid mental illnesses. The suit notes, "There is no other area of medicine where doctors will surgically remove a perfectly healthy body part and intentionally induce a diseased state of the pituitary gland misfunction based simply on the young adolescent patient's wishes."[40]

In Oregon, Camille Kiefel has filed suit against her social worker, Amy Ruff, her mental health therapist, Mara Burmeister, and two Portland-based trans health centers, Brave Space Oregon and The Quest Center.[41] Kiefel has a long history of mental health issues, which she says were ignored by those to whom she entrusted her care. She claims that she had a one-hour Zoom meeting and a forty-minute video call with Ruff and Burmeister, who then recommended she "undergo chest-reduction surgery". In August 2020, she underwent a double mastectomy, which she now regrets.

There have also been some custody cases, such as those of Jeffrey Younger of Texas and Ted Hudacko of California. Younger lost custody of his twin boys because he

[40] Zachary Stieber, "Girl Sues Hospital for Removing Her Breasts at Age 13", *The Epoch Times*, June 15, 2023, updated June 22, 2023, https://www .theepochtimes.com/girl-sues-hospital-for-removing-her-breasts-at-age-13 -post_5335492.html?welcomeuser=1

[41] James Reinl, "Oregon Woman, 32, with Long History of Mental Health Problems Now Sues Carers for Green-Lighting Her 'Woman-To-Man' Double Mastectomy That Was FAST-TRACKED after Brief Zoom Sessions", *Daily Mail*, November 7, 2022, https://www.dailymail.co.uk/news/article -11399015/Oregon-woman-sues-trans-care-team-abhorrent-misdiagnosis-left -MUTILATED.html.

refused to affirm the decision of one of his sons to transition. Texas courts gave most of the parental rights to the children's mother.[42] Ted Hudacko, another father, lost custody of his son Drew for the same reason. In 2021, he discovered that "a puberty-blocking implant had been inserted in Drew's arm and that the boy had begun a course of cross-sex hormones. The combination would likely soon sterilize Drew, if it hadn't already. No one had obtained Ted's permission."[43] Ted has not been declared an unfit parent and has visitation with his other son, but he has not been allowed to see Drew for several years, giving the impression that in Drew's case the ruling was ideologically driven.

Fortunately, for Ted, Chloe, Camille, and others, victory in the courtroom may come soon thanks, in part, to Jamie Reed, who in conscience could no longer stay quiet about what she observed as a case manager at the Washington University Transgender Center at St. Louis Children's Hospital. What she describes in her affidavit to the attorney general of Missouri should shock the country. She claims that parents of patients were lied to about the risks and the experimental nature of trans treatment for children and that she observed ethical breaches in the failure to obtain proper informed consent when children were being put on puberty blockers and cross-sex hormones. When she tried to alert her superiors about her concerns, she says she was told to "get with the program, or get out".[44]

[42] Anne Georgulas vs. Jeffrey Younger, memorandum ruling, 301st Judicial District Court DF-15-09887 (August 3, 2021), https://www.courthousenews.com/wp-content/uploads/2021/12/trans-child-memorandum.pdf.

[43] Abigail Shrier, "How a Dad Lost Custody of Son After Questioning His Transgender Identity", *New York Post*, February 26, 2022, https://nypost.com/2022/02/26/dad-lost-custody-after-questioning-sons-transgender-identity.

[44] Affidavit of Jamie Reed, February 7, 2023, https://ago.mo.gov/docs/default-source/press-releases/2-07-2023-reed-affidavit---signed.pdf.

One incident described by Reed involved a seventeen-year-old girl who was on testosterone as part of her "transition care". This young woman called the center because she was bleeding heavily from her vagina. She was instructed to go to the emergency department where it was discovered that her "vaginal canal had ripped open" during sexual intercourse because testosterone in high doses in the female body thins the vaginal tissue. Surgery was needed to repair the laceration.

By 2019, Reed became aware of desisters (people who only socially transition and then desist) and detransitioners. She recalls being troubled that one young girl, who was from an unstable home and had a history of drug abuse, was put on cross-sex hormones at sixteen and had a double mastectomy at eighteen. Three months later, says Reed, the young girl called the surgeon and said she was taking back her given name and that her pronouns were "she" and "her". Then she said, "I want my breasts back." Fighting for the safety of children drove Reed to ignore advice from colleagues to keep quiet.

The detransitioners suing the medical professionals who injured them will also find support from a growing number of physicians questioning the claim that cross-sex hormones improve the well-being of youth with gender dysphoria. In a letter to the *Wall Street Journal*, Dr. Stephen Hammes, president of the Endocrine Society, argued that this claim is backed up by more than two thousand studies.[45] He was promptly contradicted by a letter from twenty-one clinicians and researchers from nine countries, who wrote:

---

[45] Stephen Hammes, "Endocrine Society Responds on Gender-Affirming Care" (letter), Wall Street Journal, July 5, 2023, https://www.wsj.com/articles/trans-gender-affirming-care-endocrine-society-evidence-fdb8562c?mod=article_inline.

Every systematic review of evidence to date, including one published in the *Journal of the Endocrine Society*, has found the evidence for mental-health benefits of hormonal interventions for minors to be of low or very low certainty. By contrast, the risks are significant and include sterility, life-long dependence on medication and the anguish of regret. For this reason, more and more European countries and international professional organizations now recommend psychotherapy rather than hormones and surgeries as the first line of treatment for gender-dysphoric youth.[46]

The evidence of real harm being done to minors is the reason physicians such as Drs. Paul Hruz, Quentin Van Meter, and André Van Mol object to the "gender-affirming care" model put forth by professional medical societies such as the American Academy of Pediatrics (AAP) and the Pediatric Endocrine Society (PES). These physicians argue that doctors' rights of conscience will be violated if the government begins to mandate that physicians provide affirmation-only therapy.[47]

In our view, physicians are the ultimate gatekeepers. Puberty cannot be blocked without the authorization of a physician. Cross-sex hormones cannot be given without a prescription from a physician. "Top surgery"—which for women is the amputating of healthy breasts—cannot be performed without a surgeon, and the same is true for the different kinds of "bottom" surgery. Although every doctor in America takes some variation of the Hippocratic

[46] Riittakerttu Kaltiala et al, "Youth Gender Transition Is Pushed without Evidence" (letter), *Wall Street Journal,* July 24, 2023, https://www.wsj.com /articles/trans-gender-affirming-care-transition-hormone-surgery-evidence -c1961e27?mod=article_inline.

[47] Ryan Colby, "Doctors Challenge Harmful Transgender Mandate", Becket Law, August 4, 2022, https://www.becketlaw.org/media/doctors-challenge -harmful-transgender-mandate.

Oath, it has become a meaningless pledge. Are young physicians today still connected to the oath's rich tradition—the physician's fiduciary responsibility to "do no harm"?

If the weight of responsibility falls on physicians, what can be done to turn medicine back to ethical care? As Nigel Cameron writes in *The New Medicine: Life and Death After Hippocrates*:

> If modern, post-Hippocratic medicine is to be reformed, and the covenantal, philanthropic enterprise to survive and flourish again, that is a prerequisite. These must be twin goals of Hippocratic medicine today: firstly, to maintain the tradition, to keep Hippocratic medical practice alive at all costs (and they may prove to be high); and secondly to work for the recovery of the Hippocratic medical culture.[48]

It may take time, and it may take lawsuits, as Dr. Paul McHugh predicts, or the passing of laws that protect children, such as those in Arkansas and Texas. Just recently, the Florida state boards of medicine and osteopathic medicine have taken the approach of Scandinavia and England: they forbid the use of puberty blockers or cross-sex hormones for those under eighteen. Leor Sapir writes, "Rather than imposing legislative actions that put politicians between the doctor and the patient, Florida decided to invoke the existing mechanism for the regulation of health practices, putting the decision in front of state medical boards."[49]

While the mainstream media has generally been remiss by failing to report on the risks and harms of medical gender

---

[48] Nigel M. de S. Cameron, *The New Medicine: Life and Death After Hippocrates* (Wheaton, IL: Crossway Books, 1991), 163.

[49] Leor Sapir, "Reason and Compassion on Gender Medicine", *City Journal*, November 4, 2022, https://www.city-journal.org/floridas-reason-and-compassion-on-gender-medicine.

treatments, on November 14, 2022, the *New York Times* published an article entitled "They Paused Puberty, But Is There a Cost?" The summary lede reads: "Puberty blockers can ease transgender youths' anguish and buy time to weigh options. But concerns are growing about long-term physical effects and other consequences."[50] This crack in the narrative of "gender-affirming care" helps prepare the way for legal cases alleging medical abuse. Raising awareness was the first step to common recognition of Nazi medicine's human rights violations, the abusive Tuskegee experiment in Alabama, the harm done by lobotomy, and the brutality of mass involuntary sterilizations—all atrocities committed at the hands of physicians, who are charged with healing, not harming, their patients.

[50] Megan Twohey and Christina Jewett, "They Paused Puberty, but Is There a Cost?", *The New York Times*, November, 14, 2022, https://www.nytimes.com/2022/11/14/health/puberty-blockers-transgender.html.

ACKNOWLEDGMENTS

Acknowledgments from Jennifer

I count myself one of the privileged few who get to do work I've been called to do—work that brings me great joy. Projects like making movies and writing books are not for the faint of heart, but with the right people holding up your arms, like Aaron and Hur did for Moses, the task seems manageable and even fun.

Thank you, Vivian Dudro, for your vision of turning *The Detransition Diaries* film into a book, and for trusting us to write this book. Laura Shoemaker, you were so thorough and patient in your help along the way so that we could deliver a manuscript that meets Ignatius Press' high standards.

Gary Powell, your friendship over the years has been a great gift to me. We've shared many moments of camaraderie as we collaborate to protect women and children. When you, an Oxford graduate with years of teaching experience, offered to read chapters along the way, it was as if manna from heaven had fallen upon us. Thank you for your steady hand, for being a stickler for the facts and the truth, and for your impeccable command of the English language. We shall have a toast soon, I hope, on one side of the pond or the other!

Brandon Showalter, you have always been generous with your time and expertise, praying for doors to open so that our message reaches the largest possible audience. You have been on the frontlines, reporting the hard, ugly facts of trans ideology for years. I know when you get to heaven those jewels will be so plentiful in your crown, your neck just might break. Thank you for writing the foreword, knowing you could have easily written this book yourself, and for carefully reading the chapters to keep us on course.

Donovan Cleckley, your assistance with the manuscript was invaluable. It's been a pleasure to work with you again on such an important project. When we were stuck, we knew just the person to help us push this book across the finish line. The world is a better place because of people with skills like yours when it comes to the written word and a calm that can bring rest to harried writers.

To all the young people who have been harmed by this transgender cult, may this book encourage you as you hear from others like yourself and see how they survived, overcame, and even flourished in their detransition. To others who are hearing, and perhaps even believing, you were "born in the wrong body", may I say to you that you are wonderfully and perfectly made, just the way you are.

There are countless men and women, mothers and fathers, fighting on the frontlines to protect our young people. Please know: we see you, and your work is not in vain. Even when you think you are not making a differ- ence, or not winning, you are. Even though many mock you, you won't and often can't back down, especially when you are fighting to save your own children. The fruits of your labors may show up today, or next year, or later down the road, but know you are doing exactly what is necessary.

To the young people in this book, and to the many others like Helena, Grace, Nick, Cat, Chloe, Torren, and Rachel, who could have been in this book but are speak- ing out: thank you for your bravery and courage, especially as we know about the hatred and vitriol heaped on you to try to silence you—or even worse, to try to destroy you. I have nothing but respect, admiration, and love for you.

Finally, last but certainly not least, is my strong and supportive husband, Dan. You have always been my biggest and best cheerleader, having more faith in me than I often have in myself. You are a great sounding board, and you give solid and helpful advice and criticism, always aiming to help me do the best possible work. Thank you for encouraging me to add this book to my plate. Your wonderful encouragement stands behind every word in this book.

Acknowledgments from Kallie

Years ago, as a struggling twenty-something, I came upon Elisabeth Elliot's charge to "do the next thing". When I was feeling overwhelmed with challenges that seemed too much to bear, these simple words echoed deep within my young heart and soul. The call to "do the next thing" became a lifeline for me to cling to when the days seemed too short and the to-do list too long. Co-writing this book, my first book, was an answer to that call, and it wouldn't have been possible without the love and support of each of you whom I mention here. Each of you has helped me to "do the next thing", and from the depths of my heart, I thank you.

Vivian Dudro's email was the spark that ignited the flame. If not for her, this book wouldn't be in your hands. After the announcement of our forthcoming documentary, *The Detransition Diaries: Saving Our Sisters*, Vivian emailed to say: "*The Detransition Diaries* would make a great book. Do you have any interest in pursuing such a book?" Thank you, Vivian, for supporting and watching our film, and for seeing the potential in us to write this book. Thank you for seeing what the next thing was!

I'd like to thank each of the editors at Ignatius Press as well as Gary Powell for your proofreading and ability to edit proficiently. I would also like to thank Donovan Cleckley for his enthusiasm for this project and help with making sure all of our references and quotes were properly cited. You are the unseen laborers who deserve high praise.

Thank you, Laura Shoemaker, for making this process so painless. Your guidance every step of the way has been tremendous. Thank you, Ignatius Press, for giving me the opportunity to write my first book and fulfill a dream I have had for years. Working with you and your team has been a wonderful experience.

There were a lot of wonderful people who inspired this work and who contributed to it either directly or indirectly. Each of you deserves more praise than I am able to give in this small chapter of acknowledgments. My gratitude toward each of you far exceeds the brevity of the words I offer. Rachel, thank you for caring for my daughter in a way that allowed me to focus on my work without concern or worry. Thank you, Brandon Showalter, for writing a beautiful foreword and for being such a cheerleader for us and for children around the world. Dr. Van Mol, Dr. Hruz, and Dr. Van Meter: Thank you for being such wonderful examples of ethically exemplary doctors. Thank you for making time in your already full schedules to sit down and talk with Jennifer and me. Thank you, Kellie-Jay Keen, Libby Emmons, and Natasha Chart! Living all around the globe, through your own unique influences, you are making an impact on the lives of women and children—even if it feels exhausting and overwhelming. Keep doing the next thing! Thank you to those who weren't afraid to admit that you had been bamboozled by those who were supposed to protect and heal you. Helena, Grace, Nick, Cat, Chloe, Torren, and Rachel: You are the heroes of this book. Thank you for your bravery and your strength and for sharing your personal stories with the world. I'd like to leave you, and all of the other women, men, and children who have been harmed by the gender-identity industry, with this quote from an unknown author: "When some time has passed us and the story can be told, it will mirror the strength and courage of your soul."

Jennifer, you are a force and a friend. Before I went off to college, people would ask me what I wanted to do. I would reply, "Change the world." Working with you for the organization you started, I get to do that. Thank you for taking me under your wing and co-writing this book with me. Thank you for showing me and teaching me how "to do the next thing" every single day.

Mom, thank you for being my biggest cheerleader and sounding board. Thank you for raising me to think for myself and not to be afraid to say or do the right thing—however difficult the right thing is. Thank you for always answering my calls and for allowing me the space to come to you for insight, for wisdom, or just to chat.

Chris, thank you for your never-ending, steadfast love and support. You and my mom are the two people who never doubt my ability to accomplish whatever God has set before me. Thank you for letting me read to you "just one more thing, real quick". Thank you for helping me to find the time and space I needed to finish this book along with all the other responsibilities on my plate. I love you, and I am grateful for you.

Zella, my Cherie Amour, thank you for giving me the inspiration to "do the next thing". I pray that, whatever work I do, it is a blessing to you and yours.

INDEX

60 Minutes, 17, 86–87

AAP (American Academy of Pediatrics). *See* American Academy of Pediatrics (AAP)
adolescent girls: fear of being female, 159–63; higher incidence of gender dysphoria in, 145–49; importance of helping, 85; lack of understanding of experiences of, 85; peer or social contagion, 152–59; rise of gender confusion in, 75; rush to gender-affirmation care, 166–74; same-sex attraction, 164–66; trauma and, 149–52; unresolved mental health diagnosis, 149–52
adolescents: Dutch Protocol and, 42–43; lack of understanding of experiences of, 75–76
adverse childhood events (ACEs), 150–52
affirmation only approach, 216
Aharon, Alix, 36
American Academy of Pediatrics (AAP), 123; gender-affirmation model of, 224; WPATH Standards of Care and, 42
American Association for the Advancement of Science, 57
American Psychological Association (APA), 149, 152, 176
Anderson, Erica, 146, 157, 166, 175–76
Arkansas gender-affirming care ban, 219, 225
artificial reproductive technology industry, 9–10
Ashworth-Hayes, Sam, 219
autism, 162; gender dysphoria and, 114–115, 149; gender transition and, 213; informed consent and, 65

bad medicine/faulty science, damage from, 199–202
Bailey, Andrew, 18
Banks, Jim, 218–19
Baylor University Medical Center, 23–24
Bell, Keira, 213–14
Belly of the Beast (2020 documentary) (PBS), 210
Belmont Report, 54
Benjamin, Harry, 24–27, 34
Biden, Joe, 220
Big Fertility (film) (Lahl), 10

Biggs, Michael, 43, 183,
     184–88
Bilek, Jennifer, 173
biological sex: pronoun usage,
     20; queer theory and, 34; as
     real and innate, 19–20. See
     also sex
body dysmorphia: gender
     problems and, 77, 78, 79;
     informed consent and, 65
Boston Children's Hospital:
     Dutch Protocol and, 42–43;
     gender clinic in, 36
bottom surgery: damage,
     188–93; gatekeeping over,
     224; as irreversible, 41.
     See also hysterectomies;
     oophorectomy
Brave Space Oregon, 221
breast binding, 41, 115, 117–18
breast reconstructive surgery,
     85, 121
breast removal surgeries. See
     mastectomies
Breeders (film) (Lahl), 10
Buck, Carrie, 59
Buck v. Bell, 59
Bullough, Vern L., 28
Burmeister, Mara, 221
Butler, Judith, 34

California: custody cases in,
     221–22; safe havens for
     transitioning youth, 122–23,
     220
Carnegie Institution, 47
Cass, Hilary, 215–16
The Cass Review, 215–16
Cat, 100–113; eating disorder,
     149; gender stereotypes

and, 160, 162, 163; Reddit
     detrans group, 177; trauma
     and, 148
Center for Bioethics and
     Culture Network, 15
Center for Transgender and
     Gender Expansive Health
     (Johns Hopkins), 33
Chart, Natasha, 162–63
Chelmno death camp, 207
chest masculinization surgery,
     41, 72, 188–89. See also
     mastectomies
Chloe, 11, 114–23; gender
     stereotypes and, 160, 163;
     lawsuit against Kaiser
     Permanente, 220, 222;
     Reddit detrans group,
     177; social media and, 148,
     156–57, 160; unresolved
     mental health diagnosis, 148
"cisgender", term usage, 111
clinical psychologists, lawsuits
     against, 212, 213
clinical trials, England's limit of
     puberty blockers in, 217
Clinton, Bill, 52, 209
coercion: coerced sterilization
     policies, 56–62; in Tuskegee
     study, 53, 54
Cohen-Kettenis, Peggy, 42–43
Colapinto, John, 31
Cole, Chloe. See Chloe
comfort care, 41
comorbid issues: gender
     dysphoria and, 114–15, 132,
     149–50; informed consent
     and, 65; as unassessed or
     treated, 221
conversion therapy, 119

The Corrosive Impact of Transgender Ideology (Williams), 168
Cotton, Tom, 218–19
Council for Choices in Health Care (CCHC) (Finland), 63–64, 203–4
COVID-19 pandemic, 16
cross-dressing, 22, 171; hypergender dysphoria and, 36
cross-sex hormones, 96, 221; AAP (American Academy of Pediatrics) and, 42; age guidelines for, 41–42; custody cases and, 222; damage, 184–88; effects of, 81, 184–88; as experimental, 63; fertility preservation and, 194–96; Florida ban on, 225; Forcier on, 37–38; gatekeeping over, 224; informed consent and, 222; Jorgensen and, 26; lawsuits against manufacturers and promoter of, 212; legal issues over, 18; long-term physical effects, 84; National Academy of Medicine (France) on, 218; PES (Pediatric Endocrine Society) and, 42; physicians questioning use of, 223–24. *See also* estrogen; testosterone
custody cases, 221

damage: bad medicine/faulty science, 199–202; bottom surgery, 188–93;

cross-sex hormones, 184–88; infertility, 193–96; as lasting and irreversible, 175–78; medicalized for life, 204–5; mental health issues, 196–99; puberty blockers, 178–84; reproductive regrets, 193–96; return to informed consent, 202–4; social transitioning and, 178; top surgery, 188–93
data on medical transitioning, 217, 218
Davenport, Charles, 47–48, 57
Day, Elizabeth, 55–56
decision-to-transition regrets, 217
depression: cross-sex hormones and, 80; gender and, 66, 67, 92; gender dysphoria and, 149
desisters, defined, 223
The Detransition Diaries (2022 documentary) (Lahl), 9, 15, 17, 19, 114
detransitioners: defined, 16–17; Littman study on, 74, 148–50, 164; mental health issues of, 10–11; physical injuries of, 10–11; realization moment, 72–73, 77, 83–84, 96–97, 108, 121, 131–32; Reed on, 223; regrets of, 65, 73, 75, 81, 82; support for, 73, 99, 223–24; TERFs and, 109–10; testimonies of, 17, 85, 86–87, 97–98, 121–22, 140; underlying anxiety of, 80, 81; understanding of behaviors by, 74–75

detransitioning, meaning of, 73
Dhejne, Cecelia, 197
Dillon, Kelli, 210
disorder of assumption, 32–33
Down syndrome, 62
drug abuse: comorbidity of,
    223; familial drug abuse, 150
Dully, Howard, 55–56
Dutch Protocol, 42–43;
    gender-affirmation
    movement, 42–43
dysphoric symptoms, uterine
    transplants and, 22

eating disorders: gender and,
    66; gender dysphoria and,
    149
Edwards-Leeper, Laura, 175–76
egg freezing, 16
Eggsploitation (film) (Lahl), 10
Elbe, Lili, 22. See also
    Wegener, Einar
El-Hai, Jack, 209
Emmons, Libby, 161, 163
Endocrine Society, 223
endocrinology literature, 11
endometriosis, 140–41
England, legislative bans in, 225
ERO (Eugenics Record
    Office) (Cold Harbor
    Springs, NY), 47, 57, 59
Esses, James, 40–41, 174
Estabrook, Arthur, 59
estrogen, effects of, 96, 130,
    132
ethics: of cross-sex hormones
    for children, 15; guidelines
    for human participation in
    research experiment, 53;
    Hippocratic Oath, 224–25;
    informed consent and, 222;

medical abuse and, 45–46,
    142–43; in Nazi Germany,
    48–51; Nuremberg Code,
    208; of puberty blockers
    for children, 15; in research
    experimentation, 53;
    surgeries on minors with
    gender dysphoria and, 15;
    Tuskegee Health Benefit
    Program, 208–9. See also
    research experimentation
ethnic cleansing, 208
eugenics, 46–48, 56–58
Eugenics Record Office
    (ERO) (Cold Harbor
    Springs, NY), 47, 57, 59
Evans, Sue, 169–70, 214
evidence: NBHW on
    insufficiency of, 217;
    standards of care and, 43;
    Yogyakarta Principles
    and, 44

facial masculinization surgery,
    72, 83
Family Policy Alliance, 219
family-background issues,
    88–89, 150
fear of being female, 159–63
femininity: feelings of, 22, 33;
    perceptions of, 23
feminist critics: gender ideology
    and, 111; of transsexualism,
    35–36. See also Raymond,
    Janice
fertility preservation
    technologies, 172;
    medicalization and, 10;
    offered to transitioning
    children, 16
Finland, 63–64, 203–4

Florida, legislative bans in, 225

forced sterilizations: Forced or Involuntary Sterilization Compensation Program, 211; opposition to, 210–11. *See also* coercion

Forcier, Michelle, 37, 180

Freeman, Walter, 55–56

Friedmann, F. F., 25

Galton, Francis, 46, 47, 56

Gay and Lesbian Alliance Against Defamation (GLAAD), 17, 35–36, 173

gender: deconstructing of, 78; gender activists, 40; gender confusion, 36; gender incongruence, 216; gender roles, 29, 111–12, 126; gender stereotypes, 160–63; gender theories, 43; queer theory and, 34; term usage, 40; traditional assumptions about, 34

gender dysphoria: adolescent girls and, 19, 85; Benjamin's views on, 26; clinical management of children/ young people with, 216; informed consent and, 65; NBHW's revised guidelines on, 217; during transition, 98–99; understanding problem of, 19, 85–86, 142; Yogyakarta Principles and, 44

gender identity: affirmation of self-conception of, 10; defined, 29; Yogyakarta Principles and, 44

Gender Identity Clinic (Johns Hopkins), 29, 31–32

Gender Identity Development Service (GIDS) (UK), 214, 217

gender ideology: beginnings of, 21; future of, 207; as parasitic, 10; political gain and, 48; real costs of, 10. *See also* gender-affirmation movement

Gender Trouble (Butler), 34

gender-affirmation model: *Interim Cass Report* on evidence based for, 216; physicians objecting to, 224

gender-affirmation movement: Dutch Protocol, 42–43; future of, 207; gender-affirming care for children, 36–39; investigative journalism on, 212; ovarian tissue cryopreservation (OTC) and, 117; rise of, 21; WPATH (World Professional Association of Transgender Health), 39–42; Yogyakarta Principles, 43–44. *See also* Benjamin, Harry; Butler, Judith; Jorgensen, George "Christine"; Kinsey, Alfred; Money, John; Raymond, Janice; Wegener, Einar

gender-affirming care: bans on, 219–20; for children, 36–39; concerns about, 225–26; on-demand service of, 213; gender stereotypes and, 159–63; rights of conscience and, 224; term usage, 9

Gender-Affirming Health Care
Act, 122–23
The Gender Mapping Project,
36, 167
genetics, 46, 50
genital tucking, 41
GLAAD (formerly Gay and
Lesbian Alliance Against
Defamation), 17, 35–36, 173
GnRH therapy, 64, 178–79,
194
Grace, 77–87; on detransition,
17; eating disorder, 149;
Reddit detrans group, 177;
reproductive regrets, 195;
social media and, 156–57;
unresolved mental health
diagnosis, 147
Green, Jack (Jackie), 41
Green, Susie, 40–41
Grossman, Miriam, 33

Hacsi, 197
Hammes, Stephen, 223
Harlow, Harry, 120–21
harms: mainstream media's
failure to report on,
225–26; truth and treatment
without, 20
Harry Benjamin International
Gender Dysphoria
Association, 39. See
also WPATH (World
Professional Association of
Transgender Health)
Hawley, Josh, 18
Health Care Challenges for
Transgender Youth (2020 TV
program) (60 Minutes), 17
Helena, 66–76; eating disorder,
149; Reddit detrans group,

177; social media and,
156–57, 158, 161; trauma
and, 147–48; unresolved
mental health diagnosis,
149, 156–57
Heller, Jean, 208
Herron, Ritchie, 214–15, 219
Higdon, Sara, 122
Hippocratic Oath, 45, 224–25
Holmes, Oliver Wendell, Jr.,
59
homophobia, 164–65
hormone blockers, 96. See also
puberty blockers
hormone therapy: gaps in
research base and, 11;
Interim Cass Report on, 217;
lawsuits over, 213, 219
Hruz, Paul, 11, 38–39, 176,
177, 179–80, 185–86,
193–94, 199, 202, 203, 224
Hudacko, Drew, 222
Hudacko, Ted, 221–22
Human Rights Campaign, 35,
173
human rights violations:
physicians and, 226;
Yogyakarta Principles and,
43. See also involuntary
sterilization; lobotomy
experiments; Nazi
Germany; Tuskegee
experiment
hypergender dysphoria, 36
hysterectomies: lawsuits over,
213; risks of, 192

infertility: cross-sex hormones
and, 84–85; damage, 193–
96; transitioning therapies
causing, 16

informed consent: components
of, 202–4; criteria for,
65; as minimal, 80;
misinformation and, 86
*Inquiries into Human Faculty and
Its Development* (Galton), 46
Institute for Sex Research, 28
Institutional Review Board, 53
Interim Cass Report, 216–17
International Military Tribunal
(IMT), 51
investigative journalism, 211–12
involuntary sterilization,
210–11, 226
irreparable injuries: of
detransitioners, 65;
Nuremberg Code of Ethics
on, 65
Irreversible Damage (Shrier),
153–54
Isolation and gender, 66, 67

Jane, Layla (Kayla Lovdahl),
lawsuit filed by, 220–21
Jenner, Bruce, 36–37
Johns Hopkins: Center for
Transgender and Gender
Expansive Health, 33;
on phalloplasty surgeries,
190; in sex-reassignment
surgeries, 31–33
Johnson, Christine, 209–10
Jones, James H., 28
Jorgensen, George "Christine,"
24–27
Journal of the Endocrine Society,
224

Kaiser Permanente, lawsuit
filed against, 220
Karolinska Institute (Sweden), 32

Keen, Kellie-Jay (Posie Parker),
110, 174
Kiefel, Camille, lawsuit filed
by, 221, 222
Kinsey, Alfred, 11, 27–29, 33,
34
Kinsey, Sex, and Fraud
(Reisman), 28–29
Kinsey Reports, 27–28

Lambda Legal, 35
Langadinos, Jay, 213
lasting and irreversible, damage
as, 175–78
Laughlin, Harry H., 48, 57–58
lawsuit against Kaiser
Permanente, Chloe, 222
lawsuits: class action suits, 212–
13; medical community's
response to, 212
legal issues: custody cases,
221; gender-affirming
care bans, 219–20; against
Kaiser Permanente, 220;
Langadinos lawsuit, 213;
malpractice lawsuits against
practitioners, 219; need
for lawsuits, 212, 225;
Nuremberg Code of Ethics,
51–52; U.K. judicial review
on gender reassignment,
213–14; unstainable
liabilities, 18; Washington
University Transgender
Center, 222–23; Yogyakarta
Principles and, 43
LGB (lesbian, gay, and bisexual)
organizations, 35–36
LGBT+: introduction to issues
of, 89, 91; Raymond on,
36; therapists and, 79

Lidinsky-Smith, Grace, 12. *See also* Grace

Littman, Lisa, 74, 136, 148–50, 153, 155–56, 159

lobotomy experiments: discrediting of, 209–10; lessoned learned from, 62, 63; raising awareness about, 226; research experimentation, 54–56

Lovdahl, Kayla (Layla Jane), lawsuit filed by, 220–21

Malone, William, 181

mastectomies: effects of, 81, 82, 118–20; inadequate evaluations for, 118; increase in, 37; lawsuits over, 213, 221; regrets over, 77, 83, 120–21; SOC8 on, 41. *See also* top surgery

Mayo Clinic, 187

McHugh, Paul R., 31–32, 40, 212, 225

medical abuse, 45–46; coerced sterilization policies, 56–62; conclusions based on, 207; lawsuits over, 220–21, 226; lessoned learned from, 62–65; medical ethics, 45–46; medical ethics and, 45. *See also* research experimentation

medical institutions: lawsuits against, 220–21; lawsuits over, 222–23

medical personnel: encouragement to transition by, 70–72, 142–43; inadequate evaluations by, 152; medical malfeasance, 10

medicalization: fertility preservation measures and, 10; of gender, 9; of gender dysphoria as exploitative, 11; medicalized for life, 172, 204–5, 216; of transgenderism, 35. *See also* gender-affirming care

Mengele, Josef, 50–51

menstruation, 23, 115, 116, 117, 143, 160, 161, 163, 182

mental health issues: comorbidity of, 70–71, 72, 92, 132, 149–50, 221; damage, 196–99; of detransitioners, 10–11, 147; informed consent and, 65, 137; as unresolved, 78, 147, 198–99

Mermaids (advocacy group), 40, 168, 169, 173

Metzger, Daniel, 195

misgendering, 41

misogyny, 101, 110, 159, 160, 163

Missouri: lawsuit in, 222–23; legal issues in, 18

Money, John, 11, 29–33, 34, 39, 40. *See also* WPATH (World Professional Association of Transgender Health)

Moniz, Egas, 54–55, 209, 210

Mortensen, Helen, 56

My Lobotomy (Dully), 55–56

NAMBLA (North American Man Boy Love Association), 30

National Academy of Medicine (France): on insufficiency of research, 218; on puberty blockers/cross-sex hormone usage, 218

National Board of Health and Welfare (NBHW) (Sweden), revised gender dysphoria guidelines, 217

National Health Services (NHS) (UK), 40, 145, 214–16

National Research Act, 53

National Socialist German Physician's League, 49

Nazi Germany: ethnic cleansing program, 208; extermination camps, 207; medical ethics and, 48–51; raising awareness about, 226; research experimentation in, 46–52; U.S. eugenics movement and, 48

Neisser case, 49

Netherlands, 216–17

New York safe havens for transitioning youth, 220

Newsom, Gavin, 123, 211

Nick, 88–99

Nobel Prize, 54–55, 209–10

nonbinary: dating as, 84; identifying as, 40, 68, 78, 83, 108

Nuremberg Code of Ethics, 51–52, 63, 65, 208

Nuremberg Trials, 51, 53, 62–63, 208

Obedin-Maliver, Juno, 184–85, 187

O'Flaherty, Michael, 44

Oliven, John F., 25

oophorectomies, 213

oppression/privilege hierarchy, transgenderism and, 67–68

Oregon, lawsuit in, 221

ovarian tissue cryopreservation (OTC), 117

ovary removal surgeries, 213

Page, Ellen, 37

parents: accepting of transitions, 79, 93–94; encouraged to allow transitions, 37–38, 116; lack of support for, 16; lied to about suicide, 19; negative reactions of, 69, 110, 131; online groups for, 73–74; parental consent, 70; role in transgenderism, 94

Pediatric Endocrine Society (PES): gender-affirmation model of, 224; WPATH Standards of Care and, 42

pedophilia, 29–30, 33

peer contagion, 152–59

Person, Ethel Spector, 25

phalloplasty surgeries, 82, 83, 190–92

pharmaceutical companies, 110, 212

physical injuries of detransitioners, 10–11

physicians: class action suits, 213; encouragement to transition by, 116, 139; as gatekeepers, 224; Hippocratic Oath, 224–25;

physicians (*continued*)
human rights violations and,
226; inadequate evaluations
by, 104–5, 119, 137, 152;
lawsuits against, 212,
220–21; in Nazi Germany,
48–50; in support of
detransitioners, 223–24
Planned Parenthood, 69–70,
72, 104
polycystic ovary syndrome
(PCOS), 186
pornography: addictions to,
95; exposure to, 147–48;
normalizing of, 68–69
Posie Parker (Kellie-Jay Keen),
110, 174
prenatal testing, 62
pronoun usage, 20
Protecting Minors from
Medical Malpractice Act of
2022, 218–19
psychological therapies:
importance of, 64;
transsexualism and, 26
psychological trauma: ignoring
of, 66; informed consent
and, 65
psychologists, encouragement
to transition by, 69
psycho-social adjustments, after
sex-reassignment surgeries,
32
puberty blockers, 221; AAP
(American Academy of
Pediatrics) and, 42; age
guidelines for, 41–42;
custody cases and, 222;
damage, 178–84; data
from Netherlands, 216–17;

data from U.K., 216–17;
Dutch Protocol and,
42–43; effects of, 178–84;
as experimental, 63; Florida
ban on, 225; Forcier on,
37–38; gatekeeping over,
224; GnRH therapy, 64;
informed consent and,
222; *Interim Cass Report*
on, 216; lawsuits against
manufacturers and promoter
of, 212; lawsuits over,
213–14; legal issues over,
18; Lubron as, 116, 117;
National Academy of
Medicine (France) on, 218;
PES (Pediatric Endocrine
Society) and, 42; risks of,
64; in U.K., 40

queer theory: defined, 34;
development of, 34. *See also*
Butler, Judith
The Quest Center, 221

Rachel, 134–44; concerns
about cross-sex hormones,
184; gender stereotypes and,
161, 162; Reddit detrans
group, 177; trauma and,
148, 160, 165–66
rapid-onset gender dysphoria
(ROGD), 74, 136, 148–49
Raymond, Janice, 35–36
Reddit detrans group, 177
Reed, Jamie, 17–18, 222–23
Reimer, Brian, 30–31
Reimer, Bruce (Brenda
Reimer), 30–31
Reisman, Judith, 28

reproductive regrets: cross-sex hormones and, 84–85; damage, 193–96; Grace, 195

research: lack of sound research, 11; National Academy of Medicine (France) on insufficiency of, 218

research base: gaps in, 11; *Interim Cass Report* on gaps in, 216

research experimentation: ethical guidelines for, 53–54, 63; lobotomy experiments, 54–56; in Nazi Germany, 46–52, 50, 63; trans treatment as, 222; Tuskegee experiment, 52–54

rights of conscience, 224

Ringelblum, Emanuel, 207

risks: of breast reconstructive surgery, 85; of cross-sex hormones for children, 64; *Interim Cass Report* on, 216; long-term physical effects, 226; mainstream media's failure to report on, 225–26; parents lied to over, 222; of puberty blockers for children, 64; risk-to-benefit calculations, 38

ROGD (rapid-onset gender dysphoria), 74, 136, 148–49

Rowling, J. K., 157

Ruff, Amy, 221

same-sex attraction and adolescent girls, 135, 164–66

Sapir, Leor, 225

Scandinavia, legislative bans in, 225

Schnarrs, Phillip W., 151–52

school personnel, encouragement to transition by, 69, 162

secular media interviews. *See* 60 Minutes

SEGM (Society for Evidence-Based Gender Medicine, 43, 159, 181, 203

self-harming behavior, 66

semantic contagion, 156

sex: sexual orientation, 44; traditional assumptions about, 34. *See also* biological sex

sex-reassignment surgery: AAP (American Academy of Pediatrics) and, 42; age guidelines for, 41–42; Jorgensen and, 26–27; for men, 22; PES (Pediatric Endocrine Society) and, 42; psycho-social adjustments after, 31–32. *See also* surgical interventions for gender dysphoria

Showalter, Brandon, 9–13

Shrier, Abigail, 145–46, 153–54

social anxiety, gender dysphoria and, 149

social contagion, 152–59

social justice ideology, 67–68, 77

social media: influences of, 77, 115–16, 123, 128, 148, 156–61; peer contagion and, 152–54; social contagion

social media (*continued*)
    and, 156; trans activists and,
    170–72; transgenderism and,
    66–69
social transitioning, 178
social workers: encouragement
    to transition by, 70; lawsuits
    against, 221
Society for Evidence-Based
    Gender Medicine (SEGM),
    43, 159, 181, 203
St. Louis Children's Hospital,
    222–23
Stahl, Lesley, 86–87
standards of care: Dutch
    Protocol, 42–43; *Interim
    Cass Report* on, 216; of
    WPATH (SOC8), 39, 41,
    42, 218
"Standards of Care for the
    Health of Transgender and
    Gender Diverse People"
    (SOC8), 39, 41, 42, 173,
    174, 218
state medical boards, 225
Station for Experimental
    Evolution (Cold Spring
    Harbor, NY), 47
Steinach, Eugen, 26
sterilization: coerced sterilization
    policies, 56–62; opposition
    to forced, 210–11
Stoller, Robert J., 29n30
suicide: gender dysphoria and,
    149; parents lied to over, 19,
    118; post-surgery feelings
    of, 82; as reason cited for
    transitions, 80; transitioning
    and, 138, 197–98
surgical interventions for
    gender dysphoria: as

experimental, 63; gaps in
    research base and, 11; long-
    term physical effects, 84;
    malpractice lawsuits against
    practitioners performing,
    219; organizations funding,
    72. *See also* bottom surgery;
    top surgery
surrogate mother experiments,
    120–21
Sweden: Karolinska Institute
    study in, 32; National
    Board of Health and
    Welfare (NBHW), 217

Tanner stage II of puberty, 42,
    178–79
Tavistock Clinic (England),
    157–58, 167, 170, 215
testosterone: dangers of, 139,
    223; effects of, 80–81, 83,
    106–8, 117, 137–38, 141–
    42; testosterone blockers,
    96; treatments, 69–71,
    105–6, 116
Texas: custody cases in,
    221–22; gender-affirming
    care ban, 219, 225
Thailand, 41
therapists: encouragement to
    transition by, 67, 92, 96,
    116, 129; gender therapists,
    137, 138; inadequate
    evaluations by, 137;
    inexperience of, 79–80;
    lawsuits against, 221
Thoughtful Therapists, 174
top surgery: anxiety over,
    81–82; criteria for,
    80; damage, 188–93;
    gatekeeping over, 224;

as irreversible, 41; regrets over, 77. *See also* mastectomies

Torren, 124–33

trans activists: agendas of, 110–11; influences of, 81–82; misinformation from, 74; promotion of transgenderism by; 35–36, 168–69

Trans Mission (2021 documentary) (Lahl), 10, 15, 16, 17, 37, 156, 176, 197, 212

trans-exclusionary radical feminists (TERFs), 109–10, 140

TRANSform to Freedom podcast, 122

Transgender Trend (U.K.), 165

transgenderism: promotion of, 168; term usage, 25; tipping point of, 36–37

transitioning: age and, 36–39, 148–49; dangers of, 140–41; gender-affirmation movement, 36–39; parents lied to over, 19; regrets over, 18, 81; term usage, 19–20

The Transsexual Phenomenon (Benjamin), 25, 26

transsexualism: American institutions promotion of, 34; Benjamin's approach to, 26; feminist critics of, 35–36; term usage, 24–25; transphobia, 80, 138–39, 140; Yogyakarta Principles and, 43

transvestite, defined, 22

trauma, 65, 149–52, 160, 165–66

truth: acceptance of, 20; dangers of denying, 20; voices speaking the, 21. *See also* Esses, James; Hruz, Paul; Raymond, Janice

Turban, Jack, 145–46, 200–201

Tuskegee experiment: investigations into, 208–9; lessoned learned from, 62, 63; raising awareness about, 226; research experimentation, 52–54

United Kingdom: data from, 216–17; England's limit of puberty blockers in clinical trials, 217; eugenics in, 46, 47; judicial review on gender reassignment, 213–14; Mermaids (advocacy group), 40, 168, 169, 173; National Health Services (NHS), 40, 214–16; Tavistock Clinic (England), 157–58, 167, 170

United Nations, Yogyakarta Principles and, 44

United States, eugenics in, 46–48, 47, 56–62

United States Public Health Services, 52, 208

University Medical Center (Utrecht), 42–43

uterine transplants, 22–24

uterus removal surgeries. *See* hysterectomies

vaginal atrophy, 141, 184, 185, 186–87, 223

vaginoplasty, 26, 33, 41,
    192–93
Van Meter, Quentin, 11,
    39–40, 150–51, 154, 178,
    182, 187–88, 195–96, 200,
    205, 212, 224
Van Mol, André, 11, 156, 160,
    165, 168, 171–72, 178,
    181–82, 184, 185, 186, 193,
    196–97, 198–99, 200, 202,
    203, 212, 224
Vandenbussche, Elie, 164

Walsh, Matt, 173–74
Walsham, Charlie, 169
Washington University School
    of Medicine (St. Louis),
    17–18, 38–39

Wegener, Einar, 21–22, 24
Wegener, Greta, 19
Williams, Joanna, 168
Williams Institute (UCLA
    School of Law), 219
WPATH (World Professional
    Association of Transgender
    Health), 39–42, 79, 173–74,
    176, 195, 218; gender-
    affirmation movement,
    39–42
Wright, Colin, 159

Yang, Wesley, 154–55, 162
Yogyakarta Principles,
    43–44; gender-affirmation
    movement, 43–44
Younger, Jeffrey, 221–22